Contents

Preface

In the history of English literature most outbursts of intense productivity are known by labels which place them chronologically, such as 'Elizabethan' literature or 'Victorian' literature; but the upsurge of creativity which occurred between the late 1780s and the early 1830s is given a name, 'Romanticism' or 'The Romantic movement', which indicates a special cohesion and inter-relatedness in the literary output itself. Not all manifestations of this cohesion and inter-relatedness possess literary significance only. Some reflect developments that were taking place in other arts. Many give body to urgent contemporary debates over political, social, and moral issues. The aim of this present book is to explore the literature in question, clarifying what are the essentials, in substance and style, which characterise 'Romanticism'. While due attention is given to the major writers whose works form the backbone of academic syllabuses in courses on Romanticism, the critical net has been extended here to take in contemporary writers who, in their own day, were no less conspicuous in the public domain than the great names best known to us today. The method adopted for this survey, of exploring Romantic poetry, the Romantic novel, Romantic prose, and Romantic drama in turn, means that in some cases individual writers come up for consideration more than once.

Part 1

Introduction:
historical background

The Industrial Revolution

Historians use the phrase 'The Age of Revolution' when surveying events in the years during which the Romantic writers flourished in Britain. They have especially in mind the French Revolution, which broke out in 1789, and the Industrial Revolution, which brought immense changes during the decades from 1780 to 1830. The Industrial Revolution was in the first place a British development, and the outbreak of new artistic thinking and creativity which we call 'Romanticism' can be understood only by reference to the changes in the physical background to life which the Industrial Revolution had brought about. Although much of the theoretical stimulus for political, social, and ideological reform in the United Kingdom took its source from what happened in France and Germany, the practical conditions at home provided a crucial impetus too.

The Industrial Revolution involved a drift of population from country to town and the breakdown of the last vestiges of a predominantly rural social structure. Its basis was the development of new technologies which lifted the lid off processes of production and transport. Although this freeing of the economy to multiply goods and services only reached its peak in the Victorian age with the construction of the railways and the fuller expansion of heavy industry, the great breakthrough into the industrial age came when steam-power enabled mass-production in factories to replace clumsy individual productivity in cottages and small mills. The invention of the steam engine by the Scotsman James Watt (1736–1819) and the various improvements he made to it in the early 1780s led to the widespread use of steam, first for pumping, then for driving factory machinery. Erasmus Darwin (1731–1802), grandfather of the great evolutionist, recognised the significance of the new developments from the start. Thus he hailed the giant power of steam in *The Economy of Vegetation* (1792):

> Here high in air the rising stream he pours
> To clay-built cisterns, or to lead-lin'd towers;

Fresh through a thousand pipes the wave distils,
And thirsty cities drink the exuberant rills . . .
Soon shall thy arm, UNCONQUER'D STEAM! afar
Drag the slow barge, or drive the rapid car . . .

At the same time that technology was expanding industrial output, the effect of various Enclosure Acts was to expand agrarian output. Land formerly regarded as 'common' and shared among individuals was allotted to private owners of large estates, with the intention of bringing capital investment into play which could increase production. One consequence of this was to turn much wild and neglected terrain into fruitful acres for growing cereals or rearing cattle, but in many cases a cruel price was paid in detaching poor people from the soil and squeezing out small farmers.

The Romantic period was thus an age of rapidly expanding productivity, rural and urban. The publication of *The Wealth of Nations* (1776), a study of political economy by the Scottish economist Adam Smith (1723–90), had provided a theoretical justification for *laissez-faire* economics. Smith recognised self-interest as the mainspring of economic development. He argued that the wider public interest will be served indirectly by the general pursuit of individual interest and the accumulation of wealth.

The negative consequences of these developments were lamented by many writers. In particular the use of child-labour in factories provoked angry condemnation from progressive thinkers. In his *Letters from England* (1807) the poet Robert Southey records a conversation between himself and a wealthy Manchester mill-owner who is displaying the merits of his cotton factory. The tone is heavily ironic as the mill-owner proudly shows his child-labourers at work:

'There is no idleness among us; — they come at five in the morning; we allow them half an hour for breakfast, and an hour for dinner; they leave work at six, and another set relieves them for the night; the wheels never stand still.'

As Southey surveys the youngsters, dexterously busy amid the noise and movement, he keeps his reflections to himself.

I thought that if Dante had peopled one of his hells with children, here was a scene worthy to have supplied him with new images of torment.

This mechanisation of production did not everywhere increase the opportunities for employment. It proved unfortunate that progressive mill-owners were introducing labour-saving machinery into the textile industry just at the time when the war with France was shutting off the

European export market and decreasing the demand for finished goods. The threat of unemployment aroused men to band together to destroy machinery before it could be brought into use. The 'Luddites', as they were called, would fall by night upon convoys transporting new machinery to their workplaces. (The name 'Luddite' was chosen in disparagement, for Ned Ludd was a feeble-minded Leicestershire boy who destroyed stocking-frames in a fit of angry frustration.) There were outbreaks of 'Luddite' riots in Yorkshire and the Midlands in 1811 and 1812, and again in 1816.

The French Revolution

In May 1789 financial straits drove King Louis XVI to summon a meeting of the long-defunct French parliament, the States-General. Once in session, the third estate asserted itself against the clergy and the nobility. They adopted the title of the National Assembly and determined to make a new constitution. Meanwhile the people of Paris rose and stormed the Bastille, the prison that represented the power of the throne in its most tyrannical aspects. The National Assembly issued its Declaration of the Rights of Man, and privileges of rank were abolished. But the phase soon passed in which it seemed possible that a moderate system under a constitutional monarchy might be made permanent. Extremists led by the Jacobin Maximilien Robespierre (1758–94) formed an increasingly powerful faction. In 1792 the National Convention proclaimed a republic; in 1793 Louis XVI was executed, and Robespierre's Committee of Public Safety inaugurated a reign of terror which finally culminated in Robespierre's own execution in July 1794. Reaction led to the formation of the Directory in 1795, and this lasted until Napoleon Bonaparte (1769–1821) emerged as First Consul in 1799. In 1804 he crowned himself emperor, but his spectacular continental conquests, designed to break the power of Britain, gradually turned into reverses, and he was finally defeated by the Duke of Wellington (1769–1852) at the battle of Waterloo in 1815. By this time, apart from a short-lived period of official peace after the Treaty of Amiens in 1802, England had been at war with France since 1793.

As there was a natural impatience with the status quo in England, which was stimulated into action by what seemed positive in the French Revolution, so there was a natural humanity which was horrified by the massacres into which the Revolution degenerated. Moreover, it must be remembered that the aid given by France to the American colonies during the War of Independence had not endeared her to the British. Thus the French Revolution had the effect in Britain of stimulating demand for reform by progressives and resistance to reform by reactionaries. The conviction, 'We do not want a comparable blood-bath here', had its influence on many moderate people. The consequence was that crucial reforms sought in the last decades of the eighteenth century were delayed. For instance, there was a failure to deal with the issue of parliamentary representation, even though the system was unjust and outmoded. The practice was for landowners to select Members of Parliament for the constituencies over which they held sway. Small coteries of borough electors could be bribed or intimidated. In the 1780s, in a population of some 8 million, there were only 300,000 with the right to vote. The younger William Pitt (1759–1806) made a series of unsuccessful attempts to bring the question of parliamentary representation under review.

The American Declaration of Independence (1776) had finally been accepted by the British government in 1783. Its noble words about the inalienable rights of human beings could ring ironically in the ears of many in the home country, where pressure for the removal of disabilities from Roman Catholics only slowly led to the Catholic Emancipation Act of 1829, where pressure for electoral reform only slowly led to the Reform Bill of 1832, and where the universities even then remained closed to nonconformists. Small wonder that, when the new National Assembly in France issued its Declaration recognising the equal rights of all citizens, enlightened British public opinion should have warmed to the prospects for greater freedom that were now opening up. In November 1789 Richard Price (1723–91), a Unitarian minister, delivered an enthusiastic address expressing high hopes from the ardour for liberty displayed by the French:

> Be encouraged all ye friends of freedom, and writers in its defence . . . Your labours have not been in vain. Behold kingdoms, admonished by you, starting from sleep, breaking their fetters, and claiming justice from their oppressors! Behold, the light you have struck out after setting AMERICA free, reflected to FRANCE, and there kindled to a blaze that lays despotism in ashes, and warms to illuminate EUROPE!

This stung Edmund Burke (1729–97), the distinguished statesman, to a riposte, and he published his *Reflections on the Revolution in France* (1790). Price had declared the people's right to get rid of their monarch if they chose. Burke defended the inherited rights enshrined in the British constitution and lamented the crude antics of those who rebelled supposedly in the name of light and reason.

> Atheists are not our preachers; madmen are not our law-givers . . . We fear God; we look with awe to kings; with affection to parliaments; with duty to magistrates; with reverence to priests; and with respect to nobility.

It was in reply to Burke that Thomas Paine (1737–1809) published *The Rights of Man* (1791), disputing the notion of inherited constitutional obligation, and arguing, after Rousseau, that only by determination of the people can government be legitimised.

It is not among the least of the evils of the present existing governments in all parts of Europe, that man, considered as man, is thrown back to a vast distance from his Maker, and the artificial chasm filled up by a succession of barriers, or a sort of turnpike gates, through which he has to pass.

Paine then cites Burke's authorities listed above — kings, parliaments, magistrates, priests. These are the 'turnpike gates'. Man's duty is not 'to pass by ticket from one to the other', but singly to serve God and his fellow men.

Thus attitudes to the French Revolution became a deeply divisive issue in British society. Attitudes to the rise of Napoleon were no less a source of bitter dispute. For some he was a bold saviour who had brought order out of chaos. For others he was an unscrupulous adventurer who had built a new tyranny on the ruins of the noble efforts for liberty. Meanwhile France remained an enemy nation. Small wonder, perhaps, that we shall find a government agent spying on Coleridge and Wordsworth. The authorities were apprehensive, and bodies interested in reform came under official suspicion, as we shall see in the case of Thomas Holcroft and the Corresponding Society. Nevertheless Jacobinism failed to take root in Britain. The reason is neatly summed up by E. J. Hobsbawm in *The Age of Revolution: Europe 1789–1848*:

In Britain 'Jacobinism' would undoubtedly have been a phenomenon of greater political importance, even after The Terror, if it had not clashed with the traditional anti-French bias of popular English nationalism, compounded equally of John Bull's beef-fed contempt for the starveling continentals (all French in the popular cartoons of the period are as thin as matchsticks) and of hostility to what was, after all, England's 'hereditary enemy', though also Scotland's hereditary ally.

It is easy now to understand why, in spite of all the excitement and tension of this period, revolutionary fervour failed to quicken up the various movements for reform in Britain. Competitive cross-currents of interest and ideology were so powerful and complex that no single thrust of revolutionary action could possibly have materialised. It was the educated people of England — and of other European countries — who were most stirred to enthusiastic sympathy when the French Revolution broke out. Wordsworth and Coleridge, Southey and Blake were among them. But of course it was men and women such as they, with a warm sense of human brotherhood, who were most horrified by the bloody excesses which the Jacobins perpetrated. Similarly it was people such as they, devoted to ideals of peace and tolerance, who reacted most sharply against Napoleon's aggressive conquests and dictatorial pretensions.

Tory administrations were in power through most of the Romantic age, yet even among Tory statesmen on the one hand, and Whig statesmen on the other, there were conflicting attitudes to the war with France and the need for reform at home. William Pitt the Younger, who was Prime Minister for most of the years between 1784 and his death, and who had brought about the Union with Ireland in 1800, resigned in 1801 because of the king's opposition to legislation for Catholic emancipation. He was back in power in coalition with Charles James Fox (1749–1806) in 1804. Fox, a fervent Whig, was an ardent disciple of Edmund Burke. Burke had urged conciliation with America and had been a supporter of Catholic emancipation; but he saw the French Revolution as wholly evil. He labelled the rebels 'a swinish multitude'. Their doings swung him against reform, and Fox broke with him.

Another statesman who resigned with Pitt in 1801 over the issue of Catholic emancipation was Viscount Castlereagh (1769–1822). Born in Dublin, he had started his political career in the Irish Parliament and supported the Act of Union. As Secretary for War from 1805 and Foreign Secretary from 1812, he was a key figure in the struggle against France. A fellow minister under Pitt, George Canning (1770–1827), who was Foreign Secretary in 1807, was so violently opposed to Castlereagh's handling of the war that the two fought a duel in 1809. They were to find themselves in hotly opposing positions again later when Castlereagh, a rigid reactionary, supported King George IV's proposal to divorce Queen Caroline, and Canning supported the queen.

Castlereagh remained prominent in the early days of the administration officially presided over by Lord Liverpool (1770–1828), which took office in 1812 after the assassination of the Prime Minister, Spencer Perceval (1762–1812) in the lobby of the House of Commons. (The assassin was a merchant bankrupt as a result of the war.) The student of English literature is unlikely to form a very favourable impression of Castlereagh. Byron mocked him as the 'intellectual eunuch Castlereagh' in the introductory stanzas to Don Juan. Shelley also castigated him:

I met Murder on the way —
He had a mask like Castlereagh —

So Shelley wrote in 'The Mask of Anarchy' (1819) shortly after the Peterloo massacre at Manchester. The occasion was a meeting held in Manchester on 16 August 1819 by agitators for reform of parliamentary representation. The site was St Peter's Field. When the military, including cavalry, were ordered to break up the meeting, eleven people were killed and many injured. The adoption of the word 'Peterloo' for the slaughter (in echo of 'Waterloo') helped to give the event a lasting symbolic status. There was an ominous sequel a few months later, in February 1820, when a conspiracy to murder Castlereagh and other ministers, set fire to London, seize the Bank, and proclaim a provisional government was revealed to the police by one of the conspirators. The ring-leaders, who met in Cato Street, Edgware Road, were rounded up and hanged or transported. Their venture became known as the 'Cato Street Conspiracy'.

George IV as Regent and king

With hindsight it is perhaps remarkable that threats of disorder were few and far between. The Romantic period coincided with the reigns of two monarchs of various degrees of unfitness for their roles. George III (1738–1820) succeeded to the throne in 1760. His stubbornness at home in seeking to extend the sovereign's authority over successive governments, and his stubbornness abroad in pursuit of the defeat of the American colonies made his reign an unfruitful one, though his honesty and his virtue as a family man won him a certain esteem. He had a period of insanity between 1788 and 1789, and his reason finally gave way in 1811. His son George was appointed Regent and remained so until he succeeded to the throne in 1820. George IV (1762–1830), first as Regent, then as king, thus represented monarchy to the British public for nearly twenty years at a time of political unrest and widespread poverty. George III had been neither a wise nor even a very sensible king, but his defects, of simplicity rather than of selfishness or greed, were not of a kind to rouse resentment among the masses, and he proved a generally popular monarch. George IV was gifted with a good deal more understanding and taste than his father, but he forfeited respect by his extravagance and his dissipations.

His sex life in particular became a public issue. He was only twenty-one when he fell in love with Maria Fitzherbert, a widow of twenty-seven who had lost two husbands. She was a Roman Catholic and she genuinely loved the prince. The couple were secretly married in 1785. The marriage could be neither public nor official. It was invalid without the king's consent because the prince was under twenty-five. Moreover, under the Act of Settlement of 1689, to marry a Catholic was to forfeit the right of accession to the crown. In personal terms the unofficial marriage was a happy one for a long time, but the prince's extravagance produced a load of debt which the king was prepared to settle only if the prince married Caroline of Brunswick. The prince never liked her and she was quite unsuitable, but he married her in 1795 and their daughter Princess Charlotte was born a year later. There followed a separation and the return of Mrs Fitzherbert to the prince. The story of the prince's subsequent mistresses is too complex to pursue here. But the treatment of the queen became a public issue, helping to make George highly unpopular as Regent and as king. He tried in vain to divorce her, and on the day of his coronation he ordered her to be refused admission to Westminster Abbey.

There were many who had high hopes when George first came to power as Regent. This was partly because he had differed from the king in politics, favouring the Whigs and having Fox and Sheridan among his associates. But George veered round to the Tories, and expectations that he would be less zealous over the war and more zealous over Catholic emancipation and other matters of reform were disappointed. It was partly because the Whigs found themselves still consigned to the opposition that they espoused the cause of Queen Caroline in retaliation. But the Regent had charm and intelligence. He had had a good education in the classics and could speak French, German, and Italian fluently. Moreover, he was interested in the arts and sciences. He won Byron's admiration, so that long after he paid the prince a notable tribute in *Don Juan*:

There, too, he saw (whate'er he may be now)
A Prince, the prince of princes at the time,
With fascination in his very bow,
And full of promise, as the spring of prime.
Though royalty was written on his brow,
He had *then* grace, too, rare in every clime,
Of being, without alloy of fop or beau,
A finish'd gentleman from top to toe.   (Canto XII, stanza 84)

Shelley the anti-monarchist naturally hated the Regent, but it was claimed that the prince had more than once read William Godwin's radical novel *Caleb Williams*. In 1812 he gave a knighthood to Humphry Davy (1778–1829), the inventor of the miner's safety lamp. And when he made Walter Scott a baronet in 1820 he boasted, 'I shall always reflect with pleasure on Sir Walter Scott's having been the first creation of my reign.' Scott in return praised him for his ease and elegance, his accomplishments and his good nature. 'I am sure that such a man is fitter for us than one who would long to lead armies, or be perpetually meddling with *la grande politique*.'

The Regent was also a man of musical culture. The England of the 1790s was the England which twice, in 1790–2 and 1794–5, enthusiastically welcomed the composer Joseph Haydn (1732–1809), whom Oxford honoured with a Doctorate of Music. The Prince of Wales entertained him graciously. 'He is the most handsome man on God's earth,' Haydn exclaimed, and the composer cheerfully accompanied on the harpsichord while the Duchess of York sat at his side to sing and the prince performed on the 'cello. As George IV, he asked the Italian composer Rossini (1792–1868) to the palace when the latter visited England in 1823, and again indulged his penchant for accompaniment, this time with apologies for his slips in tempo. 'There are few in your Royal Highness's position who could play so well,' Rossini replied, and afterwards spoke highly of the king's appearance and demeanour. The Regent was also interested in the arts, and patronised Thomas Gainsborough (1727–88), as well as Sir Joshua Reynolds (1723–92).

Above all he was an enthusiast for architecture. The architect John Nash (1752–1835) had distinguished himself by work on provincial buildings and country houses when the Prince Regent became his friend. Not all Nash's work on such places as the Regent's Park area, Regent Street, Cumberland Terrace, and Carlton House Terrace has survived, but where it has it gives London buildings of exquisite proportions and simple grandeur. In 1784 the prince purchased a farmhouse in the village of Brighthelmstone (now Brighton) on the Sussex coast and had it enlarged by the architect Henry Holland into a substantial house, or 'Pavilion'. He decided to enlarge it further and improve it in oriental style, and Nash was called upon to remodel it. The magnificence of such rooms as the Music Room and the Banqueting Room cannot be questioned, although from the start criticism was made of the excess of ornamentation and the incongruous fancifulness of the 'Indian' and 'Chinese' idioms. But the element of theatrical extravagance is certainly an aspect of Romanticism. So too is that taste for the exotic found also in contemporary drama and poetry. The bulbous minarets of the Brighton Pavilion perhaps smack of the 'stately pleasure dome' of Coleridge's 'Kubla Khan'. The Pavilion is not, however, basically complex or eccentric in design, and if in detail it forsakes the simplicity of Regency ornament at its best, it appeals by the sheer frankness of its luxuriance. 'Regency', in reference to architecture and furniture, remains a term with associations of disciplined elegance.

Romanticism in France

Jean-Jacques Rousseau (1712–78), though he died before the Romantic movement proper may be said to have begun, initiated a number of trains of thought which were to become hallmarks of Romanticism. It is characteristic of many Romantic writers that their lives, as well as their works, bear the stamp of a fresh, uninhibited persona. We may think of Sir Walter Scott building his massive pseudo-Gothic baronial residence at Abbotsford, or of Wordsworth turning his back on a career to live on milk and potatoes in a cottage at Grasmere, of Byron storming out of his home country in high dudgeon and then taking up arms for the liberty of Greece, or of Shelley sweeping successive young ladies off their feet into dreams of paradisal freedom for the senses and the heart. In all cases the personality and output of the creator are bound together in such a way that the reader feels the vitality of the one pulsating through the other. This is not to say that all the works of the Romantic writers call for interpretation on a subjective as well as an objective basis. We may need to know something of Wordsworth's life in order to get the most out of *The Prelude*, but we should not necessarily get anything more from *The Heart of Midlothian* from a knowledge of Scott's career.

Rousseau the man makes himself vividly present behind Rousseau the writer. He was born in Geneva, the son of a watchmaker, and his mother died at his birth. Throughout his life, the wandering existence that he embarked on in boyhood was only fitfully interrupted by periods when he was temporarily taken into the care of helpful ladies or befriended by distinguished thinkers, such as Voltaire and Diderot in France, and David Hume in England. But he too often bit the hand that aided him. Restless by temperament, hungry for affection, afflicted with a disturbing sense of guilt, addicted to morbidly obsessive sexual passions, and increasingly the victim of a persecution complex, he pursued his hag-ridden way, the clouds broken for him intermittently by phases of comparatively settled life which seemed, in retrospect at least, peaceful and idyllic. 'Self-torturing sophist, wild Rousseau, / The apostle of affliction' Byron called him in *Childe Harold* (Canto III, stanza 77), adding, 'He . . . threw / Enchantment over passion'. Rousseau had a lasting relationship with the kitchen-maid Thérèse Levasseur, with whom he fell in love in 1746. He tells in his *Confessions* (written between 1766 and 1770 and published posthumously, and a not wholly reliable record) how she bore him five illegitimate children and how he deposited them as babies each in turn at a Foundling Hospital, a criminal offence for which he suffered much remorse. The probing psychological analysis laid bare in the *Confessions*, with its sharp emphasis on the distinctiveness of the individual, bears the unmistakable Romantic stamp.

Rousseau's influence emanates in the first place from this keen sense of individual autonomy, the autonomy of 'natural man'. He rejected the eighteenth-century assumption that progress in science and culture necessarily increases mankind's happiness. Civilisation corrupts, for it overlays the natural state with artifices which erode the individual's intuitive feeling for divine benevolence. Rousseau carried this emphasis into the political field in *The Social Contract* (1762) where he argued that no individual can claim authority over another. Governmental power derives from a voluntary social contract entered into by the people, who mandate power to the sovereign of the State and have the right to revoke it, should the need arise. Rousseau's political and philosophical thinking bore fruit for both good and ill in the coming age of revolution, and indeed has had repercussions in our own age. His educational thinking, expounded most notably in the novel *Émile* (1762), emphasises the need to adjust educational demands to the changing stages of the young pupils' development and not to treat them as though they were adult. 'God makes all things good; man meddles with them and they become evil,' Rousseau begins, but he does not urge a crude *laissez-faire* approach, for the child has to be defended against 'all the social conditions into which we are plunged' which would 'stifle nature in him and put nothing in her place'. *Julie, or the New Héloïse* (1761) is an epistolary novel advocating frankness and directness between individuals in their personal relationships. Virtue will flourish best in an environment where the soul can be inspired and ennobled by contact with nature. Thus from Rousseau derives a stream of thought exalting natural man, decrying moral conventions as hypocritical, and equating passion with virtue.

Rousseau's disciple Bernardin de Saint-Pierre (1737–1814) wrote a celebrated romance, *Paul et Virginie* (1787), describing how two fatherless children on the Isle of France (Mauritius) are brought up wholly uncorrupted by contact with civilisation, and fall idyllically in love in their paradisal home. The sentimental portrayal of youthful innocence against a lush tropical background extended the Rousseauist influence somewhat naïvely.

Although France, through the work of Rousseau and through the effects of the Revolution, was the inspiration of much in the English Romantic movement, the great figures of French Romanticism proper post-date those of English Romanticism. It may be argued that the French had other matters to preoccupy them between 1789 and 1815 than artistic production. At any rate Wordsworth, Scott, and Coleridge were all born between 1770 and 1772, Byron, Shelley, and Keats between 1788 and 1795, but the major figures of French Romanticism were born after the turn of the century. Victor Hugo (1802–85) was at once Romantic poet, Romantic novelist, and Romantic dramatist. An artist with a sense of the poet's prophetic role, he was also master of a lyric vein rich in personal emotion, and he could work with the fantastic and the macabre on the edge of reality. There is a melancholy grandeur about his novels, and a taste for melodrama is evident also in his plays. His humanitarian compassion for society's victims emerges notably in the great novel *Les Misérables* (1862), with its study of an ex-convict. The historical novels of Alexandre Dumas (1802–70), such as the celebrated *The Three Musketeers* (1844), belong chronologically, like Hugo's work, not to the age of Scott and Byron but to the age of the Brontës and Dickens. And a key figure in European Romanticism, the novelist George Sand (1804–76), brought out her first successful novel, *Indiana* (1832), in the year Scott died. Separated after an arranged marriage, George Sand (whose real name was Aurore Dupin) had notorious liaisons with the poet Alfred de Musset

(1810–57) and the composer Frédéric Chopin (1810–49), and in her novels she proclaimed the right of free love.

In histories of English literature the 'Romantic' period gives place to the 'Victorian' age well before these notable French 'Romantics' published their great works. Even the Frenchman Emile Legouis in his standard work *A Short History of English Literature* (1934) labels successive chapters 'Romanticism 1798–1830' and 'The Victorian Era 1830–80'. Yet a recent French scholar, Francis Claudon, in *The Concise Encyclopedia of Romanticism* (1980), includes Dickens, the Brontës, and the Brownings, not to mention Verdi and Wagner, in his survey. This illustrates how widely the 'Romantic' spirit was diffused in nineteenth-century art after the great central figures of the English Romantic movement had died.

Goethe and the artistic revolution

It is evident that our understanding of the English Romantics is more likely to be aided by attention to writers who preceded them or lived contemporaneously with them than by attention to writers who succeeded them. And in this respect perhaps the only European writer of comparable significance to Rousseau was the German Wolfgang von Goethe (1749–1832). Scott translated Goethe's drama *Götz von Berlichingen*, the study of a noble hero at loggerheads with corrupt society, in 1799, and nearly thirty years later, in 1825, Goethe and Scott exchanged mutually adulatory letters. Byron dedicated his play *Werner* to Goethe in 1823, and a comparable exchange of letters followed. Shelley was deeply influenced by Goethe. 'I have been reading over & over again Faust, & always with sensations that no other composition excites,' he wrote in 1822.

Goethe is one of the giants of European literature, of the stature of Dante and Shakespeare. His short novel *The Sorrows of Young Werther* (1774, revised 1787) studies a young man of artistic sensitivity, enquiring intellect, and deep emotions, whose fantastic dreams and hopeless love lead him to suicide, and the book produced a number of suicides among its young readers. His rambling novel *Wilhelm Meister's Apprenticeship* (1796) traces the career of a young German who is attracted to the world of the theatre and learns that it is not for him. It is a novel of personal growth and development, of education through struggle between what appeals to dreamy, self-indulgent inclinations and the demands of duty and self-discipline. Though Goethe turned away for some time from the kind of emotionalism that made *Werther* so influential, he never lost his sense of human tragedy, of the demonic powers threatening man's course, of the struggle between passion and social convention, and of the healing power of love. Out of struggle comes growth. Goethe's *Faust* (1808) universalises the theme of the restless human pursuit of experience and understanding, with the evil it produces as well as the divine impulse it

evidences; and sees the latter as its justification. Goethe's early enthusiasm for Shakespeare, for Ossian, and for Samuel Richardson, as well as
his appreciation of Byron and Scott, involve him in a two-way relationship
with English literature.

A comparable creative giant of the period was Ludwig van Beethoven
(1770–1827), who gave to music that disturbing volcanic character which
marks so much of Romantic literature. While adopting the basic forms
of the classical eighteenth-century tradition, Beethoven so extended their
outlines as to enable them to give voice to an inspiration, an emotional
range, and a degree of passionate assertiveness that were totally new in
music. He was a man of revolutionary sympathies, who tore off the
manuscript page dedicating his 'Eroica' symphony to Napoleon when he
heard that Napoleon had become emperor. Instead it became 'Symphonia
Eroica in memory of a great man'. Beethoven was scornful of social
formalities and aristocratic privileges. He had the artist's absent-minded,
sensitive, and excitable temperament, and the deafness which overtook
him gives a tragic grandeur to his character. It seems an exact exemplifi-
cation of the formulas of Romanticism that a personality so dynamic
should have stretched and moulded the established frameworks of sonata
form and symphonic structure into flexible subservience to the demands
of his musical will. The collision of the creator with his medium, of
the individual with destiny, explodes into pulsating rhythms, while an
escalating tussle with potent melodic figures touches nerves that are
sensitive to pain or paean, anguish or jubilation.

The burst of musical productivity of a more passionate and dramatic
brand, more alert to human dreams and griefs, and more sensitive to
the inspiration of nature continued with the work of Franz Schubert
(1797–1828) who was born in Vienna. His melodic gift turned him into
perhaps the finest song-writer of all time. A climactic orchestral statement
of French Romanticism was the *Symphonie fantastique* (1830) by Hector
Berlioz (1803–69), which gave expression not only to the composer's
love for the Irish actress Harriet Smithson, but also to the artist's
transfiguration of personality and experience. A recurring, ruminative
theme represents the artist's pursuit of the ideal, while his brain is teased
and tormented by memories of a ball, a country idyll, and a nightmare
that culminates in death at the guillotine.

There is the same sort of connection between life and art, and the
same taste for the dramatic and the grandiose, in some of the contemporary painters. The massacre of 20,000 Greeks by the Turks in 1822
inspired the French painter Eugéne Delacroix (1798–1863) to paint his
epoch-making picture 'Massacre at Chios' in 1824. The canvasses of
Delacroix vibrate with excitement as he catches moments of crisis in
bold colouring and dramatic pose — such as the bare-breasted figure of
France, red flag aloft in her hand, leading a mob of revolutionaries over

piled-up corpses in 'Liberty Guiding the People' (1831). Literature too inspired him to paint 'The Death of Ophelia' (1844) and the melodramatic 'Abduction of Rebecca' (1858), based on an episode from Scott's *Ivanhoe*. The great English Romantic artist J.M.W. Turner (1775–1851) has a subtlety of colour and composition far removed from the strident melodramatics of Delacroix. His Byronic picture 'Childe Harold's Pilgrimage in Italy' is a disturbing study in which the human groups are seen against a wide natural background, hazy, remote, and melancholy as Harold's own persona. Turner's taste for the dramatic in such pictures as 'Hannibal and his Army Crossing the Alps', and more notably still 'The Burning of the House of Lords and the House of Commons' (1834), sacrificed clarity of detail to a manipulation of light and shade. In the latter, vivid streaks of red and yellow against a sombre sky and a hazily realised bridge and riverscape make a sharp assault on the imagination. Fascinated by weather and skyscapes, Turner became obsessed with the effects of luminosity, and in his later pictures imagery fades into insubstantiality, bathed in shimmering translucencies almost preternatural in their suggestiveness.

Romanticism and Classicism

Attempts to define 'Romanticism' easily lead to confusion rather than clarification because the term covers such a vast range of artistic developments which are themselves tied to philosophical and political developments too. In the arts the contrast between the Classical and the Romantic is a valid one in that it distinguishes, on the one hand, respect for restrained formalities of balance and proportion, and on the other hand, zest for unfettered expression of emotion and inspiration. In the extreme case the Romantic principle leads to exaltation of the primitive over the civilised, the emotional over the rational, of what is spontaneous over what is contrived or inhibited. Belief in man's natural goodness breeds trust in his instinctive urges and what can only be called reverence for the individual's emotional experiences. Alongside this sense of the almost sacred value of individual self-expression there is the belief, or at least the suspicion, that it is the corrupt effect of civilisation in perverting human desires, stimulating greed and materialism, fettering native impulses, and producing the exploitation of man by man, that has stifled the human spirit.

Accompanying the Romantic respect for the emotions — which tends to equate virtue with reliance upon the feelings — there is a Romantic veneration for the imagination even in its wildest claims. Thus the Romantics escape the mundane realities of the present by trying to recapture the supposedly richer and more colourful life of the past — the Middle Ages perhaps especially. They also like exotic oriental backgrounds. And they remove rational constraints from their imagination in exploring the fantastic and the preternatural. The taste for the wonderful is another aspect of the Romantic claim for the unfettering of individual potential. It reaches its peak in the groping after sublimity, a groping which may invoke the diabolical in the Faustian figures of Byron, but which is transfigured by moral discipline into something prayerful and purifying in the poetry of Wordsworth.

In a celebrated couplet in his *Essay on Criticism* the Augustan poet Alexander Pope (1688–1744) wrote:

> True Wit is Nature to advantage dressed,
> What oft was thought, but ne'er so well expressed.

In a similarly concise manner the novelist Jane Austen (1775–1817) opened a novel thus:

> It is a truth universally acknowledged, that a single man in possession of a good fortune, must be in want of a wife.

To either of these sentences the response of the reader is one of pleasure deriving from satisfaction. 'How neat!' the reader thinks. 'How exact, how perceptive, how true!' Something has been perfectly achieved in the tidy encapsulation of experience, and the reader's response is of delight in that perfection. 'There is no more to be said,' he thinks.

By contrast Wordsworth, the first of our Romantic poets, writes:

> . . . and when the deed was done
> I heard among the solitary hills
> Low breathings coming after me, and sounds
> Of undistinguishable motion, steps
> Almost as silent as the turf they trod.   (*Prelude*, I, lines 320–4)

Here the response of the reader is totally different. He does not say to himself, 'There is no more to be said', for his response is not satisfaction at something perfectly achieved. His sense of mystery has been awakened. There is certainly no delight in a neat clarification of experience. Indeed, instead of being so delighted, the reader is disturbed. Instead of finding an aspect of experience forever perfectly enshrined in words, the roof has been lifted off his mental world. Classicism seems to complete a process; Romanticism starts one. Classicism satisfies; Romanticism disturbs.

Precursors of Romanticism in English literature

The characteristics of Romanticism did not, of course, explode freshly into public view when those writers whom we call the 'great Romantics' first put pen to paper. Those characteristics are to be found scattered throughout English literature from the days of the Anglo-Saxons. No one could deny that Chaucer's *Troilus and Criseyde* and Shakespeare's *Romeo and Juliet* contain ingredients of 'Romanticism'. And although the corpus of Romantic literature represents a sharp contrast to the literature of the eighteenth century, with all its polish, its poise, and its urbanity, yet voices began to be heard in the later eighteenth century which broke thoroughly with the canons of Augustan propriety and decorum. These were the voices of writers whom we can now recognise as precursors of the full-blown Romantic movement.

Among the most widely influential was the Scottish poet James Mac-pherson (1736–96). He had some acquaintance with Gaelic poetry and he had an enormous success when he published what purported to be translations of poetry by the ancient Gaelic bard, Ossian, derived from both oral and manuscript sources. Though Dr Johnson for one derided the claim as fraudulent, the pseudo-primitive Celtic tales of heroic warriors, noble yet humane, acted out against a sombre natural background of cloudy skies and roaring streams, snow-capped hills and silent woods, made an instant appeal both at home and on the Continent. The mixture of gentle archaisms with simple rhetorical devices in an incantatory, prose-like verse proved infectiously popular.

The same taste for the antique was ministered to more authentically by Bishop Thomas Percy (1729–1811), whose various volumes, *Reliques of Ancient English Poetry*, came out between 1765 and 1794, presenting ballads and metrical romances which Percy had derived from a seventeenth-century manuscript. The impetus this collection gave to interest in the old ballads clearly had its influence on Scott, Coleridge, and Wordsworth. A sadder episode in the revival of taste for the antique was the story of Thomas Chatterton (1752–70) who, after delving in a Bristol church library, manufactured pseudo-medieval poems and presented them to the public as the work of one 'Thomas Rowley'. The poems were works of considerable ingenuity and indeed of sensitive verbal artistry, but Chatterton killed himself at the age of eighteen and turned himself into a symbol of youthful promise tragically thwarted.

Two other poets, of much greater stature, broke away from eighteenth-century literary conventions to foreshadow the achievements of the Romantics. One was William Cowper (1731–1800). In his hymns he struck a new note of evangelical fervour at once authentic, powerful, and generally free of sentimentality. The sturdiness of his vocabulary, the simplicity of the imagery, and the directness of utterance together convey a depth of individual emotion disturbing in its impact. Robert Burns (1759–96) from Ayrshire escapes inclusion among the Romantic poets proper only because his dates plant him firmly in the eighteenth century. The image of the ploughman poet, lyrically hymning the bonnie Scottish maiden and the bonnie Scottish banks and braes, while hurling ironic invective at the hypocrisies of the over-pious and the pretensions of the over-wealthy, guaranteed a fervent public response. Burns sang like nature's own prodigy, celebrating honest poverty, the simple life, and the homely virtues with a rhythmic fluency that tugs at the heart.

There were prose writers who in other ways heralded the outburst of innovation which marks Romanticism. The Scottish novelist Henry Mackenzie (1745–1831) mined a vein of tender sensibility in his novel *The Man of Feeling* (1771), which anticipates the romantic identification of virtue with emotion. The 'man of feeling' himself, one Mr Harley, a country gentleman, exists primarily as the possessor of a soul oozing benevolence, whose pity overflows upon the afflicted. Innovation of a vastly different kind came from the pen of Horace Walpole (1717–97), who built an extravagantly Gothick mansion at Strawberry Hill. Having dreamed one night of a gigantic hand in armour appearing above the staircase of an ancient castle, he wrote his novel *The Castle of Otranto* (1764), an excursion into a sphere of medievalism replete with trap-doors and subterranean passages, rocks and caverns, knights and hermits, walking skeleton and bleeding statue. And where Walpole prepared the ground for Ann Radcliffe and the horror novelists, William Beckford (1760–1844), who constructed a monstrous Gothick edifice, Fonthill Abbey, with massive tower and transepts, vast galleries and vistas, opened up a new literary vein of opulent exoticism in his novel *Vathek* (1786), an excursion into colourful orientalism, steeped in magic and mystery.

Part 2

Romantic poetry

William Wordsworth

William Wordsworth (1770–1850), the greatest of the English Romantic poets, was born at Cockermouth in Cumberland. Here his father, John Wordsworth, as main business manager for Sir James Lowther, a wealthy landowner, occupied a fine house in the main street, which belonged to the immense Lowther estate. His mother Ann came from a trading family in Penrith. William had three brothers and a sister, Dorothy. Richard, the eldest, succeeded to the family estate at Sockbridge, Westmorland. John went to sea and was drowned in 1805. Christopher rose to be Master of Trinity College, Cambridge. The children's mother died in 1778 and their father in 1783, so that William had lost his mother by the time he was eight and his father by the time he was thirteen. The loss of the father left the family with an irritating financial problem, in that Sir James Lowther had neglected to settle accounts with his steward and owed him over £4000. In spite of legal action against him, the debt was not repaid until after his death in 1802, when Sir William Lowther succeeded to his vast wealth and sorted out his affairs.

By a series of fortunate circumstances William enjoyed great freedom in his childhood and youth. His mother allowed the children to make their own amusements. After her death he was sent to the Grammar School at Hawkshead. There he and his brothers had lodgings in the cottage of Ann Tyson, who seems to have permitted her charges to roam the fells or wander round Esthwaite Water at any hour of the night. The house in Hawkshead known to generations of tourists as 'Ann Tyson's Cottage' was for long believed to be where William lodged. But Beatrix Potter (the writer of children's stories such as *The Tale of Peter Rabbit*) discovered that Wordsworth's descriptions of the cottage and its sur-roundings do not fit this site. The Tysons at some point moved out to a cottage in the nearby hamlet of Colthouse and boarded the schoolboys there. Wordsworth was profoundly thankful for the early freedom he enjoyed. His poetic gift could never have developed, he declared, if in childhood 'We had been followed, hourly watched, and noosed' (*Prelude*,

V, 238). He was doubly grateful, firstly that he had been brought up in an area of such scenic beauty as the Lake District, and secondly that

From the restraint of over-watchful eyes
Preserved, I moved about, year after year,
Happy . . .   (*Prelude*, VIII, lines 328–30)

The tracking of Wordsworth's inner life is the main substance of some of his best poetry. But a few details of his external circumstances need to be known if this record is to be understood. The orphaned children were naturally much thrown on the hands of uncles and aunts. The maternal relations at Penrith were not sympathetic to William, and he seems to have endured much misery when staying there. Nevertheless the childhood he looks back upon in his later years is a happy one, often blissfully so. The five-year-old infant at Cockermouth, with the towering mass of Skiddaw and the Lake District mountains visible to the east and the river Derwent running along the bottom of the garden, sometimes 'Made one long bathing of a summer's day' (*Prelude*, I, 290). The schoolboy at Hawkshead loved boating, fishing, skating, riding, and roaming the hills half the night, snaring woodcock or just marvelling at the stars.

When Wordsworth went up to St John's College, Cambridge, in 1787, his relations naturally expected him to be ordained or to enter a profession. In fact he sat lightly to his academic studies, and not less significant than these in his development as a poet were his lonely walks and his vacation tours. One of these took him with Robert Jones to France and Switzerland in 1790. He returned to France in 1791–2 to become a warm friend of Michael Beaupuy, an officer of good family who put himself at loggerheads with his companions by his enthusiasm for the Revolution. Wordsworth was swept into a mood of exultant rapture by the aspirations of the early reformers and their seeming determination to abolish poverty and injustice, and to bring in an age of universal brotherhood and peace. He was also swept off his feet by a sudden passion for Annette Vallon, the twenty-five-year-old daughter of a surgeon and member of a firmly royalist family. It seems that Wordsworth intended to marry her, but it became unsafe for him to linger in France; he returned to England, probably in November 1792, and Annette bore his child, Caroline, in December. England's declaration of war against France in February 1793 broke off communication between the lovers. Such was the status of Wordsworth on his death in 1850, a pillar of godly respectability, that his family suppressed all material information about his youthful escapade and his illegitimate daughter. Only in our own century has the story been brought to light. Wordsworth himself practised no concealment. He and his sister Dorothy paid a month-long visit to Calais to meet Annette and Caroline nearly ten years later in 1802, just before his marriage.

One of the remarkable things about the Romantic poets, Wordsworth, Coleridge, Shelley, and Byron, is the extent to which they moved about. All four of them had extensive experience of life on the Continent, and were in varying degrees sensitive to the influence of writers such as Rousseau and Goethe. We tend to picture Wordsworth leading a settled existence in the Lake District, enjoying the scenery and writing verse. In fact he was over thirty before he went to live at Grasmere, and even then he continued to be frequently on the move. A crucial relationship was that with Samuel Taylor Coleridge (1772–1834). The intimacy began in 1797–8, when Wordsworth and his sister Dorothy were staying near Coleridge's cottage at Nether Stowey, Somerset. The two poets went to Germany together in the winter of 1798–9. The friendship continued after Wordsworth made the great decision of his life, in 1799, to settle at Dove Cottage, Grasmere, with Dorothy and to devote himself to poetry. This decision was made possible by the generosity of a friend, Raisley Calvert of Windybrow, Keswick, who died early of consumption and left Wordsworth £900 capital because he believed in the young poet's vocation and his need for independence. Coleridge followed Wordsworth north, settling at Greta Hall, Keswick. This fine house represented a totally different social position from that represented by the modest cottage at Grasmere. The twelve miles between Keswick and Grasmere were frequently trodden as the two poets visited each other.

Wordsworth married Mary Hutchinson in 1802. She joined William and Dorothy at Dove Cottage, the limited accommodation of which must often have been stretched to near breaking-point. Sara Hutchinson visited her sister there. Scott, as well as Coleridge, were among those who sampled the hospitality of the cottage. So frugal were the meals that Scott was driven to stick a chair under the door knob of his bedroom, climb out of the window, and dash up to the Swan Inn for a supplementary breakfast.

The gathering of literary personalities in the Lake District became a celebrated feature of the Romantic movement. Southey and Coleridge had married sisters, Edith and Sara Fricker, and the Southeys eventually moved into Greta Hall alongside the Coleridges. But the tale of Coleridge's relationship with Wordsworth ceased eventually to be a happy one. Coleridge's marriage to Sara Fricker did not suit him for long. Sara seems to have been the ideal wife for a conventionally steady and respectable husband such as Coleridge could never be. The constant interchange of visits between Coleridge and the Wordsworths left her by choice and temperament out in the cold. To make matters worse Coleridge fell deeply in love with Mary Wordsworth's sister, Sara Hutchinson. The emotional cross-currents disturbing the Wordsworths and the Coleridges were thus at times intense. The mutual devotion between Wordsworth and Dorothy itself involved a rare degree of fervour and, on Dorothy's part, of possessiveness. On William's wedding day she hid herself in her room miserably. That she and Mary became such firm friends is testimony to the fundamental good sense and integrity of both. Of course they had a common aim in ministering to William's needs — and Sara Hutchinson was happy to make a third in this ministry. No literary man was ever served more devoutly. 'I saw him,' Coleridge wrote, 'living wholly among *Devotees* — having every the minutest Thing, almost his very eating and drinking, done for him by his Sister or Wife.'

Though Coleridge and Wordsworth held each other in high regard and were a source of inspiration to each other, Coleridge's habits as a guest eventually put an intolerable strain on those who gave him hospitality. As he grew more dependent upon opium and, to counter its effects, upon brandy, indolence and moodiness possessed him. He indulged in jealousies and imaginary slights. No doubt at bottom he was deeply envious of the devotion Wordsworth received from his womenfolk. In 1810 the friendship was broken for a time by his resentment.

Five children were born to the Wordsworths in the first seven years of their marriage, two girls and three boys. The growing family necessitated a move from Dove Cottage in 1809, and after a few years at two different addresses in Grasmere, the Wordsworths moved in 1814 to Rydal Mount where William and Mary lived for the rest of their lives. Wordsworth's financial position was made more secure in 1813 when he was given the office of Distributor of Stamps for Westmorland, a post which involved exercising control over the collection of Inland Revenue. The couple had their share of grief, losing two children in childhood and their daughter Dora, by then married, in her early forties. Dorothy's health began to fail in 1829, and six years later her mind gave way. For twenty years she lingered, hugging a warm fire throughout the year, sometimes taxingly querulous, sometimes contentedly calm. She died in 1855, five years after William.

Wordsworth's thirty-six years at Rydal Mount turned him into a national institution. The young radical of the turn of the century became the literary patriarch of the early Victorians. Tourists walked round his grounds. Sometimes as many as five sets of visitors might call in one morning. He became Poet Laureate on the death of Southey in 1843, and by April 1845 he could be seen as a guest at the Queen's Fancy Ball in cocked hat and full court dress, a sword at his side. But only those who have not studied carefully the development of the poet's thinking and the impact upon it of contemporary events and personalities would be tempted to mock the transformation of the young radical into the aged conservative.

Nevertheless the great poetry belongs mostly to the earlier years. The intimacy with Coleridge in the late 1790s sparked off a burst of rich productivity. Coleridge had already made a friend of Southey. Indeed the two of them had planned to establish a 'Pantisocracy' in America. The idealistic purpose was that a dozen men and women should go and set up a communistic colony in which a minimum of necessary work equally shared would support them, leaving plenty of time for talk, study, and education. (The delicate question whether to allow divorce by consent had not been settled.) The one practical upshot of this collaboration was that Coleridge made the mistake of marrying Southey's sister-in-law Sara Fricker. Coleridge's connection with what was regarded as a dangerous Jacobin circle led to rumours which the odd wandering habits of the Wordsworths strengthened, and the Home Office sent a spy, Walsh, to observe the activities of the suspicious companions.

The mutual admiration and affection that warmed the hearts of Wordsworth, Coleridge, and Dorothy as they talked and rambled together stimulated both poets, and they collaborated in the publication of *Lyrical Ballads* in 1798. The collection includes poems by Wordsworth which were intended as 'a natural delineation of human passions, human characters, and human incidents', and substituted a 'language of conversation in the middle and lower classes of society' for 'the gaudiness and inane phraseology' of much contemporary verse. So Wordsworth wrote in the Advertisement to the first edition.

There are narrative poems of country life of ballad-like simplicity. 'The Idiot Boy' tells the story of Betty Foy's distress when her sick neighbour, Susan Gale, is in grave need of a doctor one night in March. Unwilling to leave the invalid's bedside, Betty adopts the desperate expedient of sending her loved idiot son on his pony to fetch the doctor. The boy is incapable of comprehending his mission. When Johnny fails to return by the early hours, Betty's worry about him sends her running out in search of him. Eventually reaching the doctor's door, she knocks him up to ask whether her son has been there. The mother's distress is now such that she completely forgets the original mission and makes no mention of Susan Gale's illness. Returning to her search, she at last sees the pony feeding perilously near a waterfall with Johnny on its back.

> She looks again — her arms are up —
> She screams — she cannot move for joy;
> She darts, as with a torrent's force,
> She almost has o'erturned the Horse,
> And fast she holds her Idiot Boy.

The most ironic touch of all, however, is provided by Susan Gale. So worried in mind has she been for Betty and her son that the sickness is forgotten. She gets up to search for them and meets them in a joyous reunion.

In contrast to the sunniness ultimately lighting this tale of trouble, a pall of gloom hangs over 'The Thorn', which tells how a seduced and betrayed girl was left pregnant. No one knows whether a child was born alive or dead. But the girl, Martha Ray, repeatedly climbs up a mountain to cry 'Oh misery!' while sitting beside a thorn bush, a little pool, and a 'hill of moss' where villagers suspect the baby is buried.

The collection also contains two delightful poems, 'Expostulation and Reply' and 'The Tables Turned', in which the quiet drinking in of the influence of nature or exploration of her delights in field and wood are recommended as more fruitfully educative than book-learning.

> One impulse from a vernal wood
> May teach you more of man,
> Of moral evil and of good,
> Than all the sages can.   ('The Tables Turned')

But the most astonishingly mature poetic achievement in *Lyrical Ballads* is 'Lines composed a few miles above Tintern Abbey on revisiting the banks of the Wye during a tour, July 13, 1798'. The second visit after a space of five years causes the poet to look back. He realises that recollections of the previous visit have nourished him restoratively in inner tranquillity and indeed in mystical suspension of physical pressures and self-consciousness. Thus he is aware now that, looking again at the scene, he is storing up resources of 'life and food / For future years'. A survey of his own development in response to nature then follows, which was to be explored with greater depth and detail in later works. There was a time in childhood when nature's forms and colours were in themselves a satisfaction, a passion, and a rapture of unreflecting intensity. Then he began to hear in nature's presence 'the still sad music of humanity', chastening and quietening his responsiveness. Moreover, he became conscious of a seemingly divine presence in nature, dwelling in sky and sea and sunset and in the human mind too. Thus he now recognises in sensitivity to the natural world an anchorage for personal integrity. Indeed 'Nature never did betray / The heart that loved her'. She can strengthen us in a 'cheerful faith' in ultimate goodness, invulnerable to the evidence of human selfishness, malice, scorn, or the tedium of daily life.

The blank verse of 'Tintern Abbey' has a naturalness, a dignity, and a fluency that show Wordsworth at his best. Whether he is picturing a scene, defining his inner responses, or analysing the subtleties in the relationship of man to his natural environment, his grasp of vocabulary and cadence remains sure and unfaltering.

When a second edition of *Lyrical Ballads* was called for and came out in 1800, Wordsworth wrote an extended Preface defending his attempt to write verse using 'the real language of men in a state of vivid sensation' and describing 'incidents and situations from common life'. 'Humble and rustic life was generally chosen, because, in that condition, the essential passions of the heart find a better soil in which they can attain their maturity, are less under restraint, and speak a plainer and more emphatic language.' He defends his work against charges of triviality and meanness, arguing the primacy of moral purpose. 'All good poetry is the spontaneous overflow of powerful feelings,' Wordsworth declares, and presents a lofty view of the poet's vocation. 'He is a man speaking to men'; but a man possessing more than ordinary sensibility, enthusiasm, tenderness, knowledge of human nature, and indeed having 'a more comprehensive soul'. He is not just a man of rare imaginative creativity and capacity for self-expression; he is also a man 'pleased with his own passions and volitions, and who rejoices more than other men in the spirit of life that is in him'. 'Poetry is the breath and finer spirit of all knowledge . . . it is as immortal as the heart of man.'

Wordsworth early arrived at a lofty concept of his own poetic vocation, and he never lacked knowledgeable acquaintances to corroborate his confident aspirations. Coleridge pressed him to undertake a masterpiece, Raisley Calvert left him money to pursue his calling; later Sir George Beaumont gave him an estate near Keswick. We may doubt whether there was ever any great artist more blessed in the mental and material support he received from his nearest and dearest and from sympathetic admirers. It would be easy to mock the adulation, but it was a remarkable integrity of personality and purpose that called it out and indeed that ultimately fully justified it.

The gems of Wordsworth's output are scattered over a wide variety of poems, but it is *The Prelude* that takes us to the heart of his personality and his vocation, and, ironically enough, it was published only posthumously. Wordsworth planned a long philosophical poem, 'The Recluse'. In preparation for the task he set about tracing his own development in an introductory poem. From this vast project what emerged was *The Excursion* (1814) and *The Prelude* (1850), the latter being the preparatory autobiographical survey which had been expanded to the proportions of an epic in fourteen books.

The Prelude is an uneven work, but its finest passages have a rare vividness in narrative and self-exploration. Books I and II deal with childhood and school-time. Wordsworth tells how he was 'fostered alike by beauty and by fear', for when as a boy he stole a bird from someone else's trap at night he heard 'low breathings' and footsteps pursuing him among the hills, and when he slyly borrowed a boat to row out over Ullswater a huge black peak towered threateningly between him and the stars, and strode after him 'like a living thing'. Wordsworth records how nature, at first an incidental source of background pleasure to his boyish games, became a direct delight to his senses and his mind. It gave him moments of half-realised rapture which stimulated spiritual aspiration. Moreover, from a source of imaginative energy in himself he conferred 'new splendour' on external things. In climax he experienced a sense of mystical communion with the created world in adoration and love of the Uncreated.

The Prelude is not a tidily organised autobiography. It is not in arrangement an orderly historical record. It reflects the manner of its composition, for Wordsworth worked at it intermittently, drawing into it what seemed relevant. He returns to childhood memories, for instance, in Book V and Book XII. Nevertheless there is a rough chronological progress through successive books, 'Residence at Cambridge' (Book III), 'Summer Vacation' (IV), 'Books' (V), 'Cambridge and the Alps' (VI), and 'Residence in London' (VII). Books IX, X, and XI cover Wordsworth's experiences in France. He records how he welcomed the Revolution as a movement which could put an end to poverty and injustice:

> All institutes for ever blotted out
> That legalised exclusion, empty pomp
> Abolished, sensual state and cruel power,
> Whether by edict of the one or few.　　　　　(IX, lines 525–8)

On his return to England, war was declared on France, and Wordsworth found himself rejoicing in defeats inflicted on his countrymen. A forceful account of the Terror succeeds, and disillusionment sets in, not with the principles of the Revolution but with the treachery to them. The rise of Napoleon completes his disillusionment. Wordsworth, who on the outbreak of the Revolution had cried:

> Bliss was it in that dawn to be alive,
> But to be young was very Heaven!　　　　　(XI, lines 108–9)

sees a Pope summoned to crown an emperor. The French people

> That once looked up in faith, as up to Heaven
> For manna, take a lesson from the dog
> Returning to his vomit.　　　　　(XI, lines 362–4)

The last three books of The Prelude record how Wordsworth's lost faith and balance were restored to him by the influence of his sister Dorothy and in renewed sensitivity to nature. And he dedicates himself to explore:

> How oft high service is performed within,
> When all the external man is rude in show.　　　　　(XIII, lines 227–8)

The Prelude was addressed to Coleridge, who repeatedly urged Words-worth to work on his magnum opus. The Excursion cannot but disappoint if The Prelude is really taken seriously as an introduction to it. Its nine books present a loosely constructed sequence built around three characters, the speaking Poet, the Wanderer, and the Solitary. The Poet joins the Wanderer, a philosophically minded man of quiet faith, independence, and individuality, who has chosen to spend his life as a pedlar in close contact with the living world of nature and with the simple folk he serves. He introduces the Poet in particular to the Solitary, a man whose early good fortune was destroyed by the death of his wife and who has turned sour and cynical. The conversations between these three are extended, and the argument against the Solitary is further strengthened when the Village Pastor joins their discourse. It soon becomes evident to the reader that the Poet, the Wanderer, and the Solitary are but three projections of William Wordsworth, recording various aspects of his experience and his thought. The most impressive section of the work is the story of Margaret in Book I. Her worthy, hard-working husband, a cottage-weaver, is broken in health, then ruined by a period of famine, of war, and of failing demand for his work. The couple have two children, but poverty ruins the man's temper, and one day he disappears to join the army. The elder child goes to work on a farm, the younger one, a baby, dies. Dispirited by years of waiting for her husband's return, Magaret becomes abstracted and inconsolable. The cottage and garden decay by neglect, and she dies. The episode breathes a deeply felt sympathy and carries a forceful social message through the sheer undemonstrativeness of its telling.

Wordsworth achieved excellence in many different poetic genres. His 'Ode: Intimations of Immortality from Recollections of Early Childhood' (1807) handles the elaborately structured form with an ease and freshness that testify to sheer virtuosity. The poem is at once a bright celebration of childhood and an acutely penetrating investigation into what the growing boy's gradual, and often tentative, adjustment to his environment signifies. The 'visionary gleam', the 'glory and the dream', tasted in nature in our earliest days and then lost, testify to the loosening of contacts with our eternal origin.

> But trailing clouds of glory do we come
> From God, who is our home.

The child has to acquire, under nature's guidance, an adaptability to his new world, and one may wonder at his eagerness to embrace its shackles. Nevertheless Wordsworth bursts into joy at the recollection of the child's early faltering contact with his new world, for it evidences his lingering hold on his eternal origins.

Far different in temper and technique are the poems in which simple encounters and incidents in rural life provoke moral reflections on the human lot. In 'Resolution and Independence' (1807), for instance, the poet tells how a bright morning followed a stormy night and he walked on the moor in high spirits until a sudden change of mood overtook him. Through indulging joy in his own well-being he is led to reflect on the price poets have seemingly paid later in life for their early raptures.

Chatterton (who committed suicide at the age of eighteen) and Robert Burns come to mind:

We Poets in our youth begin in gladness;
But thereof come in the end despondency and madness.

In this disturbed state of mind the poet comes across an extremely aged and bent man, leaning on a staff and staring into a moorland pool. He is a leech-gatherer, making what he can from roaming the moors, and finding shelter where he may. Leeches have lately become much harder to come by, the man says, but he struggles on as best he can. His cheerfulness and kindness cause the poet to laugh himself to scorn for his self-indulgent worries. In 'Michael' a touching narrative unfolds from the description of a heap of stones in Greenhead Ghyll above Grasmere. They are the remains of a half-built sheepfold to which attaches the story of Michael, a simple shepherd, his wife, and son. They lived in calm toil and contentment until they were suddenly ruined by Michael's long-standing financial guarantee of a nephew who had failed. Michael's attachment to his fields is such that he cannot bear to mortgage land. The only recourse is for their loved son Luke to go and earn money elsewhere. Luke falls into evil ways in the city, and his father's heart is broken. The sheepfold they started to build together is never completed. The old couple die and the estate is sold. The social message here is again all the more forceful for being unuttered. In blank verse of rare directness and limpidity the moving human drama is unfolded, and the reader is left to his reflections.

If Wordsworth is one of our great narrative poets, our great philosophical poets, and our great lyrical poets, he is also one of our great sonneteers. Outside the works of Shakespeare and Milton there is nothing to match the blend of dignity and feeling, of flexibility and fervour, achieved by Wordsworth in the sonnet form. There are sonnets of description such as the one composed on Westminster Bridge in 1802 ('Earth hath not anything to show more fair'). It has that strange potency which permeates verse where every phrase, every word, once received, seems inevitable. There are sonnets lamenting the current national materialism ('The world is too much with us', published in 1807) and selfishness ('Milton! thou shouldst be living at this hour', written in 1802). There are times when personal emotion breaks through with irresistibly unaffected frankness, as in 'It is a beauteous evening, calm and free', recording a seashore walk at Calais with his daughter Caroline. There are more public sonnets commenting on recent history, such as 'I grieved for Buonaparte' (1802).

To pick out such shining examples of Wordsworth's skill with the sonnet is to remind ourselves that the same poet wrote 132 'Ecclesiastical Sonnets' tracing the history of Christianity in Britain in three parts, and bearing all the marks of a mechanical determination to write whether inspired or no. But the proportion of first-rate poems in Wordsworth's total production, if calculated arithmetically, would present a misleading picture, for Wordsworth's total production was so vast. No reader can survey his work without recalling numerous poems that clamour for attention as treasures of our literary inheritance. We have scarcely touched here on the mass of lyrics recording Wordsworth's responsiveness to the natural scene and to those who live close to it. There are many which, once known, can never be forgotten: 'My heart leaps up when I behold / A rainbow in the sky' or 'Behold her, single in the field, / Yon solitary Highland Lass' or 'I wandered lonely as a cloud' . . . such poems keep their freshness, however often repeated. In these, and in the group of poems about 'Lucy', elemental feelings are stirred to the depths as the magic and the insight reach us through language of unaffected simplicity and cadences of irresistible grace.

Samuel Taylor Coleridge

Wordsworth's sister Dorothy was a perceptive and vital influence upon both her brother and Samuel Taylor Coleridge (1772–1834). The nature of this influence can be detected here and there in the work of both poets, for critics have put their fingers on observant descriptive touches in their poems which can be paralleled in Dorothy Wordsworth's *Journals* or in her Letters. 'She gave me eyes, she gave me ears,' Wordsworth said of her. Though Coleridge's heart was given to Sara Hutchinson, there is no doubt that he and Dorothy shared a deep mutual sympathy and under-standing. And although Dorothy's frequent references to him in her *Journal* and in her Letters naturally veil her friend's failings, they show how much suffering Coleridge's failings caused those who loved him.

Like Wordsworth, Coleridge early stirred up admiration for his gifts. He too was the recipient of practical help in the form of an annuity granted him by Thomas and Josiah Wedgwood. The son of the vicar of Ottery St Mary in Devonshire — his thirteenth offspring and the third of his second marriage — Coleridge lost his father at the age of eight and was sent off to school at Christ's Hospital, where Charles Lamb was an admiring fellow-pupil. From there Coleridge went to Jesus College, Cambridge, but two years later suddenly enlisted as a dragoon (calling himself 'Silas Tomkyn Comberbacke') and had to be bought out of this totally unsuitable career by his elder brother. A meeting with Southey led to a walking tour with him in Wales and to the excited plan to establish a Pantisocracy. Twelve 'gentlemen' and twelve 'ladies' were to embark for America. Adam Smith had argued that there is only one productive man in every twenty. The logical deduction was that if each of them worked a twentieth part of the time, there would be enough produce to meet all the colony's needs. The young idealists had not got to the stage of formulating what should be the exact regulations governing the commerce of the two sexes in this communistic society. Coleridge's unfortunate marriage to Sara Fricker blighted his life in one respect. In another respect recourse to opium, at first as an escape from toothache and other pains, and to brandy as a counter-stimulant, also blighted his life.

From residence in Bristol where Southey lived, and at Nether Stowey in Somerset where the friendship with Wordsworth flourished, Coleridge moved in 1800 to Greta Hall, Keswick. This large house, which at first he shared with its builder, was shared with Southey from 1803. The two families formed a lively household, but Coleridge could not for long live comfortably with his wife; he went to London in 1801, stayed then for periods with the Wordsworths, and in 1804 departed for Malta. He went in search of health, but packed a plentiful supply of opium. He reached Valetta in April, and served for a year or so as secretary to the Governor, Sir Alexander Ball. Neither the work nor the social scene proved congenial enough to weaken Coleridge's addiction, and he left Malta for Italy in September 1805. After some months in Rome, during which he was advised that articles he had written about Napoleon for the *Morning Post* rendered him an object of official suspicion, he sailed home and was back in England by August 1806. His subsequent wanderings included further periods of time spent with the Wordsworths, and he finally came to rest in 1816 at Highgate, in the house of a physician, James Gillman, who looked after him till his death.

'No man was ever yet a great poet,' Coleridge averred, 'without being at the same time a great philosopher.' Coleridge's literary theory gave the same lofty status to the poet that the theories of Wordsworth and Shelley did. That is an aspect of his 'romanticism', as is his emphasis on what he called the 'esemplastic' power of imagination, by which he meant its capacity to mould material into a unity. Alongside the inspirational insight and enthusiasm Coleridge brought to the study of poetry, there is a unique precision in his analytical method, nowhere more obvious than in his study of Wordsworth's poetry in his *Biographia Literaria* (1817). He categorises Wordsworth's qualities as 'purity of language', 'weight and sanity of Thoughts and Sentiments', 'the sinewy strength and originality of single lines and paragraphs', 'perfect truth to nature' in image and description, the human sympathy and sensibility which accompany his 'deep and subtle thought', and above all the sheer 'imaginative power' which links him with Shakespeare and Milton. Coleridge also lists Wordsworth's defects as an occasional '*inconstancy*' (incongruity) of style, a laboriously detailed '*matter-of-factness* in certain poems', 'an undue predilection for the *dramatic* form' in certain poems, where sometimes only the poet is thinking 'and then it presents a species of ventriloquism', prolixity and repetition arising from 'intensity of feeling disproportionate' to the subject, and finally what Coleridge calls 'mental' (as opposed to verbal) 'bombast' — 'a disproportion of thought to the circumstance and occasion'. 'This, by the bye,' Coleridge adds, 'is a fault of which none but a man of genius is capable.'

Thus Coleridge combines qualities of analytical subtlety, of imaginative sensitivity, and of philosophical grasp which give him a place among the most distinguished of England's literary critics.

It was contact with Wordsworth which inspired Coleridge the poet to his finest work. The plan for the *Lyrical Ballads*, Coleridge tells us in *Biographia Literaria*, was that he should tackle subjects 'in part at least supernatural' while Wordsworth dealt with subjects 'chosen from ordinary life'. Coleridge's 'Rime of the Ancient Mariner' is much the longest poem in the volume. In ballad form the mariner tells how his ship was driven by storm into desolate Antarctica. An albatross comes flying through the fog like a messenger of hope. The sailors feed it, the ice splits, a south wind springs up, and the ship returns northward with the bird accompanying them. The mariner shoots the bird and a dreadful retribution follows. The ship is becalmed in the Pacific.

Day after day, day after day,
We stuck, nor breath nor motion;
As idle as a painted ship
Upon a painted ocean.

There is water everywhere, but not a drop to drink. The crew, parched with thirst, hang the dead albatross around the mariner's neck. The mariner sees a spectral ship approaching, and the crew are at first delighted. But horror soon returns. How can a ship sail steadily towards them thus without breeze or tide? In fact it is a skeleton ship with a crew of two, Death and Life-in-Death. They cast dice, and it is Life-in-Death who wins the mariner. One after another his crewmates drop down dead with a silent curse upon the mariner. Their souls fly away audibly. The solitary agony of the mariner takes a turn when he sees water-snakes gambolling in the sea, and he is stirred to bestow an unconscious blessing upon them. He finds he can pray; the dead bird drops from his neck. He sleeps, and then it rains. A storm breaks, and in the tumult the dead crew rise and manage the ship, corpses indwelt by angelic spirits who sing sweetly. Eventually the mariner reaches home, but the curse remains with him in that he must wander ever after from land to land, seizing upon people and compelling them to hear his tale.

'The Ancient Mariner' is one of the most vivid, most unforgettable poems in the language. Had Coleridge written nothing else it would have given him the status of a poetic genius. The compulsive rhythmic pulse of the verse, the bold clarity of the descriptive imagery, the unnervingly adept atmospheric manipulation of the weird, the awesome, and the uncanny, together with a sure dramatic power revealed in narrative presentation, will always make readers marvel at Coleridge's gifts.

This mastery of rhythm and of atmosphere was to emerge again in his unfinished poem 'Christabel', in which Coleridge exploited four-foot lines with a maximum of syllabic freedom and variety. The poem tells the story of Lady Christabel. Her mother has died, and a seeming enchantress, Geraldine, lays a spell on her. The background is a rich tapestry of medievalism ('romanticised medievalism') such as Keats exploited in 'The Eve of St Agnes'. Christabel encounters Geraldine in the forest, a maid supposedly torn from home by ruffian knights, and takes her home for safety. Ominous events alert the reader: the howl of the castle dog and Geraldine's inability to cross the threshold without being lifted over it, not to mention her appearance when she undresses:

Behold! her bosom and half her side —
A sight to dream of, not to tell!
O shield her! shield sweet Christabel.

Soon it is clear that Geraldine is possessed. Part I of the poem has all the charm of subtly managed archaism and suggestive preternaturalism. But in Part II, when the story develops more naturalistically into one based on a past quarrel between Christabel's father, Sir Lionel, and Geraldine's father, Lord Roland de Vaux of Tryermaine, the incantatory spell of the first part, strongly dependent as it is on the suggestive and the undefined, is less surely sustained.

Another even more remarkable fragment is 'Kubla Khan'. One day in Somerset in 1797 Coleridge fell asleep under the influence of opium while he was reading *Purchas his Pilgrimage*. When he awoke he realised that he had composed a poem in his sleep. He began to write it down, but was interrupted by a 'person from Porlock', whose visit drove the rest of the poem from his memory. The fragment we have has the same compulsive fluency as the best of 'Christabel' and 'The Ancient Mariner'.

In Xanadu did Kubla Khan
A stately pleasure-dome decree:
Where Alph, the sacred river ran
Through caverns measureless to man
Down to a sunless sea.

A series of vivid archetypal pictures follows, of chasm and fountain and river and 'a damsel with a dulcimer', the whole shot through with streaks of verbal paintwork mesmeric in their colourfulness.

The impact of these three visionary poems has naturally detracted attention from Coleridge's more sober output. But there is a handful of poems which bring one close to Coleridge in his own proper person with touching directness. There is 'Frost at Midnight', 'This Lime-tree Bower my Prison', and above all the harrowing 'Dejection; an Ode', a call *de profundis* with a personal appeal to Sara Hutchinson.

Robert Southey

Robert Southey (1774–1843) had something of Coleridge's youthful pre-cocity. In his early teens he planned to finish Spenser's *Faerie Queene*, studied the text for evidence of how it should be done, and wrote three cantos accordingly. He was a precocious rebel too, taking up the ideals of the French Revolution and getting himself expelled from Westminster School for publishing an attack on flogging. It was in a mood of disillusionment with English society that he planned the Pantisocracy with Coleridge. He also wrote a brief radical play, *Wat Tyler*, which his enemies resuscitated to his distress in 1817, long after his views had changed. It is impossible not to feel sympathy for Southey. After he settled in Keswick in 1803 he soon found himself responsible for Cole-ridge's family as well as his own, and worked arduously with his pen to support them. He may have lost his youthful radicalism, and he was made Poet Laureate in 1813, but he was no time-serving opportunist. In his time he turned down a lucrative post on *The Times*, a seat in Parliament, and a baronetcy offered by Sir Robert Peel.

Southey's massive narrative poems won praise in his own day, but their reputation has not survived him. *Thalaba the Destroyer* (1801) tells of a courageous Arabian hero and his perilous quest to destroy a race of evil magicians. It is a tale of victory won at the cost of the hero's life. *Madoc* (1805) traces the career of a medieval Welsh prince who takes a body of emigrants to America and has fierce battles with the Aztecs. *The Curse of Kehama* (1810) derives from Southey's study of Hindu mythology. The evil Raja Kehama's son, Arvalan, is killed by Ladurlad, the father of a peasant girl he has tried to rape. Kehama in revenge condemns Ladurlad to a life of torment and to permanent immunity from death that might end it. As in *Madoc*, it is only in the after-life that the good and the evil fully reap their due reward. *Roderick, the Last of the Goths* (1814) tells how Count Julian called upon the Moors for vengeance when King Roderick raped his daughter. This brought about the eighth-century Moorish invasion and conquest of Spain. (See the later reference to Landor's play on this subject.)

Southey's exotic tales are presented in elaborate stanzas with a surface vigour of rhythm and rhetoric which somehow fails to ring consistently true. There is a lot of noisy language and feverish declamation, a great deal of manufactured urgency and excitement, yet the lines stay obstinately cold on the page. Southey seems to be trying too hard, though in fact he was a writer of excessively alert sensitivity, to whom composition was costly in nervous tension. His heart would throb and his face would burn as he penned the lines we judge so coolly. It is all the more ironic that the poems do not register a felt personal involvement of the poet with his characters.

If these extravagant epics, by their far-off backgrounds, their large-scale heroic adventures, and their supernatural dimensions, display one aspect of Southey's Romanticism, he also wrote verses of simple homely directness which illustrate a converse aspect of Romanticism. Indeed his verses 'After Blenheim' have never lost their appeal. In simple ballad form an evening dialogue is conducted between old Kaspar and his two little grandchildren, Peterkin and Wilhelmine. The children have turned up in their play what Kaspar recognises as a skull left over from the battle of Blenheim — 'the great victory'. The innocent questions of the children about the battle, its cause, its evident wickedness, and its fruitlessness, probe so deeply that Kaspar's reiterated 'It was a famous victory' acquires devastating ironic overtones. The other gem of Southey's to last — though in a bowdlerised form — is his children's story of the Three Bears whose home is invaded, in Southey by an old woman, in the now current version by 'Goldilocks'. These two still popular pieces demonstrate Southey's imaginative range, but it was largely history and biography, journals and essays, polemic and translation which kept the wolf from the door of Greta Hall. Of this vast output *The Life of Nelson* (1818) is still read.

Southey's most disastrous mistake was, as Laureate, to overdo things in his poem on George III's death, *A Vision of Judgment* (1821). He prefaced his poem with an attack on the 'Satanic school' of contemporary poets for their lasciviousness, their audacity, arrogance, and impiety. Southey's main target was Byron, for whose satiric wit the poem provided ideal material to ridicule. See, for instance, Southey's account of George III's entry into heaven.

Lift up your heads, ye Gates; and ye everlasting Portals,
Be ye lift up! For lo! a glorified Monarch approacheth,
One who in righteousness reign'd, and religiously govern'd his people.
Who are these that await him within . . .?

Who indeed? None other than William III, Charles I, Elizabeth, Edward VI, the Black Prince, Edward III, Richard I, and Alfred the Great.

Byron took his revenge and found a weak spot in Southey's shift from youthful radicalism to Toryism.

He had written praises of a regicide;
He had written praises of all kings whatever;
He had written for republics far and wide,
And then against them bitterer than ever.

For pantisocracy he once had cried
Aloud, a scheme less moral than 'twas clever;
Then grew a hearty anti-jacobin —
And turn'd his coat — and would have turn'd his skin.

(The Vision of Judgment)

Sir Walter Scott

Sir Walter Scott (1771–1832) reviewed Southey's *The Curse of Kehama* for the *Quarterly Review* and told George Ellis (1753–1815) in a letter that he had done his best to draw attention to the 'beautiful passages' and 'to slur over the absurdities'. He thought the poem offered 'cruel openings' for hostile critics. Ellis had translated some Middle English verse in *Early English Metrical Romances* (1805) about the same time that Scott's *Minstrelsy of the Scottish Border* (1802–3) came out in three volumes. Percy's *Reliques* had set Scott off exploring the Border country and collecting at first hand ballads preserved only in oral tradition. Scott (whom as a novelist we shall consider more thoroughly in a later section) then turned to original verse with its roots in ancient balladry.

The Lay of the Last Minstrel (1805) is a narrative poem in six cantos with a total of about 3000 lines. The tale is told by an aged 'last minstrel'. Set in the sixteenth century, it is a complex story of feud and combat, of disguise and trickery, and of love across the barriers of enmity. The lofty atmosphere is spiced with a supernatural theme concerning a magic book buried at Melrose Abbey in the tomb of Michael Scott, the wizard. The form which Scott adopted is the rhyming four-foot line, made flexible by the maximum variety in the number of syllables.

The feast was over in Branksome tower,
And the Ladye had gone to her secret bower,
Her bower that was guarded by word and by spell,
Deadly to hear, and deadly to tell —
Jesus Maria, shield us well!
No living wight, save the Ladye alone,
Had dared to cross the threshold stone.

This is in fact the metrical system adopted by Coleridge in 'Christabel', and indeed it has come to be known as the 'Christabel metre'. Coleridge did not publish 'Christabel' until 1816, long after the composition of the *Lay*, but it is known that Scott had heard the first part of 'Christabel' read aloud before he began to write his poem, and Lockhart records that he was inspired by its 'music' to use a 'similar cadence'. Scott himself argued on the basis of Pope's translation of Homer's *Iliad* that four-foot lines might be more natural to English, since English pentameters (five-foot lines) often contained an unnecessary foot.

Achilles' wrath to Greece, the *direful* spring
Of woes unnumbered, *heavenly* goddess, sing.

Scott argued that scrapping the fifth foot, represented by the italicised adjectives, could remove a load of 'bolstering' and make the verse more 'forcible and animated'.

Scott's choice of metre certainly justified itself. The *Lay* was an immense success, and Scott exploited it by writing further narrative poems in the same genre. *Marmion* (1808) is set in the reign of Henry VIII. Marmion, an English nobleman who is capable of forgery and faithlessness, is finally killed at the battle of Flodden. A knight who disguises himself as a palmer, and a nun, Constance de Beverley, who has broken her vows in pursuit of her lover only to be walled up alive in her convent, add drama to what is generally agreed to be Scott's finest work in this field. Certainly the surge of the verse and the sweep of the action make some of the poem's peak passages powerfully impressive. The battle scenes are charged with vigour and excitement.

No thought was there of dastard flight;
Link'd in the serried phalanx tight,
Groom fought like noble, squire like knight
    As fearlessly and well;
Till utter darkness closed her wing
O'er their thin host and wounded King . . .

Scott seems to accomplish with maximum ease what Southey failed to accomplish with maximum effort and strain. He mined the vein again and again, in *The Lady of the Lake* (1810), *Rokeby* (1813), *The Bridal of Triermain* (1813), *The Lord of the Isles* (1815), and *Harold the Dauntless* (1817), and then surrendered the profitable field to Lord Byron. There are numerous incidental beauties in the narrative poems. They include noble outbursts such as:

Breathes there the man with soul so dead,
Who never to himself hath said,
'This is my own, my native land' . . .

which opens Canto VI of *The Lay*, touching and tender ballads such as 'Rosabelle', also in *The Lay*, and the stirring 'Lochinvar', as well as the song 'Where shall the lover rest' in *Marmion*. Poems such as these and fragments from the narratives at their best might in themselves have made the reputation of a major poet.

Lord Byron

It was only in the late Victorian age that Wordsworth came to be generally accepted as the archetypal Romantic poet. By being so recognised he displaced George Gordon Lord Byron (1788–1824) — at least in England. Byron's reputation on the Continent was and remains higher than his reputation at home. His career involved so much of the extraordinary and the sensational that no account can be given of it which does not sound extravagant. How far his behaviour can be accounted for by heredity and upbringing the psychologists must decide. On his father's side the Byrons seem to have had their fair share of rakes and roisterers. Captain Jack, his profligate father, ran quickly through two wives' fortunes. Augusta, Byron's stepsister, was the daughter of Jack Byron's first wife, Byron himself of the second. This second wife had plenty to complain about and found herself gravely reduced in circumstances when her husband died in 1792. Byron was then four years old. He had been born with a club foot, nurtured first by a hell-fire-breathing Calvinist nurse, and subjected by his unstable mother to alternate bouts of fawning caresses and furious insults, especially about his supposed resemblance to his father and about his lameness. Some critics have laid emphasis on the abnormalities of Byron's upbringing, his embarrassingly dislikeable mother especially, and explored teasing titbits of biographical information. For instance, when Byron was a child of nine his nurse's mature sister used to 'come to bed to him and play tricks with his person'. When he went from Harrow School to Cambridge, and later too, he formed passionate attachments to boys without any suggestion of homosexual practice. It has become fashionable therefore to speak in knowing terms about Byron's career of womanising as at once revenge upon womanhood and the effect of repressed homosexuality.

It seems more natural to assume that here was a handsome, over-sexed, gifted young aristocrat who, at a time of fashionable sexual laxity, was subject to few inhibitions, social or moral, and made the most of his opportunities until he was satiated. His biography indeed records a succession of occasions on which he fell in love and of other occasions when he believed he had fallen in love and in fact had not. The deaths first of a cousin, the direct heir, and then of his great-uncle, had turned him in 1798 into Baron Byron of Rochdale, with a romantic family seat at Newstead Abbey, Nottinghamshire. Mary Chaworth, a near neighbour, was an early object of his love. The number of women with whom he actually had liaisons was considerable. A most damaging affair was that with Lady Caroline Lamb, wife of William Lamb, the future Lord Melbourne and Queen Victoria's Prime Minister. Caroline was a self-willed individualist, headstrong and utterly careless of social convention. 'Mad, bad, and dangerous to know' she first wrote of Byron in her journal, but once he had conquered her, she was the madder, throwing discretion to the winds, and turning herself and Byron into the talk of fashionable London. Once when Byron was entertaining a rival she disguised herself as a carman to get inside his house and confront him.

When Byron began to grow tired of her, she could not reconcile herself to the loss and pursued him with an almost insane abandon.

The Byron whose affair with Caroline Lamb scandalised London society had become the literary lion of the year after the publication of *Childe Harold's Pilgrimage*, Cantos I and II, in 1812. For, after leaving Cambridge, Byron had embarked on a two-year continental tour (1809–11). This took him to Spain, Portugal, Malta, Greece, and Turkey. While going through the Dardanelles, Byron fulfilled a romantic ambition by swimming the Hellespont as Leander had swum it to be with Hero long ago. Though his lameness prevented him from dancing and kept him from many sports, he was proud of his accomplishments as a swimmer. The first cantos of *Childe Harold* were the literary product of this tour. Harold takes leave of England as one weary of dissipation:

> For he through Sin's long labyrinth had run,
> Nor made atonement when he did amiss.

He is something of an outcast, disillusioned with women, and afflicted by strange inner pangs. The moody pose and the bold rhetoric of description proved a recipe for instant popularity.

With this achievement behind him, Byron turned to challenge Scott as a narrative poet, offering a brand of romanticism shot through with veins of voluptuousness and oriental exoticism which the minstrel of the Border could not match. *The Giaour* (1813) tells in rhyming octosyllabics how the Turkish lord Hassan takes one of his harem, Leila, who is in love with the Giaour, and throws her, bound, into the sea to drown. The Giaour takes a bloody revenge on Hassan before entering a monastery to seek forgiveness and peace. ('Giaour' was a term used scornfully by Turks of Christians and other non-Moslems.) *The Bride of Abydos* (1813), another Turkish tale in the same metre, centres on Zuleika. Her father, a Pacha, determines that she shall marry a rich, ageing Bey she does not know. She seeks comfort from her beloved brother Selim, who reveals that he is really her cousin. Her father brought about his father's death by poison. He confesses his love for her but is killed by the Pacha. Zuleika dies of grief. (The implicit incest theme is to be noted.) In *The Corsair* (1814) Byron uses a longer, five-foot line to tell the story of Conrad, a pirate chief. He takes leave of his beloved Medora to set out from his island headquarters and forestall an attack upon it by the Turkish Pacha. He tries to pass himself off as a dervish escaping from the pirates, but when the Pacha's galleys are seen to be in flames he is recognised as a spy and imprisoned. The chief slave of the harem, Gulnare, falls in love with him and offers him the chance to plunge a dagger in the Pacha while he sleeps. When he refuses to do so dastardly an act, she kills the Pacha herself and escapes with Conrad, but back at the island Medora has died of grief, believing Conrad dead.

The Corsair has a particular interest in that it builds up to full proportions the figure of the Byronic hero, as already roughly sketched in the first two cantos of *Childe Harold* and in the figure of the Giaour. In Conrad there is little of conventional handsomeness. The high pale forehead, the profuse black hair, the rising and curling lip, the smooth voice and the surface facial charm all seem to be hiding something —

As if within that murkiness of mind
Work'd feelings fearful, and yet undefined.

He was not a man by nature given to evil ways, 'to war with man and forfeit heav'n'. He has been 'warp'd by the world in Disappointment's school' —

Fear'd, shunn'd, belied, ere youth had lost her force,
He hated man too much to feel remorse.

He knows he is detested, but knows too that those who detest him fear him. He is beyond affection and beyond contempt. Alone, bitter, an outcast, a brooding, suffering egotist mastering his own deep passions with iron control, he has but one softer feeling, his love for the fair Medora.

The narrative poems sold in their thousands. The Byron whose affair with Caroline rocked London drawing-rooms was the sensational author of the glowing, feverish romances which everybody was reading and talking about. And for reasons which biographers conspicuously fail to plumb, he suddenly married Annabella Milbanke, a sober, rather prim, perhaps even prudish young woman. Had he had enough of high-spiritedness, unconventionality, and instability at the hands of Caroline? If the marriage seems to be built on a mystery, Annabella's sudden determination to leave her husband a year later, taking their daughter with her, is also something of a mystery. Not because no causes can be adduced, but because too many have been canvassed, and there is evidence both to support them and to bring all of them under question. Were Byron's unpredictable black moods and bitter outbursts intolerably brutal and crude? Did Annabella seriously feel that she had tied herself to a madman? Was she deeply shocked by Byron's affection for his stepsister Augusta Leigh? Did she know that it was an incestuous relationship and that Augusta's child (called 'Medora') was Byron's daughter? Did she suspect him of homosexuality? Did Byron subject her to anal intercourse late in her pregnancy? There were rumour-mongers in Byron's own day to canvass these theories which spread like wildfire in London. Byron began to be ostracised, and when he left England, agog with his scandalous doings, in 1816, it was for the last time. The amours did not cease, of course. Claire Clairmont, stepsister of Mary Shelley, threw herself at him, and a daughter, Allegra, was born. There was Marianna Segati, wife of a Venice draper, and Margerita Cogni, wife of a baker. The tale of promiscuity was not ended until Byron fell in love with Teresa Guiccioli (Countess Guiccioli) whose husband, the Count, was prepared to let him fill the role of *cavalier servente*, and Byron settled down at last. This was in 1819.

We see the full-grown Byronic hero in the dramatic poem *Manfred* (1817) and in the third and fourth cantos of *Childe Harold*, published in 1816 and 1818 respectively. Manfred is a doomed outcast of Faustian complexion. His Gothick castle is in the Higher Alps. He summons spirits of the universe and requests of them the gift of forgetfulness. It is not within their power to oblige. Manfred is tortured by remorse for some seemingly unspeakable sin. It is his 'fatality to live', to be his 'own soul's sepulchre'. He is prevented by a hunter from jumping to his death from a cliff. Offered wine, he sees blood on the rim of the vessel and the character of the nameless sin is revealed:

I say 'tis blood — my blood! the pure warm stream
Which ran in the veins of my fathers, and in ours
When we were in our youth, and had one heart,
And loved each other as we should not love.

From castle gallery to cliff, to cottage, to cataract, and to mountain summit the scene changes as the agony is rehearsed, until in the Hall of Arimanes the phantom of Manfred's beloved Astarte rises before him to foretell his death on the morrow. 'I could not tame my nature down,' Manfred laments. 'I disdain'd to mingle with / A herd, though to be leader.' He is one of those who became old in their youth. He has been his own destroyer. He has scorned religion and suffered 'the innate tortures of that deep despair / Which is remorse without the fear of hell'.

This is the Byronic disillusionment at its most sombre. The projection of whatever guilt Byron felt for his love of Augusta has a larger-than-life intensity which confers Satanic dimensions on the figure of Manfred.

By thy cold breast and serpent smile,
By thy unfathom'd gulfs of guile,
By that most seeming virtuous eye,
By thy shut soul's hypocrisy;
By the perfection of thine art
Which pass'd for human thine own heart;
By thy delight in others' pain,
And by thy brotherhood of Cain,
I call upon thee! and compel
Thyself to be thy proper Hell!

The catalogue of guilt assumes mountainous proportions. Romantic intensity and romantic excess submerge the individual in the dye of wholesale diabolical wickedness.

Far more approachable is the hero of Cantos III and IV of *Childe Harold*. Though he has quaffed 'life's enchanted cup' too quickly and found the dregs wormwood, he has risked returning to the social scene, protected by 'guarded coldness' and an 'invulnerable mind'. But he soon learns again that he is the 'most unfit / Of men to herd with Man'. He will yield the domain of his mind to no one; so he sets off again on his wanderings in Europe, and explores the historical and literary associations of the spots he visits. Childe Harold as a character is gradually forgotten, and the poet begins to speak in his own voice. The hint of Spenserian pastiche which we had at the beginning of Canto I is left far behind. But the Spenserian stanza is managed with a far more flexible sentence structure and with an increasingly rich variety of tone. There are memorable stanzas inspired by the battlefield of Waterloo, with a dramatic reconstruction of the Brussels Ball before the fatal day which tore doomed young soldiers from the scene of gaiety. The public at home were no doubt eager for news from the countries so long cut off by war, and here was dramatic reportage from the scene of the recent slaughter which brought the long tale of bloody events to its climactic conclusion. Moreover, here too was analysis of the mentality of the fascinating tyrant, Napoleon, whose power had kept a continent in awe.

The scene shifts to the Rhine, to Switzerland, and to Italy. The sight of Lake Leman provokes reflection on a figure as dynamic in his own way as Napoleon: Rousseau. Byron recognises him as a man of comparable historic significance. Did not he and his like make a 'fearful monument' by their literary assault upon established opinions and institutions? Thus the bold descriptive writing is spiced with reflections on the master-spirits of the age, and of course with the intermittent running commentary on the poet's own private agonies. He has neither loved the world nor been loved by it; he has never fitted into the crowd; he has always shrouded himself from others in his private thoughts. But an address to his loved daughter, torn bitterly from his keeping, seems designed to remind the reader of his right to sympathy. The exploration of Italy in Canto IV touches the nerve of many different emotions. In surveying the Coliseum Byron turns to picture the death of a gladiator with a degree of pathos and of dramatic force that inevitably moves the reader. The rhetoric is frank in its artifices and neat in its cadences. A Romantic vein is evidenced here in the sensitivity to the grandeur of ruins and in bringing out the human tragedies associated with the historical story. Regret expands into a metaphysical apostrophe to Time. So far as recent history is concerned Byron, like Wordsworth, laments that 'France got drunk with blood to vomit crime' and that vile ambition dashed all hope of freedom. And, as if anxious that no ingredient of

Romanticism should be missing from his poetic recipe, he sings the pleasures of being alone with nature, far from society, where he can 'mingle with the Universe'.

Yet there is also a Byron who scarcely seems to belong to the Romantic movement at all, a Byron who, some have claimed, was an Augustan wit born out of his due time. This Byron has latterly been far more eagerly acclaimed in Britain than the Romantic Byron exported to the Continent. He showed his temper and his skill early in *English Bards and Scotch Reviewers* (1809). Angered by hostile reviews of his collection *Hours of Idleness* (1807), Byron hit out at the contemporary literary world in heroic couplets often packed with venom. Writers of the past are praised: Pope, Dryden, Congreve, and Otway; so are some rather insignificant contemporaries. For the rest Byron lashes out. Scott is accused of foisting 'stale romance' on the public to make money. Wordsworth is ridiculed as one

> Who, both by precept and example, shows
> That prose is verse, and verse is merely prose.

Coleridge, who wrote a poem to a donkey, is 'the bard who soars to elegise an ass'. Scott was magnanimous enough to welcome Byron as a friend later. So was Thomas Moore, another of the targets, though when he first read the poem he challenged Byron to a duel in a letter which missed him because he had gone abroad.

The satiric vein turned more venomous still when Byron saw that Southey had been foolish enough to attack his work and his morals in the preface to *A Vision of Judgment*. Outraged by the seeming hypocrisy of the tribute to George III, he wrote his own *Vision of Judgment* (1822). When the king arrives at the gate of Heaven, the archangel Michael presides over his examination. Lucifer appears to claim George III as his own on the basis of his record, and when there is a call for corroboration from witnesses they come in their thousands. Then Southey is brought up for the defence, and when he starts to read his poetic tribute to the king the verses drive everybody crazy. In the ensuing chaotic tumult the king slips into Heaven unobserved.

> And when the tumult dwindled to a calm
> I left him practising the hundredth psalm.

For this poem Byron adopted the Italian stanza 'ottava rima', an eight-lined stanza rhyming *ababababcc*. It was peculiarly effective for planting a stinging barb or comic rejoinder in the final couplet. Byron revealed its enormous possibilities, using it for his comic and satiric masterpiece in sixteen cantos, *Don Juan*, which came out in four sections between 1819 and 1824.

Don Juan was an astonishing undertaking. Its sixteen cantos contain over 1900 stanzas and some 15,000 lines in all. W.H. Auden, a facile versifier, has testified that when he tried to compose in the same form he found it taxing indeed merely to write a few smooth stanzas. Yet when Byron came to write what I calculate to be his 1763rd stanza, it ended:

And never straining hard to versify,
I rattle on exactly as I'd talk
With company in a ride or walk.

The story, of course, comprises a number of amours. Don Juan is early seduced by Donna Julia and dispatched abroad by his supposedly high-principled mother, Donna Inez (based on Annabella, Byron's wife), when he is but sixteen. After shipwreck on a Greek island Juan has an idyllic love affair with his saviour, Haidée. But when her father, Lambro, returns he throws Juan into the hands of pirates. They sell him in Constantinople to a Sultana, Gulbeyaz, whose amorous eye he has caught. She has him purchased, dressed as a woman, and thus brought into her presence. But Juan is still lamenting the loss of Haidée. He repels her advances, until he is eventually softened by her tears and her humiliation. He is sent into the harem to sleep with the 'other' girls, and when the Sultan discovers him he narrowly escapes death. Soon he is with the Russian army, besieging Ismail and distinguishing himself; then in Russia, earning the favour and favours of the Empress Catherine. She eventually sends him on a diplomatic mission to England. Thus the last six cantos (XI–XVI) show Juan at large in English society, pursued again by aristocratic ladies.

Byron makes his presence felt throughout as story-teller and commentator. Once more we sense his affiliation to the eighteenth century and to writers like Fielding who sit at the reader's side and chatter in his ear. Byron will interrupt the story to shake his head over his youthful characters' innocence and inexperience, and over his older characters' tantrums and deceits. He will break in with wry, ironic or sarcastic commentary on evidences of cant or hypocrisy. He will insert a parenthetical observation to his publisher, Murray. He will pursue a digression which brings the mockery of worldly wisdom to bear upon human foolishness. He will indulge in personal reminiscences. He will insert remarks about the problems of composition — spelling, grammar, rhyming, and scanning — or even turn in mockery on a simile he has just penned. The poem has in fact the air of sustained monologue by a skilled improviser.

Yet in narrative variety and dramatic thrust it makes compulsive reading. Whether it is a romantic tryst of young lovers on a beach or a ghastly experience of cannibalism by sailors drifting in an open boat at sea, an assault upon a fortress or a night frolic at an English house party, the action is deftly presented. The management of action and dialogue within the strict fetters of the chosen stanza form has both smoothness and naturalness. The analysis of the thoughts and feelings of the characters gives depth to the human portraiture. Inevitably the narrative often demands seriousness of tone, even gravity or grief, and the commentary is not always cool or jocular. When roused by the theme of unnecessary military slaughter or by acts of tyranny and injustice, Byron displays the hot anger of the radical Whig aristocrat, the man who could forgive Southey for turning Tory, but not for attacking upholders of the radicalism he had himself abandoned.

Even into *Don Juan*, then, the serious Romantic Byron intrudes. His voice is heard in the luscious account of the love between Juan and Haidée and its consummation on the sea shore, 'Ocean their witness, and the cave their bed'. In rhythmic assurance and verbal configuration this idyll has the pulsing musical memorability of those unforgettable lyrics which have long graced anthologies as inevitably as any in our language: 'When we two parted', 'There be none of Beauty's daughters', 'The Assyrian came down like the wolf on the fold', and 'The isles of Greece'.

It was Greece that in the summer of 1823 called Byron to his death. Determined to play a part in the Greek war of independence, he died in April of the following year at Missalonghi. The attempt to turn heroic man of action, for which he equipped himself with an absurdly flamboyant Homeric helmet, ended on the bed of sickness amid rather ineffectively disunited and inadequately disciplined revolutionaries. The mixture of the tragically grand and the farcically footling was somehow characteristic of the man.

Percy Bysshe Shelley

Percy Bysshe Shelley (1792–1822) is the most problematic of the English Romantic poets. In some respects his lot had much in common with Byron's. When Thomas Love Peacock wrote to him in 1819, urging him to return from his 'exile' in Italy, Shelley averred in reply that there were perhaps only five people in his home country who did not regard him 'as a rare prodigy of crime and pollution whose look even might infect'. Such a man indeed was Shelley to his contemporaries. His grandfather was a wealthy baronet, his father a country gentleman and a Member of Parliament. As heir to an entailed estate, respectable — but not too respectable — things were expected of Shelley. When he went to Oxford his father assured him that he was prepared to provide for any number of illegitimate children, but he was not prepared to put up with a misalliance. But Shelley was nature's own rebel. It is impossible to find in the treatment he received from parents and superiors justification or excuse for the venom he displayed in living out the role of a persecuted denouncer of authority.

It is easy to understand what made him suspect in his own day. Like Wordsworth and Southey he early espoused revolutionary politics, but unlike them he never lost his radicalism. He attracted the attention of government spies. From his teens he directed his hatred and ridicule not only at kings and rulers, privilege and tyranny, but also at Christianity and the institution of marriage. His enthusiasm for proselytising, his anxiety to 'convert' ('corrupt', it could be argued) his own sisters and the various girls he fell in love with was bound to irritate the older generation.

For in vain from the grasp of Religion I flee.
The most tenderly loved of my soul
Are slaves to its hated control.
It pursues me, it blasts me! oh where shall I fly?
What remains but to curse it & die?

So he wrote in a letter to his friend and later biographer, Thomas Jefferson Hogg (1792–1862), with whom he collaborated at Oxford in publishing a pamphlet, *The Necessity of Atheism*, and distributing it as provocatively as possible. Both he and Hogg were sent down, chiefly, it would appear, for denying their authorship of it.

Shelley's reading of Rousseau inspired him with a sense of the goodness of natural man and natural feeling when not corrupted by the inhibiting institutions of society, and he was soon heatedly persuading Harriet Westbrook, a friend of his sister's, that she must escape to freedom from the social and moral conventionalities of her comfortable middle-class home. His success stopped short of converting her to free love, but the couple eloped and married in Edinburgh, Hogg joining them there, for Shelley's escapades with his loved ones generally involved third parties, not to mention fourth and fifth parties. Soon the trio were at York. Then Shelley and Harriet took a cottage in Keswick, and Hogg, who had become too passionately attached to Harriet for her taste, was left behind. In his place came Harriet's elder sister Elisa. Meanwhile Shelley had a certain amount of explaining to do to his epistolary intellectual soul-mate, Elisabeth Hitchener, for apostasy to his oft declaimed scorn of the institution of marriage. He solved the problem by a slight misrepresentation of the facts. One of the less estimable aspects of Shelley's character was his ingenuity in presenting different versions of the same events to different people. The Shelleys were forever on the move. They spent periods in Ireland, in Wales, in Devon, and in Edinburgh before returning south.

It was through cultivating the acquaintance of the social thinker, William Godwin (1756–1836), author of *Political Justice* (1793), that Shelley met and fell in love with his daughter, Mary Wollstonecraft Godwin (1797–1851). Mary was the sixteen-year-old daughter of Mary

Wollstonecraft (1759–97), the distinguished feminist author of *Vindication of the Rights of Woman* (1792), who died soon after her daughter's birth. Godwin himself rejected the institution of marriage, as Mary Wollstonecraft had done, but nevertheless married her, at her wish it appears, shortly before their daughter's birth. Since then Godwin had married a second time, acquiring thereby a stepdaughter, 'Claire' (strictly 'Jane') Clairmont, the young lady who bore Byron's daughter Allegra. Godwin was appalled when Shelley revealed that he and Mary had fallen in love. 'My attachment to you is unimpaired: I conceive that it has acquired even a deeper & more lasting character,' Shelley wrote to Harriet, explaining what had happened, and apparently assuming that she would continue to live in his household. She had already borne him a daughter, Ianthe, and was soon to bear him a son, Charles. Nevertheless in 1814 Shelley and Mary, accompanied by her stepsister Claire, escaped together to France, hotly pursued by Mrs Godwin. After some weeks they returned to England, and Shelley was soon writing to Harriet, mainly in the hope of getting his hands on some money, and then angrily denouncing her for her failure to cooperate. A month later he was writing to her again, requesting thirty pounds. And a further month later, in November, she gave birth to his son Charles.

Shelley's manner of life was such that he was constantly short of money. Although the entail on the estate guaranteed him an inheritance ultimately, he was for long dependent on the goodwill of a father he repeatedly insulted. Since his father outlived him and various legal devices were used to control his access to capital, Shelley's story was for long one of repeated manoeuvres to ward off creditors and imprisonment. He borrowed widely from friends and rashly from money-lenders on the strength of his prospects. He was unscrupulous in leaving tradesmen's bills unpaid. There are insuperable difficulties in the way of any attempt to reconcile Shelley's social and moral idealism with his personal conduct.

As with Byron, much evil scandal that was rumoured of him in his own day could be confirmed only by intimate knowledge, and after he died the Shelley family restricted access to papers they held, and exerted such pressure on his connections (his widow especially, who was dependent on them) that for over a hundred years the truth was veiled and a Shelley 'myth' was fostered which, while it could not conceal either his radicalism or his lack of moral inhibitions, nevertheless managed to present him as a beautiful, idealistic, and soulful young man whose sheer innocence and genuineness, impulsiveness and warm-heartedness led him into scrapes that more calculating and less sincere personalities would have avoided. There were tributes enough to corroborate the myth, such as Byron's claim that Shelley 'was the *best* and least selfish man' he ever knew. 'I never knew anyone who was not a beast in comparison,' he added.

The myth cannot be sustained in the face of what scholars have discovered in the last few decades through examination of surviving letters and diaries. So far as his romantic attachments are concerned, it is quite impossible to defend Shelley. Harriet's suicide in despair in 1817, when she was again pregnant by an army officer, was misrepresented as a consequence of a descent into prostitution. We now know her as an intelligent young woman baffled by her desertion and by her husband's eccentricities. Shelley drew Elizabeth Hitchener into a shared household with Harriet, only to get rid of her unkindly when they wearied of her company. He repeatedly planned communal living and the sharing of partners. One such scheme was briefly practised with Hogg and Mary (who was more content to be shared with Hogg than to share Shelley with Harriet or Claire). Shelley's relationship with Claire involved him for a time in an awkward domestic triangle. There were those who believed that an illegitimate daughter, Elena, whom Shelley registered as his in Naples in 1819, was Claire's, though the mother may have been his Swiss maid, Elise. But even more irreconcilable with the Shelley myth than the sexual freedoms practised was surely the neglect of creditors' demands. Shelley seems to have seen no inconsistency between his venomous denunciations of the privileged oppressors of the poor and his readiness to exploit his aristocratic status and his prospects from inherited wealth in building up debts at the expense of shopkeepers.

Shelley was not the only writer of the period to have to devote a great deal of energy to borrowing money, and, when able to, he certainly helped those near to him. His relationship with Godwin was soured by Godwin's reliance upon promises of money which Shelley made and which were not always fulfilled. The financial connection was such that malicious rumour could claim that Shelley had 'bought' Godwin's two daughters from their father. Shelley himself scarcely discouraged the projection of a 'wicked' image. In the register in the hotel at Chamonix he described himself (in Greek) as Democrat, Philanthropist, and Atheist, and in the 'Destination' column wrote 'Hell' ('L'Enfer').

It was in April 1816 that Claire arranged to sleep one night with Byron at an inn near London. Byron was on the point of leaving for Switzerland, and when he did so Claire won Shelley's support for following him to Geneva, where the intimacy was renewed and where Shelley's friendship with Byron began. It was not long, however, before Byron had wearied of Claire, and she became an impediment rather than an aid to the friendship. Byron was not to be moved to meet Claire again even after she gave birth to their daughter Allegra.

The Shelleys were back in England again in 1817, but in 1818 once more set out for Italy, this time never to return, for Shelley was to die tragically at the age of twenty-nine. He had moved to Pisa in 1821. A villa was found for Byron nearby. The two were planning to launch a periodical, *The Liberal*, to be edited by Leigh Hunt (1784–1859), who was due to come over and join them in July 1822. Shelley, accompanied by his friend Edward Williams, took his own sailing-boat to meet Hunt at Leghorn. On the return journey a sudden squall overtook them and they were drowned. Quarantine restrictions were such that the recovered bodies had to be burned on the shore.

The nine cantos of the early poem *Queen Mab* (1813) do not make very digestible reading. Shelley himself was later to describe it as 'a poem written by me when very young, in the most furious style, with long notes against Jesus Christ & God the Father & the King & the Bishops & marriage & the Devil knows what'. Indeed its targets are Monarchy, War, Tyranny, Commercial Exploitation, and Christianity. It was suppressed, but it was to be several times reprinted by underground presses and to become known as 'the Chartists' Bible'. Of *Alastor* (1816) Mary Shelley said, 'None of Shelley's poems is more characteristic than this.' In blank verse it tells how a 'youth is pursued to his death by Alastor, the Spirit of Solitude'. The youth, Shelley tells us in his Preface, can be 'joyous, and tranquil, and self-possessed' as long as his aspirations are directed towards the infinite in contemplating the majesties of the universe. But eventually, no longer satisfied thus, he hungers for a being who will embody all that his ideal vision comprehends. He has an ecstatic erotic experience in the dream of an Arab maiden, but the vision is lost in the waking world. 'He seeks in vain for a prototype of his conception. Blasted by his disappointment, he descends to an untimely grave.' Shelley placed as epigraph to the poem a quotation from the *Confessions* of St Augustine, meaning: 'I did not yet love, and I longed to love. Longing to love, I looked everywhere for what I could love.'

Shelley's longest poem is *Laon and Cythna* (1817), which was reissued as *The Revolt of Islam* in 1818. The subtitle to the first edition was 'The Revolution of the Golden City: A Vision of the Nineteenth Century in the Stanza of Spenser'. Shelley explained to Longman, the publisher, that 'the scene is supposed to be laid in Constantinople and modern Greece, but . . . it is in fact a tale illustrative of such a Revolution as might be supposed to take place in an European nation'. In his Preface to the poem Shelley looks back to the French Revolution as a movement to which 'the most generous and amiable natures' were most sympathetic. He accepts that the subsequent atrocities and tyrannies were terrible, but offers the excuse: 'Can he who the day before was a trampled slave, suddenly become liberal-minded, forbearing, and independent?'

The poem is in twelve cantos. After an introductory canto, much of Cantos II to IV is transfigured autobiography, featuring the young Laon and his beloved sister Cythna. Cythna initiates rebellion in the city independently of Laon, and is captured. Laon, however, storms the city and takes it in Canto V, and Cythna (now called 'Laone') escapes. Canto

VI presents the murderous counter-attack of the discomfited Tyrant. It is successful, but Laon and Cythna flee. The celebrated description of their subsequent love-making has a sensuous clarity and an imaginative intensity characteristic of Shelley's most vivid eroticism. In Cantos VII, VIII, and IX Cythna recounts her adventures, how she was captured, then imprisoned, and subjected to monstrous hallucinations; and how sailors aided her escape. She rewarded them on board by converting them to atheism, liberation of their cargo of slaves, and free love. In Canto X we return to the city, now a scene of death and pollution, famine and plague. The wretched inhabitants turn to religious prayer and penitence; and the priests demand expiation by immolation of Laon and Cythna. In Canto XI Laon returns to the city and offers his life on condition that Cythna is spared. But as he is taken up to the pyre Cythna comes sweeping in on horseback to stand smilingly at his side and share his fate. The last canto closes with Laon and Cythna sailing off to a visionary Hesperides.

The lyrical drama *Prometheus Unbound* (1820) is Shelley's major work. In the ancient myth the Titan Prometheus stole fire from heaven for the benefit of mankind, and in vengeance Jupiter chained him to a rock in the Caucasus, where an eagle consumed daily his liver which was restored each succeeding night. Shelley made of this another study in liberation from tyranny. His Prometheus represents mankind, and in Act I he is chained to a rockface. He has cursed Jupiter for his persecution, and there is a powerful ironic moment when the Phantasm of Jupiter arises to repeat Prometheus's own words of total defiance. The curse must be renounced and the defiance abandoned. Mercury brings a band of Furies to taunt Prometheus and bring him to despair by displaying how the whole world is suffering from tyranny and injustice, war and famine. Prometheus is comforted by Spirits of the Earth and reminded by Panthea, an Oceanid, of his love for her sister Asia, one of the three Oceanides. He declares:

> I would fain
> Be what it is my destiny to be,
> The saviour and the strength of suffering man.

In Act II Panthea goes to waken far-off Asia and remind her of Prometheus's love. Panthea and Asia descend to the underground realm of Demogorgon. Asia questions him. Who is the creator of the living world? Who made its evils and sufferings? The only clear answer she gets is that eternal Love is not subject to Fate and Time, Chance or Change. Love is thus identified with freedom. Panthea sees Asia transfigured, and a spirit voice is heard acclaiming her beauty in the rapturous lyric, 'Life of Life! thy lips enkindle / With their love the breath between them'. In Act III Demogorgon rises from his volcanic depths to depose

Jupiter. Prometheus is freed. 'Henceforth we will not part,' he declares to Asia, and the Spirit of the Hour foresees the world renewed.

And behold, thrones were kingless, and men walked
One with the other even as spirits do,
None fawned, none trampled . . .

Act IV is a kind of coda, a celebration of cosmic harmony with mankind in a state of perfection.

It would be absurd to pretend that there is any dramatic effectiveness in the handling of the ultimate challenge to Jupiter and the huddled account of his fall. In Shelley clarity of narrative or dramatic presentation is submerged under an over-abundance of descriptive richness and lyrical celebration of love or beauty. Instances of this astonishing lyrical spontaneity abound in a variety of metres and stanza forms. Shelley's finest poetry seems to be a by-product of his major efforts as a poet and of his emotional life as a lover of women and of natural beauty. The ode 'To a Skylark', the 'Ode to the West Wind', and those intensely fervent lyrics that overwhelm with their music and their naturalness — 'I arise from dreams of thee', 'One word is too often profaned', and 'When the lamp is shattered' — are incidental to Shelley's central ambition to storm the hearts of men with a vision of a world freed from injustice and inequality, from the fetters of Christianity, monogamy, and sexual inhibition. It may be argued that in some respects his voice sounds as much like a voice from the 1960s as a voice from the early nineteenth century.

A group of poems more substantial than lyrics have nevertheless kept their appeal. 'Julian and Maddalo; A Conversation', written in 1818 but not published until 1824, is a fascinating exercise in a form far removed from the ideal worlds of *The Revolt of Islam* and *Prometheus Unbound*. Written in regular iambic couplets with an eighteenth-century flavour, it records a discussion that takes place in Venice between Julian (Shelley), who is sceptical in religion but a hopeful progressive, seeking the regeneration of society, and Count Maddalo (Byron), who displays a cynical detachment from movements for reform. The argument is enlivened by the introduction of Maddalo's child (Byron's Allegra), representative of innocence. A visit to a maniac, whose agonised outburst against the miseries of life casts an entirely different light on the cosy theoretical reasonings of the disputants, opens up disturbing new dimensions. In the same year Shelley wrote 'Lines written among the Euganean Hills' (1818), a poem which clutches at hope in the midst of deeply meditated dejection. There is cunning use of octosyllabic couplets which are more generally associated with cheerfulness.

Many a green isle needs must be
In the deep wide sea of misery.

'Epipsychidion' (1821) was inspired by Claire's discovery of Emilia Viviani, a young woman of great beauty who was temporarily imprisoned in a convent until a husband should be found for her. Shelley once more portrays a triangular relationship in imagery which presents Mary as the moon, Emilia as the sun, and himself as the earth, needing, presumably, the alternate ministrations of both. He invites Emilia to sail with him as his 'heart's sister' to a far Eden where trouble is unknown and where she can become

The living soul of this Elysian isle,
Conscious, inseparable, one.

It was in 1821 also that the news of John Keats's death, and the story that it had been hastened by a hostile review of his work, provoked Shelley to write the elegy 'Adonais', another and a notably dignified exercise in the Spenserian stanza.

At his death Shelley was working on a poem, 'The Triumph of Life', which shows evidence of greater discipline over thought and expression. It uses the *terza rima* of Dante's *Divine Comedy* with which Shelley had experimented in the 'Ode to the West Wind'. In his dream the poet sees the Chariot of Life rolling relentlessly forward, surrounded by wildly dancing multitudes all destined to be crushed under it. Life sweeps forward, a mighty juggernaut, the powerful men of the past chained to it. There is a desolating clarity and acerbity in Shelley's picture of all those defeated by life, that is —

All but the sacred few who could not tame
Their spirits to the conqueror —

those who shunned earthly power and wealth. The greater firmness of conceptualisation and the diminishing verbal effervescence in this work seem to mark a new development in poetic control. The poet meets Rousseau, who interprets the scene before them. Perhaps nothing could illustrate the status of Rousseau for the Romantics more forcefully than this encounter does. Where Dante chooses Virgil as his guide and mentor, Shelley chooses Rousseau. The philosopher begins to recount what appears to be his own experience of love that led to disillusionment. But where the argument was tending is not clear. Shelley broke off, scribbling a note of love to Jane Williams, the last recipient of his homage — and of some delightful poems — but frustratingly out of reach, like the public he had sought for his poetry, and like the fulfilment of his social ideals.

John Keats

The personalities and the careers of both Byron and Shelley were strongly influenced by their aristocratic outlook and inheritance. In this respect

John Keats (1795-1821) stands in marked contrast. He was born in London, the son of a groom who managed a livery-stable in the city, where horses could be hired or taken care of. But the family was not poor, for Keats's father had married the daughter of his boss, John Jennings, who owned the business. Like Wordsworth, however, Keats lost his father early, for he was thrown from his horse one night when the boy was not yet nine years old. Mrs Keats married a second time, but not happily, and she eventually left her second husband who, as the law stood at the time, was now in possession of whatever money or property she had. She too died early, in 1810. The four children of her first marriage were brought up by their grandmother, Mrs Jennings.

The Keats children ought to have been adequately provided for, but Mrs Jennings made an unfortunate choice in entrusting the money destined for them into the hands of a guardian, Richard Abbey, from whom they never received what was properly due to them, so that Keats was dogged by shortage of cash all his life.

Keats was educated at a small private school at Enfield, Middlesex, where he seems to have received from an assistant master, Charles Cowden Clarke (the headmaster's son), the same kind of sympathetic literary nourishment that Wordsworth received at Hawkshead from William Taylor. Under the guardian's direction Keats was apprenticed to a surgeon and apothecary, but he kept in touch with Cowden Clarke, from whom he borrowed Spenser's *Faerie Queene*. It delighted him and was to become a crucial poetic influence. As a medical student Keats progressed far enough to gain his apothecary's certificate, but then, when Mr Abbey wanted to push him further on the road, he irritated him by his refusal. 'I mean to rely upon my abilities as a poet,' he declared.

We shall look in vain in Keats's poetry for evidence of the social radicalism of Shelley. Yet by accident he attracted the animosity of conservative critics. Cowden Clarke was an enthusiast for the poetic revolution which was urged by Leigh Hunt in his journal *The Examiner*. Hunt, himself a competent poet whom Byron was later to involve in the periodical *The Liberal*, was welcomed in Italy by Shelley before his last, fatal voyage. Hunt's enthusiasm for a more vital and imaginative poetry, freed from eighteenth-century principles of correctness in style and substance, was linked to political radicalism. Indeed Hunt's politics had already brought him a two-year gaol sentence for an attack on the Prince Regent. Hunt recognised Keats for the promising young poet he was — just as he had recognised Shelley's genius. But to be published in Hunt's periodical or to be reviewed enthusiastically by Hunt — and Keats enjoyed both these 'advantages' — was to be classed by the opponents of reform as one more of Hunt's band of upstarts labelled 'The Cockney School'. This helps to explain the virulence of the attack on Keats in the *Quarterly Review* in 1818, of which Byron wrote:

Who kill'd John Keats?
'I,' says the Quarterly,
So savage and Tartarly;
'T'was one of my feats.'

In fact Keats's early death was due to consumption. He had watched
his brother Tom die of the disease in 1818, and had tended him so closely
towards the end that his own infection was perhaps almost inevitable.
Keats's life, even more than Shelley's, may be mythologised so as to
make him the archetypal young poet, victimised, afflicted, frustrated,
and hounded to an early grave. Moreover, the story of his love for Fanny
Brawne is one of acute pathos. Five years his junior, the daughter of a
Hampstead widow, she seems to have been a lively, intelligent girl when
he met her in 1818, but she was not easily won. Whether the couple
eventually became engaged is not clear, but when Keats's terminal decline
set in he had to surrender all hope of her, and indeed destroyed her last
letters to him, not trusting himself to read them. By this time Keats had
been ordered to Italy to avoid the English winter of 1820–1, and he died
in Rome in February 1821.

Keats differs from Shelley, Byron, and Wordsworth in not having
completed a major poem of epic proportions. It is difficult for us to
appreciate how important to a poet's reputation at this time was the long
poem. It was not just that what mattered to the public was Shelley's
Revolt of Islam and *Prometheus Unbound* rather than those brilliantly
executed lyrics and short poems which are now the first things to come
to mind when Shelley is named. It is clear that this was also what
mattered primarily to the poet himself. Clearly neither Wordsworth nor
Shelley could have conceived of a climate of poetic opinion such as now
obtains in the twentieth century, when poetic reputations of the first
order can be made purely on the basis of short poems. Ours is as much
the age of the short poem as the nineteenth century was the age of the
long poem.

In this respect Keats's poetic career must have seemed even more
tragically blighted in his own day than it seems now. For in Keats's
volume of 1817, in his *Endymion* (1818), and in his volume of 1820 there
is such a concentration of mature poetic richness that the total output
might have represented a life-time's achievement. Yet when Keats died
he was some two years younger than Wordsworth was when he and
Coleridge first began to plan the *Lyrical Ballads*. The 1817 volume
includes two notable sonnets, the celebrated 'On first looking into Chapman's Homer' and 'Keen, fitful gusts are whisp'ring here and there'. The
two poems bring us close to the young man who could be suddenly
transported by the discovery of a poetic masterpiece — in the first case,
Chapman's translation of Homer, in the second case Milton's 'Lycidas'

Romantic poetry · 61

and Petrarch's sonnets to Laura. But the most substantial poem in this
first volume is 'Sleep and Poetry'. It is characteristic of Keats to hymn
sleep as the 'soft closer of our eyes' before turning to celebrate poetry
and proclaim his vocation:

> O for ten years, that I may overwhelm
> Myself in poesy; so I may do the deed
> That my own soul has to itself decreed.

Keats surveys the delights which can nourish the poetic imagination but
also concedes the need to pass beyond them to explore 'the agonies, the
strife / Of human hearts'.

When *Endymion* was published Keats wrote an apologetic Preface,
admitting that the work displayed 'inexperience' and 'immaturity'. Its
four books of around a thousand lines each clearly represented Keats's
first attempt at a major work. Its story comes from Greek mythology.
Endymion, a shepherd, falls in love with a maiden who has visited him
in a dream, and he determines to find her. She is Cynthia, the moon
goddess. He seeks her in the depths of the earth, and is then lifted away
by an eagle to where Cynthia is again restored to his arms in sleep. After
a further journey below the depths of the ocean, he eventually encounters
a sorrowing Indian maiden and falls in love with her. Ultimately she
turns out to be Cynthia herself. In presentation the poem is vague and
inert. Written in smooth couplets, the verse has a kind of spineless
luxuriance; we can understand why Keats felt that it suffered from
adolescent 'mawkishness'. Its opening line is one of the most frequently
quoted in the language:

> A thing of beauty is a joy for ever.

The 'Ode to Sorrow' sung by the Indian maiden is a technically brilliant
exercise with rich sensuousness in the imagery and haunting compulsive-
ness in the metre. But in the poem as a whole there is much feverish
rhetoric in the dialogue and some sickly excess in descriptive colouring.

The volume of 1820, however, is a compact treasury of works witnessing
to an astonishing level of poetic maturity. None of them is more remarkable than the narrative poem 'The Eve of St Agnes', where Keats's
mastery of the Spenserian stanza is evident. The setting is vaguely
medieval and the background that of a family feud, a grave obstacle to
the lovers, Porphyro and Madeline. On St Agnes's Eve maidens dream
of their lovers if they observe certain simple traditions. A ball is being
held in Madeline's home: Porphyro steals to her bedroom and hides until
she is in bed. Then, when she lies dreaming of him, he awakens her to
carry her off to his home. Never did poet display more subtle verbal
virtuosity in the manipulation of atmosphere than is found here in the
portrayal of the winter evening, the distant revelry, the sensuous loveliness

of Madeline, and the passionate devotion of Porphyro. Keats has a unique capacity to play upon the reader's senses one by one, to brush the tips of our imaginative antennae and tease our sensibilities by the sheer magic of verbal conjuration.

Alongside 'The Eve of St Agnes' is a second narrative poem, 'Isabella, or, The Pot of Basil', a story from Boccaccio. Here Keats uses the *ottava rima* form which Byron exploited for a far different purpose in *Don Juan*. Isabella has two brothers who want her to marry a nobleman, but she is in love with Lorenzo, and they murder him. His ghost, however, reveals to Isabella what has happened; she exhumes the body and takes her lover's head home to be hidden in a plant pot under basil. When her brothers see how she cherishes the pot they steal it, only to discover the macabre truth that their guilt is known, and they flee. Isabella herself mourns and dies. Delightful as much of the poem is, it does not match up to 'The Eve of St Agnes' in the blending of style and substance. Whereas at times the presentation has a Chaucerian narrative simplicity, and a faintly archaic management of incident and reflection (such as the address to Melancholy) distances and frames the story, yet a touch of melodrama in characterising the villainous brothers and a too harrowing treatment of certain gruesome details together represent a somewhat incongruous mixture.

Keats made two attempts towards a full-scale epic on the subject of Hyperion. Once more he returned to Greek mythology, this time to the story of how the ancient order of gods, the Titans, were overthrown and supplanted by the new gods of Olympus. Saturn is leader of the Titans, and Hyperion is his sun god. Book I of 'Hyperion' opens with a study of the fallen Saturn and the goddess Thea in gloom and desolation. Meanwhile Hyperion, the one Titan not yet displaced, senses the coming doom and the first loss of power. Coelus sends him to the Earth to Saturn. Book II presents a council of the fallen gods rather as Book II of Milton's *Paradise Lost* presents a council of fallen angels. A similar topic is at issue among them. Must they resign themselves to being supplanted by a race superior in beauty?

> for 'tis the eternal law
> That first in beauty should be first in might.

Should they welcome the new order or seek revenge on their supplanters? Hyperion arrives among them as the book closes. In Book III we leave the fallen gods for the new ones, Hyperion for Apollo (as Book III in *Paradise Lost* forsakes hell for heaven). But Keats abandoned the poem after little more than a hundred lines. The blank verse is often distinguished: there are passages which combine the old Keatsian richness with a looser rhythmic flow and a more firmly resonant rhetoric than found earlier; but the matter at issue lacks dramatic potential. What we have is a series of static pictures rather than a compelling unfolding action. And the dependence upon Milton is too close. Keats realised this when he abandoned the project.

He tackled the subject again, however, in the smaller fragment 'The Fall of Hyperion'. This time the poet tells how, finding himself in a luxuriant natural setting, he drinks a magic potion, falls into a slumber, and is led in a vision to the shrine of the prophetess Moneta, who takes him where he can look upon the fallen Saturn and Thea. The fragment includes a significant dialogue between Moneta and the poet: he stands below the steps that lead to immortality and begs to be enlightened.

'None can usurp this height,' return'd that shade,
'But those to whom the miseries of the world
Are misery, and will not let them rest.'

Such men are neither 'visionaries' nor 'dreamers', she goes on. Keats's frankness here in facing his own lack of social involvement in the causes that Shelley and his like espoused shows a touching honesty.

The 1820 volume contains one other narrative poem, 'Lamia'. Lamia is a serpent transformed by Hermes into a beautiful woman so that she can pursue and seduce Lycius whom she loves. The two betake themselves to her sumptuous palace, but at their wedding feast Lycius's wise old teacher Apollonius penetrates Lamia's disguise and cries her name. 'Begone, foul dream!' After a brief altercation she vanishes, and Lycius is found to be dead. The poem is in couplets, the narrative is neatly managed, and an air of accomplished craftsmanship prevails. It is interesting that Keats once more has recourse to classical legend. From the start Greek mythology had an irresistible appeal for him. It is only necessary to compare 'Hyperion' with its model, *Paradise Lost*, to recognise how central to Keats's thinking as a poet was pagan mythology. Christianity is not something which, like Shelley, Keats attacked. It is something he ignored.

The most solid testimony to the greatness of the 1820 volume is to be found in the odes. In the ode form Keats found (as Wordsworth did in the 'Immortality' ode) a vehicle through which he could explore his world and his response to it, dredge out from deep within himself whatever truths could be clung to in the face of life's transitoriness and his own unfulfilled aspirations. In the 'Ode to a Nightingale' the poet is drugged by his share in the happiness poured out through the bird's song. In this mood he longs for a 'draught of vintage' that would carry him away from the world of human suffering —

The weariness, the fever, and the fret
Here, where men sit and hear each other groan.

He would leave the world where the young grow pale and thin, and die, where beauty fades and love does not last. He determines to join the nightingale in its world of happiness by means of the poetic imagination, and he surrenders himself to the beauty around him. The ultimate sequence to such bliss must surely be death.

> Now more than ever seems it rich to die,
> To cease upon the midnight with no pain . . .

The nightingale at least represents one aspect of immortality, its song being heard century after century. But finally the imagination falters, and the sense of reality returns.

If surrender to the song of the nightingale provides a release from time, so too does contemplation of a work of art in 'Ode on a Grecian Urn'. The human beauty and love captured in the figures on its frieze can never fade or die as they do in real life. The pictured trees can never shed their foliage. Thus the urn remains for ever a testimony that 'Beauty is truth, truth beauty', for its silent loveliness has the profound stability of the eternal. The 'Ode on Melancholy' expresses the ultimate irony of Keats's concern with the way beauty and happiness die. Addressing the reader, the poet insists that in order to indulge the full pathos of life we must turn from what is overtly gloomy and concentrate on what is supremely beautiful and joyful, recalling that in its transience lies the heart of sadness. In these odes Keats's uncanny mastery of verbal texture and tonality is at once infused by deeply felt personal anguish and subjected to the discipline of a poetic form perfectly tuneable to his gifts.

The 'Ode to Autumn' and the 'Ode to Psyche' are more purely descriptive pieces, rich in the same fine-grained sensuousness. 'La Belle Dame Sans Merci' is an exercise in simple balladry, magically resonant with harmonics of the unnervingly preternatural. Once more it assays in miniature the theme of seductive ensnarement that leaves life's sojourner 'alone and palely loitering'. Keats became also a master of the sonnet, using it for praise of other writers (Shakespeare in 'O golden tongued Romance, with serene lute!'), for sad reflection on his own lot ('When I have fears that I may cease to be'), and at the last for a cry from the sickbed for his loved one's presence ('Bright star! would I were stedfast as thou art').

William Blake

Not all poets writing between 1790 and 1830 could be classed as 'Romantic'. Literary historians have tended to place William Blake (1757–1827), who was born in the same year as Burns, among the late eighteenth-century precursors of Romanticism. It is only what he has in common with certain others that can make a poet part of a 'movement', and there is a great deal in the work of Blake that represents a wholly unique vision. Essentially a prophet, he devoted immense effort to the composition of vast 'poetic' works which in style are frequently little more than rhetorical prose chopped up into lines, and in substance employ a private mythology which only enthusiasts have the patience to interpret. Yet if Romanticism connotes an outburst of individualism directed against received convention and accepted code, if it connotes a frontal assault upon corruptions, moral and social, that enslave, if it connotes eagerness for stylistic experiment, for the utmost exploitation either of the simple or the complex, and if it connotes total and defiant self-commitment to what inner inspiration demands of the artist, then Blake is perhaps the supreme Romantic.

It may be argued that Keats's failure with 'Hyperion' revealed classical mythology to be no longer capable of sustaining the universality of appeal needed in epic treatment. In any case Blake's need was for a degree of moral earnestness and satire which only a deeply believed religious framework could sustain. Thus the prose work *The Marriage of Heaven and Hell* (1793) is rich in aphorism and paradox which seemingly turn Christian categories upside down. Blake will not accept the duality of Body and Soul, of Energy or Evil and Reason or Good.

(1) Man has no Body distinct from his Soul.
(2) Energy is the only life, and is from the Body; and Reason is the round or outward circumference of Energy.
(3) Energy is Eternal Delight.

It is not difficult to cull from this work aphorisms that chime in with much that we have found in the major Romantic poets in the way of celebrating imagination, independence, the feelings, and the passions, such as 'Sooner murder an infant in its cradle than nurse unacted desires'. *America* (1793), which is verse with a somewhat vague metrical basis, is a prophecy and celebration of revolution. *Visions of the Daughters of Albion* (1793) is an ardent defence of natural passion, 'a great plea for sexual freedom', the poet Kathleen Raine has called it. In later prophetic books, such as *The Book of Urizen* (1794), *Milton* (1804–8), and *Jerusalem* (1804–20), Blake developed his unique mythology. What emerges repeatedly in his longer works is his hatred of the effects of the Industrial Revolution, his hatred of what he considers to be the barren rationalism represented by English thinkers such as Bacon, Newton, and Locke, his mystical openness to revelation, and his urge to project a Christianity free from codifications and self-centred rationalisations that are alien to the reality of the Divine Humanity and the authority of the inspired imagination.

Blake was artist as well as poet, and engraved and printed his own works. He had to make his living as an engraver, sometimes of worthless material. His marriage to a comparatively uneducated woman, Catherine, was a happy and companionable one, though childless. No poem is more widely known to the English than Blake's prefatory verses to *Milton*, now popularly called 'Jerusalem' ('And did those feet in ancient time / Walk upon England's mountains green?'); but what now gives Blake his decisive status as a poet is the lyric output which preceded and in some cases enriched his bigger works. In particular the dichotomies explored in depth later are evident in *Songs of Innocence* (1789) and *Songs of Experience* (1794). In the first collection Blake shows himself master of a limpid, childlike simplicity which is never naïve but rather apt to give off fitful resonances, religious or social. Such is the case in 'Little Lamb, who made thee?', where the reply is:

Little Lamb, I'll tell thee:
He is called by thy name.

Such too is the case with the portraits in 'The Chimney Sweeper' and 'The Little Black Boy'.

But in *Songs of Experience* the tables are turned. Instead of the Lamb there is 'The Tyger'. Instead of 'Who made thee?', we have:

What immortal hand or eye
Could frame thy fearful symmetry?

Instead of the little chimney sweep's dream of heaven, we have the reality of his misery. And:

For Mercy has a human heart,
Pity a human face,
And Love, the human form divine,
And Peace, the human dress.

has become:

Cruelty has a Human Heart,
And Jealousy a Human Face;
Terror the Human Form Divine,
And Secrecy the Human Dress.

Blake has a unique capacity to give resonance to the simple lyric without detriment to its simplicity; to load it subtly with irony or obliquity, paradox or metaphor, which at once disturb and delight. Consider the Epilogue to *The Gates of Paradise* (1793):

Truly, My Satan, thou art but a Dunce,
And dost not know the Garment from the Man;
Every Harlot was a Virgin once,
Nor can'st thou ever change Kate into Nan.

George Crabbe

Another prolific poet whose major output coincided with that of the Romantic poets without thereby making him fully one of their number was George Crabbe (1754–1832). Nevertheless just as Blake's prophetic role gave him a place at their side, so George Crabbe has characteristics which link him decisively with the Romantics. Crabbe was born in Aldeburgh, East Anglia, the son of a minor customs official and part-time fisherman. He was educated at Bungay and Stowmarket, and then given a medical training. But he forsook medical practice to try to live by his pen, and was fortunate to receive help and encouragement when he sent specimens of his work to Edmund Burke. He was ordained in 1781 and held various country livings. There was a gap of twenty years between the publication of the two early collections of poetry, *The Village* (1783) and *The Newspaper* (1785), and the more mature volumes which place his work firmly in the Romantic period, *The Parish Register* (1807), *The Borough* (1810), *Tales in Verse* (1812), and *Tales of the Hall* (1819).

In *The Parish Register* Crabbe makes the church's record of the year's baptisms, marriages, and funerals a starting point for a series of sketches of the characters and stories of various parishioners. For instance, the first name is that of an illegitimate child, born to Lucy, daughter of the local miller, a proud, overbearing father. She was wooed and seduced by a poor sailor whom the miller rebuffed. The miller throws out his pregnant daughter. The sailor is killed abroad. This sets the pattern of Crabbe's distinctive blend of character study and narrative.

The Borough provides another detailed survey of small-town life in a series of so-called 'Letters'. They have such headings as 'The Church', 'The Vicar — The Curate etc', 'The Election', 'Professions — Law', 'Trades', 'Amusements', 'Players', 'The Almshouse and Trustees'. In these a gallery of portraiture of life at various levels is presented with a down-to-earth directness peculiarly forceful when contained within Crabbe's crisp but fluent couplets. In some of the letters a character receives substantial narrative treatment. There is, for instance, the story of 'Peter Grimes' which was adapted to form the libretto of Benjamin Britten's opera. There is also the story of Blaney, adept at winning and dissipating fortunes and finally admitted to the almshouse, the victim of his unprincipled irresponsibility.

> Nor love nor care for him will mortal show,
> Save a frail sister in the female row.

Which brings us to the story of his fellow-inmate, Clelia, whose liaisons have brought her to the same spot. By such means Crabbe binds his material together.

Crabbe increasingly strengthened his narrative line, as is evidenced in his later volumes of *Tales*. Over his work as a whole the range of his portraiture provides fascinating documentation of the characters of professional men and labourers, tradesmen and fishermen, rogues and smugglers, the respectable and the riff-raff, all surveyed with an eye which is unsparing in the accuracy of observation of the people and their ways, yet manages never to be censorious. What most decisively gives Crabbe's later work a place on the periphery of the Romantic movement is, firstly, that he totally rejected any sentimentalisation of rurality and its dwellers. The poeticisation of the countryside and its picturesque inhabitants in which eighteenth-century poetry had often delighted was something he utterly forswore. Truth to nature was his first principle.

> By such examples taught, I paint the Cot,
> As Truth will paint it, and as bards will not.

And the second characteristic which links Crabbe with his 'Romantic' contemporaries is his analytical exploration of the psychology of his characters, especially perhaps of the unbalanced, the neurotic, the devious, and the unsavoury. There is what can justly be called a 'Wordsworthian' plainness of approach and style and a 'Wordsworthian' fascination with the lot of the unprivileged and the unfortunate.

Thomas Moore

While Shelley and Keats were little read, the works of Crabbe sold well, as did those of Scott and Byron. Thomas Moore (1779–1852) achieved comparable popularity. He was so successful that by 1812 Longman offered him £3000 for a projected oriental romance. This was the genesis of *Lalla Rookh* (1817). It sets four narrative poems within the framework of a rather slight prose tale. Lalla Rookh, daughter of the Indian emperor Aurengzebe, is promised in marriage to the king of Bucharia. She sets out from Delhi with her magnificent caravan and is beguiled on the tedious journey by the Cashmere minstrel Feramorz.

The exotic oriental background is stagily contrived and lacks authenticity. Metrically the lines too often bounce ponderously forward, rhymes chiming obtrusively and gratingly. The main effect of *Lalla Rookh* on the modern reader is to fill him with new respect for the engagingly flexible music that Scott and Byron so often sustained in their narrative romances.

Moore was born in Dublin, the son of a grocer, and educated at Trinity College. He came to England, was given an Admiralty post in Bermuda, but after a brief stay there he appointed a deputy and returned to England via America. Moore had published poems under the pseudonym 'Thomas Little' in 1801, and thus he is greeted in Byron's *English Bards and Scotch Reviewers*:

Tis Little! young Catullus of his day,
As sweet, but as immoral, in his lay!

What was then considered to be a somewhat risqué element in some of his early verse gained him a reputation and a public. In spite of the aborted 'duel' already referred to, he became one of Byron's closest friends, a correspondent over many years. Byron entrusted his memoirs to Moore but, under family pressure, Moore allowed them to be burnt. Instead he presented the public with the first standard biography of the poet, *Letters and Journals of Lord Byron, with Notices of His Life* (1830). This, along with Moore's lives of *Sheridan* (1825) and *Lord Edward Fitzgerald* (1831), give him a place among the major English biographers.

The grocer's son from Dublin who became a favourite of London society and an intimate of the noble lord possessed great charm of character. Between 1807 and 1834 he published his *Irish Melodies*. The felicitous wording, the smooth versification, and the flexible rhythms of these poems made them at once easily memorable and eminently singable. The tenderness of the love poems, the nostalgia for an idealised Ireland, and indeed the cultivation of an 'Irish' Romanticism peculiarly acceptable in English drawing-rooms and remote from revolutionary realities at home made it fashionable eventually to denigrate Moore by drawing comparison with more virile and socially aware poetry, such as that of the Scottish Burns. But Moore contributed to Irish patriotism by stirring the Irish, however sentimentally, to an awareness of their national inheritance and by supplying to succeeding decades a means of celebrating it fervently and decorously.

The uniqueness of Moore's achievement is now recognised. His verses were meant to be sung: and indeed they 'sing' in the ear before ever a note is sounded. Moreover, they have lasted and will last. Some carry their own brand of pathos from past tragedies. Moore had known Robert Emmet, the young revolutionary of 1798, when they were at Trinity College together. He paid tribute to Emmet's heroism in 'Oh! Breathe not his Name', and to the grief of his sweetheart after his execution in 'She is far from the land':

She is far from the land where her young hero sleeps,
    And lovers are round her, sighing;
But coldly she turns from their gaze, and weeps,
    For her heart in his grave is lying.

Such lyrics, like 'The last rose of summer', 'Believe me, if all those endearing young charms', 'The harp that once through Tara's halls', 'Silent, O Moyle! be the roar of thy water', and 'Let Erin remember the days of old', captivate by what is really a consummate artistry in touching the heart by frankly laying it open and doing so with a simplicity too genuine to strive always to evade the obvious.

There are those who praise Moore chiefly for his satire. But in this genre his work has been too topical to last. *The Twopenny Post-Bag* (1813) affects to present to the reader letters dropped by a postman and undelivered. By this device public figures are made satiric targets. Today, however, we find more life, and less spite, in *The Fudge Family in Paris* (1818), which makes fun of an English family on a visit abroad.

Thomas Hood

It may come as something of a surprise to discover how much comic verse was written during the Romantic period. Wordsworth provoked parodic pastiche of his work. His 'Peter Bell', in which simplicity degenerates into absurdity and doggerel, brought a mocking riposte from Shelley, 'Peter Bell the Third'. It had to be 'the Third' because a second 'Peter Bell' had already emerged from the minor poet John Hamilton Reynolds (1796–1852). In it Peter, in advanced old age, peers among churchyard gravestones, registering the deaths of various persons from Wordsworth's poems until he is eventually cheered by a more welcome inscription:

> The letters printed are by fate,
> The death they say was suicide;
> He reads — 'Here lieth W. W.
> Who never more will trouble you, trouble you.'

Reynolds was the close friend of Keats, with whom he planned a joint volume of adaptations from Boccaccio, and it was for this project that Keats wrote 'Isabella'. Reynolds, however, preferred security to poetic poverty and in 1818 sent Keats a delightful sonnet bidding farewell to the Muses. He did not forsake literature entirely however, for he collaborated with Thomas Hood (1799–1845) in the anonymous *Odes and Addresses to Great People* in 1825.

In that year Hood married Reynolds's sister Jane. Hood was born in London, the son of an expatriate Scot who had turned publisher. The *Odes and Addresses*, of which Hood had written much the larger and indeed the better part, was well received. Speculating on the authorship, Coleridge suspected it was the work of Charles Lamb. (Anonymity produced strange attributions. In 1817 Byron had repeatedly to refute his sister's suspicion that he was 'Peter Pattieson', the pseudonymous author of Scott's *Old Mortality*.) Having once amused the public, Hood found that he was expected to go on producing comic verse.

His most remarkable comic vein has two notable characteristics, the blend of the amusing with what is by nature serious, grave, even tragic or bloodthirsty, and the dependence for hilarity on outrageously clever puns. 'Faithless Sally Brown' is a ballad which turns infidelity into farce.

Ben is press-ganged into the navy and his sweetheart faints away. When he returns he finds himself supplanted by another. He chews his pigtail and dies.

His death, which happen'd in his berth,
    At forty-odd befell;
They went and told the sexton, and
    The sexton toll'd the bell.

In the same genre 'Faithless Nellie Gray' makes hilarious fun of Ben Battle, who has lost both legs in war. When his former sweetheart, Nellie Gray, refuses to have a man 'with both legs in the grave', he realises that some other man is 'standing in' his shoes and hangs himself.

Yet there was another side to Hood, which gives him a deserved place among the Romantics. His taste for the macabre is in the Gothick tradition going back to Mrs Radcliffe. 'The Dream of Eugene Aram, the Murderer' is a ballad with the compulsive neurotic ambience of Coleridge's 'The Ancient Mariner'. Aram too is burdened by the guilt of killing, and must tell his story with the maximum indulgence in its horrors and terrors. He is a schoolmaster, and he pins a boy, recounting the gory details and the appalling psychological consequences with the pretence that he has dreamed it all. After a night of agony he was drawn back to where he had thrown the corpse in a stream.

Heavily I rose up, as soon
    As light was in the sky,
And sought the black accursed pool
    With a wild misgiving eye;
And I saw the Dead in the river bed,
    And the faithless stream was dry.

The incantatory pulse of the ballad metre and the simple, emphatic rhetoric have a Coleridgean power to haunt and disturb.

An even more disturbing exercise in creating an atmosphere of mystery and terror is 'The Haunted House', where Hood conjures up a sense of tingling awe and shrinking apprehension, vibrating with overtones of menacing preternatural intrusion, as the reader is slowly conducted into the house and upstairs.

No human figure stirr'd, to go or come,
No face look'd forth from shut or open casement;
No chimney smoked — there was no sign of Home
From parapet to basement.

Towards the end of his life Hood began to use his power to work on the feelings and arouse pity and awe for a new social purpose. Thus 'The Song of the Shirt' presents the picture of a poor seamstress sitting in rags and misery, toiling ceaselessly to make what could barely be called a living.

> O! Men with Sisters dear!
> O! Men with Mothers and wives,
> It is not linen you're wearing out,
> But human creatures' lives!

Published in *Punch* at Christmas 1843, along with 'The Pauper's Christmas Carol', it soon became widely known, and was taken up by the working-classes to become part of the popular literature inspiring radical reform. A cry against a different aspect of human exploitation is voiced in 'The Bridge of Sighs', a terse, tight-lipped commentary on the lifting up of one more of those seduced and abandoned girls who threw themselves into the river to drown.

Ebenezer Elliott

A less well-known poet whose work likewise became an inspiration to the radical working-class movement was Ebenezer Elliott (1781–1849), a Yorkshireman, largely self-educated, who began work in his father's iron foundry in Rotherham and continued to deal in iron when it failed. He was active in the Chartist movement. He wrote a collection of *Corn Law Rhymes* (1831) which pulled no punches: witness this song to be sung to the tune of 'Robin Adair':

> Child, is thy father dead?
>   Father is gone!
> Why did they tax his bread?
>   God's will be done!
> Mother has sold her bed;
>   Better to die than wed!
> Where shall she lay her head?
>   Home we have none!

Elliott's pictures of poverty and misery among the labouring classes certainly link him with Hood. He was also bitter in his portrayal of the transformation of rural village life by the Enclosure policy, for it deprived villagers of their common lands in the interests of more productive and up-to-date agriculture. In *The Splendid Village* (1833), a poem highly derivative of Oliver Goldsmith's *Deserted Village* (1770), a wanderer returns to his native village, weary of roaming, and hungry to find a congenial environment for a happy retreat. Instead he finds an armed game-keeper ready to treat him as a vagabond, a brother and his wife beaten into dejection and poverty, the village school replaced by a private academy for the rich, and a squirearchy in the hands of brutal, ignorant, bloated *nouveaux riches*. The village rector is an absentee pluralist. The idyllic past is no more. The village green has gone, the common too.

> Where is the Common, once with blessings rich —
> The poor man's Common? — like the poor man's flitch
> And well-fed ham, which erst his means allow'd,
> 'Tis gone to bloat the idle and the proud!

Elliott's picture is a depressing one. 'The very children seem afraid to smile' and a 'tax-plough'd waste' replaces shepherd and sheep, hind and cow, cock and hen, and blooming milk-maid.

> But yonder stalks the greatest man alive!
> One farmer prospers now, where prosper'd five!

James Hogg

Elliott had really much more in common with Burns than with his Scottish contemporary, James Hogg (1770–1835), the 'Ettrick Shepherd'. Hogg was a largely self-taught fiddler and singer whose help was sought by Scott when gathering material for *Minstrelsy of the Scottish Border*. With Scott's assistance Hogg burst upon the literary scene to enjoy the success that had attended the lionisation of the peasant-poet, Burns. When Hogg was invited to Scott's house in Edinburgh and went there fresh from the sheep-market with its marks upon him, he was led into a room where Mrs Scott, a little indisposed, reclined stretched out on a sofa. Thinking it appropriate to adjust his manners to those of the lady of the house, Hogg stretched himself out on a sofa opposite her.

Hogg published *The Mountain Bard* (1807) and *The Forest Minstrel* (1810), collections of verse, but it was *The Queen's Wake* (1813) which proved an immense success. In it he was determined to emulate Scott as a narrative poet. The 'wake' is a celebration at Holyrood in honour of Mary Queen of Scots. A contest is held at which minstrels compete for pre-eminence. A bard from Fife presents 'The Witch of Fife', a virile, swift-moving tale of the preternatural, which yet is securely rooted in reality through the character of the witch's husband. He opens the poem, wanting to know where his wife and her colleagues have been during the last three nights. He is naturally apprehensive.

> 'It fearis me muckil ye haif seen
>   Quhat guid man never knew;
> It fearis me muckil ye haif been
>   Quhare the gray cock never crew.
>
> 'But the spell may crack, and the brydel breck,
>   Then sherpe yer werde will be;

Ye had better sleip in yer bed at hame,
  Wi' yer deire littil bairnis and me.'

His wife tells how on the first night she and the others rode hunting, drank magical beer, and saw a phantasmal being whose piping set all creatures dancing. On the second night they sailed in a cockleshell to Norway and Lapland to join a festival of fairies and genii. On the last night they flew to Carlisle and drank the bishop's wine. This news puts an end to the husband's hitherto worried remonstrances. He wants to go too. He spies on the next coven, learns the magic formula, and flies after them to Carlisle. He is found dead drunk next morning by Englishmen and only rescued from being burned to death by remembering the magic word that frees him to fly home.

The poem has great vitality, combining the narrative vividness, the concise descriptive boldness, and the dramatic thrust that come from cunning use of traditional devices. The faint ironic overtones which make the reader conscious of the need to keep his tongue in his cheek are, however, utterly absent from the best poem in the collection, 'Kilmeny', which is presented by a bard from Ern in the Highlands. This charming poem in smoothly flowing four-foot couplets tells how Kilmeny goes up the glen one day and does not return. She is transported to a visionary land of loveliness and light, inhabited by beautiful beings. She is told by one of them that he searched far and wide for a 'sinless virgin, free of stain / In mind and body', and could find only Kilmeny.

I have brought her away frae the snares of men,
That sin and death she never may ken.

She is urged, if ever she returns to the world 'of sin, of sorrow and fear', to tell of the joys waiting here. They submerge her body in a stream to make her eternally young and beautiful. They show her a vision of historic strife between Scotland, England, and France, and of ultimate peace and harmony. Then she begins to long to go back home to her own world. Her wish is granted. She returns home, bearing with her an unearthly beauty and shedding about her an unearthly tranquillity that infect even bird and beast, and draw them to her.

And all in a peaceful ring were hurled;
It was like an eve in a sinless world!

After a month and a day Kilmeny disappears again.

She left this world of sorrow and pain,
And returned to the land of thought again.

The 'land of thought' of course matches that realm of which Keats dreamed, where beauty and love can neither fade nor die.

Robert Bloomfield, John Clare

The cult of the peasant-poet was not just a Scottish phenomenon. In England at the turn of the century the collection *The Farmer's Boy* (1800) brought success to Robert Bloomfield (1766–1823). Though Bloomfield was brought up in rural Suffolk and saw farm life there, he was soon apprenticed to a London shoemaker and could not claim the extensive rural experience of a Burns or a Hogg. Nevertheless he gives a record of a farmhand's daily work which is convincingly practical and yet finely alert in its awareness of the environment. Thus, when Giles goes out at night to check on the sheep:

> From the fire-side with many a shrug he hies,
> Glad if the full-orb'd Moon salute his eyes,
> And through the unbroken stillness of the night
> Shed on his path her beams of cheering light.

Plainly Bloomfield's tone and idiom are those of eighteenth-century pastoral verse; his couplets breathe the mannered decorum of Thomson and Goldsmith, and for all his knowledge of farm life the voice could be that of a spectator.

Bloomfield had published several volumes and even his *Collected Poems* (1817) by the time John Clare (1793–1864) began his poetic career with *Poems Descriptive of Rural Life and Scenery* (1820) and *The Village Minstrel* (1821). In the meantime the Ettrick Shepherd had brought the stains of the sheep-market into the Edinburgh drawing-room. Though Clare was born of the same generation as Byron and within a year or so of Keats and Shelley, he was to live long after they were dead, and indeed his later poetry belongs outside the scope of this book. There could be no doubt about Clare's credentials as a 'peasant-poet'. Born at Helpstone in what was then rural Northamptonshire, he worked as a farm-labourer, and though his first volume of poems was a success, its chief effect on him was to make him suspect locally, and subsequent collections sold poorly. His struggle against poverty while burdened by a growing family, his frustrations as a poet, and his social concern about rural deprivation and hardship in the wake of the Napoleonic wars together helped to unhinge him, and his last thirty-four years were spent in asylums for the insane.

Clare's rural scenes breathe authenticity and understanding. His labourer rising in 'Harvest Morning', unlike Bloomfield's shepherd turning out at night, is conceived from within by one who has shared his experience.

> Cocks wake the early morn with many a Crow
> Loud ticking clock has counted four
> The labouring rustic hears his restless foe

> And weary bones and pains complaining sore
> Hobbles to fetch his horses from the moor . . .

Moreover, when 'lovely Emma' is pictured among the harvesters and her beauties described 'blooming in low life unseen', Clare finds it a harsh incongruity that she should be thus employed.

> O Poverty! how basely you demean
> The imprison'd worth your rigid fates confine.

No portraiture could be more exact, no observation of environment more detailed than Clare's in, say, 'The Woodman'. The man's toiling days, his generous humanity, his scanty leisure in the bosom of his family, and his simple faith are recounted with a sincerity which is touchingly cheerful. Yet Clare does not forget to observe that the slavish rigours of the man's life are inescapable, the doors of wealth are forever shut against his kind, and it is only by sheer good luck that he has his health and can avoid the humiliation of dependence on the parish.

Clare's output includes a large group of poems about birds as well as about flowers and animals. (The listed titles of Clare's bird poems looks like the index to an ornithological encyclopaedia.) He has an uncanny talent for pin-pointing their individual characteristics and taking vivid snapshots of them as they go about their business. The loving thoroughness with which minute avian idiosyncrasies are observed and recorded gives Clare a status as a poet of natural life that is second to no one's. Such sensitive intrusions into the familiar world of England's bird-life and beast-life are deeply moving to the responsive reader. So too are those later poems written in the asylum where Clare's cries *de profundis* acquire a mystical dimension.

Samuel Rogers, Thomas Campbell

We leap across a dozen social barriers to pay due respect to a poet whose name recurs continually in the literary memoirs of the period. Samuel Rogers (1763–1855) was a banker who could afford to play the part of a dilettante in the world of letters and art. His entrée into the circles of the great was a help to Wordsworth on his visits to town, and the ubiquitous socialite Tom Moore was forever encountering him at fashionable parties. Rogers's literary reputation was based on his highly successful poem *The Pleasures of Memory* (1792), the flavour of which can be grasped from the tone of his own introduction.

> The Poem begins with the description of an obscure village, and of the pleasing melancholy which it excites on being revisited after a long absence. This mixed sensation is an effect of the Memory. From an effect we naturally succeed to the cause; and the subject proposed is

then unfolded with an investigation of the nature and leading principles of this faculty.

The project is carried out in some 600 lines of heroic couplets, smoothly unassertive, unenlivened by anything distinctive in imaginative or intellectual content, but harking back to mid-eighteenth-century idiom:

Hark! the bee winds her small but mellow horn,
Blithe to salute the sunny smile of morn.

It was fortunate for Rogers that he so delighted in memory, for his ninety-odd years gave him ample opportunity to exercise the faculty. In his *Lectures on the English Poets* (1818) Hazlitt put his finger, if rather roughly, on Rogers's failings:

He is a very lady-like poet. He is an elegant, but feeble writer . . . and his verses are poetry, chiefly because no particle, line, or syllable of them reads like prose.

The Scottish poet Thomas Campbell (1777–1844) took a leaf out of Rogers's book when he bid for popular success (and achieved it) with *The Pleasures of Hope* (1799); but hope proved to be an unsatisfactory conceptual peg on which to hang illustrations and reflections, especially for a writer so unphilosophically minded as Campbell, and the poem is something of a hotch-potch. However, it has contributed some lines to our stock of common quotations, notably:

'Tis distance lends enchantment to the view,
And robes the mountain in its azure hue.

and

What though my winged hours of bliss have been,
Like angel-visits, few and far between?

It is to another of Campbell's poems ('Lochiel's Warning') that we owe the saying, 'Coming events cast their shadows before'.

It is ironic that Campbell's cultivation of hope led to so little in the literary field. His later work disappointed his contemporaries. Nevertheless his output contains a few poems which have made a lasting impression on our national literary consciousness. There are the tragic ballads 'Lord Ullin's Daughter' and 'The Maid of Neidpath', the awesomely compulsive battle poem 'Hohenlinden', and what is perhaps most characteristic of Campbell, the hectoringly virile exercises in rhythmic martial rhodomontade, 'The Battle of the Baltic' and 'Ye Mariners of England'. There was a time when every schoolchild would learn something of Campbell's work, if it was only 'The Soldier's Dream', an exercise in the searing pathos of dreaming of home and family on the field of battle.

Other minor poets:
Landor, Bowles, Hemans, Frere

Another writer whose longevity, like Rogers's, gives him a place in the literature of two ages, was Walter Savage Landor (1775–1864). He was still publishing in the 1840s and 1850s, but his career as a poet began as early as 1795 (with *Poems*), and his most celebrated poem, *Gebir* (1798), came out in the same year as the *Lyrical Ballads*. The contrast between these two publications could scarcely be exaggerated. Landor took the tale, 'The History of Charoba, Queen of Egypt', from *The Progress of Romance* (1787), a study by the Gothick novelist Clara Reeve (1729–1807). It tells how Gebirus comes with his army, determined to force Charoba into marriage. He is outwitted by the queen through the skilful help of her nurse, and the city he is founding is destroyed. Landor built this tale up by ramification, allusion, and lavish use of the decorative devices of the epic poet into a blank verse work of seven books and some 2000 lines. Even with the help of the prose 'Argument', which Landor inserted at the beginning of each book, the work is confusing and the progress of the narrative difficult to disentangle. De Quincey, who claimed that only two people had read the poem, to wit Southey and himself, cited a description of Gebir preparing for his first interview with Charoba as representative of the picturesqueness of Landor's portraits:

> But Gebir, when he heard of her approach,
> Laid by his orbed shield: his vizor helm,
> His buckler and his corslet he laid by,
> And bade that none attend him: at his side
> Two faithful dogs that urge the silent course,
> Shaggy, deep-chested, croucht; the crocodile
> Crying, oft made them raise their flaccid ears,
> And push their heads within their master's hand . . .

What is interesting about the work is the way it exemplifies a conception of the poet's task totally different from that entertained by Wordsworth. Like Southey, Landor was an enthusiast for what W. L. Renwick (in *English Literature 1789–1815*, *Oxford History of English Literature*, Vol. 9) calls 'the grand or historical creation that demanded elaborate construction, notebooks full of information, and sustained objective effort of the imagination'. This was not the recipe for either *The Prelude* or *The Excursion*, for either Byron's *Don Juan* or Shelley's *The Revolt of Islam*. Landor was a classicist, and his output of shorter poems includes some neatly disciplined love lyrics and some notable epigrammatic verses that reveal his gift for crispness and polish. None is so widely known as his 'Dying Speech of an Old Philosopher':

I strove with none, for none was worth my strife.
Nature I loved, and next to Nature, Art.
I warmed both hands before the fire of life.
It sinks; and I am ready to depart.

William Lisle Bowles (1762–1850), a clergyman, began his long career as a writer with *Fourteen Sonnets* (1789), and he won the admiration of both Wordsworth and Coleridge. Though his output was to include long poems such as *The Grave of the Last Saxon* (1822) and *St John in Patmos* (1832), his sonnets alone have any historical significance. In the first place, the sonnet form had been neglected during the eighteenth century, and its revival by Bowles for use in personal reflection proved important for the Romantic poets. In the second place, Bowles's sonnets were imbued with an effusion of tender sensibility and opened up a vein of ruminative emotionalism that clearly appealed to contemporaries, however cloying we may find it now.

The sonnets repeatedly tap the vein of nostalgic regret, indulging moods of gentle, tender sorrow as partings, absences, or bereavements are dwelt upon. Places are visited and the lost hopes of youth lamented.

O Time! who know'st a lenient hand to lay
Softest on Sorrow's wound, and slowly thence,
Lulling to sad repose the weary sense,
The faint pang stealest unperceived away . . .

In smooth cadences the regrets of life and its inadequate consolations are languidly laid before us:

Yet ah! how much must that poor heart endure,
Which hopes from thee, and thee alone, a cure.

The bland verbal *bel canto* undulates insinuatingly but nervelessly on the ear, the lugubrious tonality and the textural flaccidity evoking an atmosphere of soporific tedium.

There is more versatility and more sturdiness of tone and temper in the work of Mrs Felicia Hemans (1793–1835), who was fortunate enough to win the respect of Wordsworth and Scott, Shelley and Byron.

True bard and holy! — thou art e'en as one
Who, by some secret gift of soul of eye,
In every spot beneath the smiling sun,
Sees where the springs of living water lie . . .

So Mrs Hemans addressed Wordsworth when she stayed at Rydal. Sara Hutchinson and Mary found her trying. 'Her affectation is perfectly unendurable,' Sara wrote. Wordsworth, however, said, 'I took her part upon all occasions . . . there was much sympathy between us,' and he added a stanza in her praise in the verses 'On the Death of James Hogg':

Mourn rather for that holy Spirit,
Sweet as the spring, as ocean deep;
For Her who, ere her summer faded,
Has sunk into a breathless sleep.

Poets who call each other 'holy' are apt to make us wince, and it is easy to make fun of Mrs Hemans if only because her most remembered poems, 'The boy stood on the burning deck' ('Casabianca') and 'The stately homes of England', have left us with phrases over-quoted in the past and therefore readily discreditable in the present. But the modern reader who searches through Mrs Hemans's vast output will be astonished at the general level of sheer accomplishment sustained in long romantic narrative poems, Welsh airs, miscellaneous lyrics, and religious verse. *Records of Woman* is a collection of nineteen poems in various metres, celebrating historical and legendary figures, and beginning with Arabella Stuart. James I separated her from her husband and imprisoned her because of the threat she represented to the succession as a descendant of Henry VII.

The genuineness of Mrs Hemans's response to what is beautiful or worthy, tender or pathetic, shows a romantic sensibility which, if neither bracing nor imaginatively adventurous, somehow escapes the soporific debilitation of Rogers and Bowles. In introducing an edition of her work to the Victorian public in 1873, W.M. Rossetti declared:

She is a leader in that very modern phalanx of poets who persistently coordinate the impulse of sentiment with the guiding power of morals or religion. Everything must convey its 'lesson', and is indeed set forth for the sake of its lesson: but must at the same time have the emotional gush of a spontaneous sentiment.

One cannot leave consideration of the Romantic poets without noting the indebtedness of Byron to the diplomatist John Hookham Frere (1769–1846), whose talent for comic and satiric verse reached its peak in *Prospectus and Specimen of an Intended National Work Relating to King Arthur* (1817–18), reissued as *The Monks and the Giants* (1818). The poem is presented by 'Robert Whistlecraft' as the work of his late brother William. In the verse form (*ottava rima*) and its handling it was immediately imitated by Byron in his comic poem *Beppo* (1818) and in *Don Juan*. Byron admitted his indebtedness, but felt that acknowledging it might damage Frere.

After a jaunty introduction, Canto I of Frere's poem takes us to a Christmas feast held by King Arthur and his knights at Carlisle. The knights are a vigorous band:

They look'd a manly, generous generation;
    Beards, shoulders, eyebrows, broad, and square, and thick,

Their accents firm and loud in conversation,
   Their eyes and gestures eager, sharp, and quick,
Show'd them prepar'd, on proper provocation,
   To give the lie, pull noses, stab and kick;
And for that very reason, it is said,
They were so very courteous and well-bred.

The reader will recognise the use of the stanza's final couplet to give an ironic twist to what has gone before as a trick which Byron took up and used to great effect. Southey noted the connection in writing to Landor of the importation of this sportive Italian form.

Frere began it. What he produced was too good in itself, and too inoffensive, to become popular for it attacked nothing and nobody . . . Lord Byron immediately followed . . . with his 'Don Juan', which is a foul blot on the literature of his country, an act of high treason on English poetry.

Part 3

The Romantic novel

Sir Walter Scott

Sir Walter Scott (1771–1832), like Wordsworth, has a greatness that transcends his status as a 'Romantic'. Indeed though Wordsworth has at least two superiors as an English poet, Scott has none as an English novelist. He was born in Edinburgh, the son of a well-to-do lawyer. An illness in infancy, which was probably poliomyelitis, left him with a slight lameness in one leg, and on health grounds he was sent for a time from the city to his grandfather's farm at Sandy Knowe in Roxburghshire, and later in boyhood he spent periods of time at an uncle's house at Kelso. Thus his city education at Edinburgh High School and Edinburgh University was interrupted by experience of a very different kind in the Border country to which he became permanently attached. Scott was admitted to the bar in 1792, and in this profession he was to rise eventually to become Sheriff-Depute of Selkirkshire and Clerk of Sessions.

The story of Scott's life can be so presented that it has on the reader the impact of a Greek tragedy, for it involves extremes of achievement and devastation. His son-in-law, John Gibson Lockhart (1794–1854), whom we shall discuss later as a prose writer in his own right, was to make of his *Life of Sir Walter Scott* (1837–8) not just an informative documentary rich in factual interest, but also a moving portrayal of personal triumph and disaster.

It was not Scott's legal career that had the makings of drama, but his literary career and the business interests which clustered around it. While he was attending Kelso Grammar School Scott had begun his life-long friendship with James Ballantyne and his brother John. James Ballantyne became owner of the *Kelso Mail* and an accomplished printer, and Scott arranged with his publisher that Ballantyne should print his *Minstrelsy of the Scottish Border*. By the time *The Lay of the Last Minstrel* came out Ballantyne, with Scott's encouragement, had set up house in Edinburgh, and once more Scott arranged for him to be the printer. Scott put money into Ballantyne's business and became a partner with one third of the profits credited to him. Though Scott the poet and the future Scott the novelist were profitable company for any publisher or printer to keep, Scott the editor indefatigably produced works (such as the eighteen-volume edition of Dryden and the nineteen-volume edition of Swift, not to mention the thirteen-volume *Collection of Scarce and Valuable Tracts* (1809–15)) which had a habit of lingering on bookshop shelves. But no publisher could afford not to humour Walter Scott, and the career of the Scottish publisher Archibald Constable, who started *The Edinburgh Review* in 1802, became closely involved with Scott's. The complex financial arrangements which inextricably entangled Scott with the fortunes of the printing-house and thereby the publishing-house were to prove disastrous for him at the peak of his career.

Meanwhile, however, the poems made money, and soon the novels made money too. Scott was rummaging in a drawer in 1813 when he found the first part of a novel which he had begun back in 1805 and put away after receiving discouraging advice about its opening chapters. This was *Waverley* (1814), with its subtitle *'Tis Sixty Years Since*, which looks back to the Jacobite Rebellion of 1745. Scott enjoyed secrecies and mystifications. His authorship of *Waverley* was concealed. As subsequent novels appeared they were presented as 'by the author of *Waverley*', or transparent pseudonyms were used, such as Jedediah Cleishbotham who had the 'Tales of My Landlord' from one Peter Pattieson. Thus the mystery of authorship provided a national sensation.

As the novels tumbled from the press and lavish advances were forwarded from publisher to author, Scott's passion for turning himself into a beneficent feudal lord with a magnificent family home outran all caution. He had married Charlotte Charpentier, the daughter of a French royalist family, in 1797. The couple lived in Edinburgh, then at Ashiestiel on the Tweed, and in 1811 Scott purchased a property at Abbotsford, which he set about rebuilding and expanding to the dimensions and the splendour of the kind of country house that goes with inherited wealth. Neighbouring estates were purchased. Auction sales of antiques were ransacked for suitable embellishments. Scott, as laird of Abbotsford, was a beneficent master of his retainers and a genial host to both the notabilities and the personal friends who became his guests. He loved the life of the moneyed laird and rose early to do his daily stint of writing before breakfast, thereby leaving himself free later for the better things of life.

It was not, however, Scott's romantic extravagance as the would-be originator of a line of landed gentry which ruined the commercial houses he was tied to. The London money-market had suffered from one of its periodic orgies of rash speculation late in 1825 when Ballantyne and Constable crashed, Ballantyne to the tune of over a quarter of a million. Scott found himself with debts amounting to some £120,000. The heroism with which he faced his misfortune is made evident in his private Journal.

He had already settled Abbotsford on his son; his creditors allowed him to keep his library, and he determined to pay off the debt with his pen and save himself the shame of bankruptcy.

The full extent of the disaster was brought home to Scott late in January 1826, but by 5 February he was writing:

> Rose after a sound sleep, and here am I without bile or anything to perturb my inward man. It is just about 3 weeks since so great a change took place in my relations in society, and already I am indifferent to it . . . If I have a very strong passion in the world, it is *pride*, and that never hinged upon the world's gear, which was always with me — light come, light go.

He was to suffer another blow before long, for his wife died in the following May. But what he made with his pen went a long way towards paying his debts before he died.

When Scott wrote a General Preface to the collected edition of his novels (1829), he told how he had hoped as a novelist to do for Scotland something of what Maria Edgeworth had done for Ireland, introducing Scotland's 'natives to those of the sister kingdom, in a more favourable light than they had been placed hitherto'. He was determined to represent a whole people. Indeed in the first chapter of *Waverley* (1814) he wrote:

> The lowbred Scottish gentlemen, and the subordinate characters, are not given as individual portraits, but are drawn from the general habits of the period . . .

In the first chapter too, after lightly ridiculing some contemporary brands of fiction, he explains that his own novel is neither a stilted tale of chivalrous romance, nor an atmospheric mystery novel, nor yet a crime extravaganza; neither a sentimental tale, nor a society novel, for the emphasis is not on temporary fashions, but on the 'characters and passions of the actors; — those passions common to men in all stages of society'.

Edward Waverley is a young Englishman with a romantic turn of mind who has been brought up alternately by his father, Richard Waverley, a careerist Whig politician, and his uncle, Sir Everard Digby, a Jacobite. Edward's desultory reading of imaginative literature has left him with a tendency to respond to romantic aspects of a situation rather than to weigh things coolly with rational judgment. Having taken a commission in the army and been posted to Scotland in 1745, he looks up some of his uncle's connections, the Bradwardines, while on leave, and is led by curiosity into the company of a rebel Jacobite Highland chieftain, Fergus MacIvor. He falls in love with Fergus's sister Flora, a beautiful and sincere devotee of the Stuart cause. She is a mine of folklore and plays her harp in an idyllic retreat by a waterfall. Waverley compromises himself with his regiment by his visits to her. Jacobite intrigue complicates the situation, and he is imprisoned. The sense of injustice overpowers his better judgment and, when Rose Bradwardine rescues him, he joins the Jacobites. He distinguishes himself at the battle of Prestonpans, but also conveniently saves the life of Colonel Talbot, an English officer of courage and common sense for whom Fergus's followers are only a 'gang of cut-throats'. This makes possible Edward's ultimate pardon.

Scott later called his hero 'a sneaking piece of imbecility'. Nevertheless the situation of the hero who — by a peculiar sequence of circumstances — gives his support to a cause to which in reason or by the demands of loyalty he ought to be opposed, served him well in later novels. It enabled him to take his reader inside the minds and hearts of bitterly opposed ideological groups. The fact that on the one side there are the compulsions of reason and common sense, of sobriety and prudence, while on the other side there are the lures of a romantic idealism which tugs at the heart and fires the imagination can no doubt tell us something about Scott's own personal character as calculating businessman and builder of Abbotsford. The pattern of ideological conflict which tears at the conscience and heart of a sensitive young man is Scott's nineteenth-century version of the age-old pattern which places Everyman between the Virtues and Vices in the morality plays or, for that matter, Othello between Desdemona and Iago in Shakespeare.

Important as this pattern was for Scott, there are plenty of novels — including some of the best — which do not employ it. *Guy Mannering* (1815) is a tale of usurpation. The laird of Ellangowan in Dumfriesshire is reduced to poverty through his carelessness and the villainy of the lawyer Glossin. Glossin achieves the removal of the child Henry Bertram, Ellangowan's heir, to Holland by kidnappers and, having driven the old laird to his grave, he takes over the estate. Henry, however (ignorant of his identity, and called 'Brown'), lives on in the army in India. When he returns 'home' in pursuit of his commanding officer's daughter, Julia Mannering, he is recognised by the gypsy Meg Merrilies and, in spite of Glossin's use of the smuggler Dirk Hatteraick in a second attempt to kidnap Henry, she engineers a happy ending. There is about the shape of the action something strongly reminiscent of Shakespeare's *A Winter's Tale*, with the loss of the true heiress in babyhood, her survival, and her return after sixteen years. Moreover, Meg Merrilies watches over the house of Ellangowan rather as Paulina functions in *A Winter's Tale*. Both are tutelary wire-pullers. This comparison is made because Scott's achievement as a novelist can be fully understood only in the light of two literary influences, that of the eighteenth-century novelists, and that of the Elizabethan dramatists. He drew upon both sources. And it is worth noting that the chapter mottoes in *Guy Mannering* are almost all from Shakespeare — from *All's Well that Ends Well, Much Ado about Nothing, King Lear, Hamlet, Othello, Macbeth, Measure for Measure, Titus Andronicus,* as well as from several of the history plays. There are also three quotations from *A Winter's Tale* — one of them at the head of Chapter XI from the speech by Time which explains the lapse of sixteen years.

The *Antiquary* (1816) fascinates, not only because there is something of parodic self-portraiture about the study of Jonathan Oldbuck, the learned laird of Monkbarns, with his garrulity and his eccentricities, but also because of Scott's conscious policy in portrayal of the poor. In the Advertisement to the novel he echoes Wordsworth's Preface to the *Lyrical Ballads.*

I have . . . sought my principal personages in the class of society who are the last to feel the influence of that general polish which assimilates to each other the manners of different nations. Among the same class I have placed some of the scenes, in which I have endeavoured to illustrate the operation of the higher and more violent passions; both because the lower orders are less restrained by the habit of suppressing their feelings, and because I agree with my friend Wordsworth, that they seldom fail to express them in the strongest and most powerful language.

It is ironic that in this respect Scott achieved what many a noisy political radical might have been proud to achieve. For him the dignity of the poor is a moral fact and a religious fact rather than a political fact. The poverty-stricken Mucklebackits have a stoic grandeur in suffering; and they have a biting rejoinder for Monkbarns when he is surprised to see the poor fisherman repairing for sea the boat in which his son has just been drowned.

'And what would ye have me to do . . . unless I wanted to see four children starve, because ane is drowned? It's weel wi' you gentles, that can sit in the house wi' handkerchers at your een, when ye lose a friend; but the like o' us maun to our wark again, if our hearts were beating as hard as my hammer.'

In the face of the realities of human life beggars take liberties with baronets. So the philosophical old bedesman Edie Ochiltree does not rein his ironic tongue when life is at risk at a moment of dire crisis:

'Lordsake, Sir Arthur, haud your tongue, and be thankful to God that there's wiser folk than you to manage this job.'

Through the mouths of characters such as Edie, a stream of commentary runs through Scott's novels which gives a larger philosophical background to the changing aspects of human fortune, pressing home the littleness of human grandeur in family, wealth, or rank, the equality of all in the face of death, the cramping nature of attachment to worldly goods, the speed with which youth passes away, the nostalgia of age, and the ultimate futility of war.

It is in *Old Mortality* (1816) that the dualistic pattern of *Waverley* is most magnificently exploited. The story starts in 1679. Henry Morton, a young, moderate-minded Presbyterian, innocently gives shelter to an old family friend, John Balfour of Burley. But Burley, a fanatical Covenanter, has just murdered the Archbishop of St Andrews, and when soldiers under the command of the renowned John Grahame of Claverhouse arrive they arrest Morton. This injustice and the evidence of brutal oppression drive Morton to throw in his lot with the Covenanters as Waverley threw in his lot with the Jacobites. Confrontations between covenanting rebels and Royalist forces culminate in the defeat of the Covenanters at Bothwell Bridge.

The gallery of portraits on each side of the great divide is brilliantly varied. Authority and order are opposed to rampant individualism and fanatical confidence in the self's righteousness that can issue in bloody assassination. The book opens with the festival of the popinjay, a traditional compulsory feudal assembly and an occasion for sport and chivalrous exercise at which puritans grunt their disapproval in the background, an ominous indication of smouldering discontent. From this beginning the tension escalates. If the government side stands for justice, order, and reason, the Covenanters stand for freedom and the validity of the individual conscience. If the government side stands for culture, tradition, and ceremony, the Covenanters stand for asceticism and piety. But authority can be readily warped into oppression and individualism into fanatical self-righteousness. If Claverhouse's autocratic tyranny is harsh, Balfour of Burley's masking of ambition under pietistic humbug is the ultimate hypocrisy.

To formulate Scott's vision in a series of abstractions is to do scant justice to his imaginative fertility in bringing to life a host of vivid characters in whose words and deeds the vision is embodied. That vision too reflects his fascination with localities. Scott's backgrounds are related to the human stories enacted before them by means of a symbolism which gives poetic dimension to the narration and helps to universalise the vision. In the first clash of arms between Covenanters and Royalists at Drumclog (Chapter 15), the Covenanters are on their own ground —

> . . . a wide and waste country lay before them, swelling into bare hills of dark heath, intersected by deep gullies.

Wild and untamed, this background suggests

> . . . the omnipotence of nature, and the comparative inefficacy of the

boasted means of amelioration which man is capable of opposing to the disadvantage of climate and soil.

It is the appropriate setting for the lawless rebels and, in a practical sense, an aid to their undisciplined method of fighting. The Royalists herald their approach with trumpets and kettledrums, the symbols of civilised ceremony and order; the Covenanters strike up a bloodthirsty psalm with the prophetic confidence of fanaticism. Scott's historical reconstruction and his poetic enrichment of it tend to shift the central focus from the personalities of heroes such as Henry Morton and Edward Waverley. Nevertheless, in so far as their upbringing has been such that they are lured into mistaken allegiances and learn better by bitter experience, the pattern of their educative development resembles that of Goethe's Wilhelm Meister.

Political and religious ideologies play a smaller part in the next group of novels. Although they are placed in the past, and a clear sense of period is invoked, the human interest, emotional and moral, is less central to the main power game theme. Nevertheless the conflicts have philosophical dimensions. In *Rob Roy* (1817) the world of commerce is opposed to the world of romance. Francis Osbaldistone, son and heir of a wealthy London merchant, has acquired a rebellious taste for a different kind of life and at an uncle's home in Yorkshire finds not only the lovely Diana Vernon, but also a nest of intrigue; for Rashleigh Osbaldistone, a crafty, envious cousin, schemes to get his hands on Francis's inheritance and his sweetheart. Francis's trip with Bailie Nicol Jarvie of Glasgow to the Highlands takes us into the presence of the outlaw Rob Roy. The date is just prior to the abortive Jacobite rising of 1715, but the essential conflict is a moral struggle between good and evil, intertwined with a thematic contrast between the world of mystery and romantic outlawry, and the world of prudent, commercial common sense, the latter delightfully exemplified in Bailie Nicol Jarvie.

'But I maun hear naething about honour — we ken naething here but about credit. Honour is a homicide and a blood-spiller, that gangs about making frays in the street; but Credit is a decent honest man, that sits at hame and makes the pat play.'

The Heart of Midlothian (1818) opens with an account of the riots which occurred in Edinburgh in 1736 after the guard fired on the crowd on the occasion of a public execution. At this time Scots law allowed a murder charge to be brought against a mother whose child had disappeared if she had also tried to conceal the pregnancy. Under this law Effie Deans, the young half-sister of Jeanie, is imprisoned and in danger of execution. The girls are the daughters of Davie Deans, a veteran who was out with the Covenanters in the rebellion dealt with in *Old Mortality*.

Jeanie is an unselfish, self-critical, and dutiful girl who greatly loves her dear ones. She has a steadiness of temper and a firmness of resolution that distinguish her from her wilful sister. She could save Effie by claiming that her sister had confided in her that she was pregnant. Her religious scruples stand in the way.

'I wad ware the best blood in my body to keep her skaithless . . . but I canna change right into wrang, or make that true which is false.'

and later —

'It is not man I fear,' said Jeanie, looking upward; 'the God whose name I must call on to witness the truth of what I say, He will know the falsehood.'

In the event she saves her sister by walking to London and seeking a pardon from Queen Caroline.

The story is based on an actual case. Scott's management of it involves a degree of psychological penetration, emotional sympathy, and dramatically poignant presentation that make it one of the finest novels in our literature. It is significant that the basic conflict imposed on Jeanie, to choose between what is virtuous on the one hand and what will save the life of a dearly loved one on the other hand, is the conflict imposed on Isabella in Shakespeare's *Measure for Measure*. When Jeanie goes to visit her imprisoned sister in the Tolbooth for an interview of rare emotional force, Scott prefaces the chapter with a motto which makes the Shakespearean parallel unmistakable:

Sweet sister, let me live!
What sin you do to save a brother's life,
Nature dispenses with the deed so far,
That it becomes a virtue.   (*Measure for Measure*)

If *The Heart of Midlothian* may be said to be emotionally the most searching of Scott's novels, *The Bride of Lammermoor* (1819) is the most powerfully poetic. Once more chapter mottoes from Shakespeare, Heywood, and Beaumont and Fletcher point to a conscious dependence on Elizabethan dramatists. Set at the end of the seventeenth and beginning of the eighteenth century, it explores a conflict between the Master of Ravenswood, a man of ancient aristocratic lineage, and the *nouveau riche* Sir William Ashton who has advanced himself by intrigue and hypocrisy. The conflict has a political dimension, but the enmity between the two transcends politics. In Ravenswood's eyes, Ashton is the man who ruined his father, and one to whom he owes hostility by every principle of filial loyalty. The Master of Ravenswood is descended from an ancient family rooted in the neighbourhood and surrounded by the romance of legendary tradition. Sir William Ashton is a careerist, timid and calculating, who can write clever letters and make cunning speeches. He is terrified of hunting; he does not even know the walks in his own grounds. Ravenswood is frank and impetuous, a sportsman by heredity, loving every inch of the patrimonial estate which has been forfeited to this scheming hypocrite. The love between Ravenswood and Ashton's daughter Lucy is doomed. Lucy, for all her honesty and sincerity, has just too much of the Ashton spiritlessness. A scheming father and an overbearing mother are more than she can cope with. She is tricked by them into marrying their chosen suitor, and on the wedding night her mind gives way and she stabs her husband to death. The conflict in the tragic hero is finely articulated, and a fatalistic element intrudes in the various legendary prophecies about the family, in ominous flashes of lightning, and in the three old hags, reminiscent of the Weird Sisters in *Macbeth*, who thrive on death and funerals and foresee Ravenswood's doom:

'Broad in the shouthers, and narrow around the lungies — he wad mak a bonny corpse — I wad like to hae the streaking and winding o' him.'

A Legend of Montrose (1819), dealing with the Highland rising of 1644 in favour of Charles I, presents an antithesis like that of *The Bride of Lammermoor*. On the one side is the calculating master of political intrigue, the republican Duke of Argyle, a morose, ambitious, mean, and vindictive character, untrustworthy, cautious, and cowardly. On the other side the spirit of Montrose pervades the Royalist ranks. He is essentially a romantic figure, a man of iron constitution, graceful and athletic, overflowing with 'the energy and fire of genius'. He is as honourable in his dealings as Argyle is villainous. A remarkable third element in the basic scheme is introduced by Dugald Dalgetty of Drumthwacket, a mercenary for whom war is business, and who judges all his military experience in terms of the pay, booty, and provender. He is unattached by principle to either side, but the technique of war is a passionate preoccupation of his. Chivalry is nonsense; his motto is 'Fides et fiducia sunt relativa' (faithfulness and trust are relative). He is a scrupulous wage-earner who will keep his contract strictly and, when it has run out, go over to the other side without a qualm.

It was after the publication of *A Legend of Montrose* that Scott first ventured out of Scotland for his settings, but it will be convenient here to mention his other Scottish novels before leaving Scotland. *The Monastery* (1820) and *The Abbot* (1820) are concerned ideologically with the conflict between Catholic and Protestant in the years following the Reformation. The monastery of Kennaquhair was inspired by Scott's interest in Melrose Abbey. In the 1830 Introduction to *The Monastery* Scott defined his general plan as follows —

to conjoin two characters in that bustling and contentious age, who, thrown into situations which gave them different views on the subject of the Reformation, should, with the same sincerity, dedicate themselves, the one to the support of the sinking fabric of the Catholic Church, the other to the establishment of the Reformed doctrines. Scott of course had no difficulty in drawing characters representative of the opposed ideologies, but themes of usurpation, rivalry in love, and even an ambiguously conceived supernatural phantom turn the whole into one of his less successfully constructed novels.

Some amends are made in *The Abbot* whose hero, Roland Graeme, like Waverley and Henry Morton, has been subjected to a double propaganda in his youth, Catholic and Protestant, and finds himself on the 'wrong' side in civil rebellion. There is a convincing study of Mary Queen of Scots, who has her share of vanity, tenderness, courage, and sensuousness, not to mention a caustic tongue. Scott, as ever, gets behind sectarianism to underlying conflicts between reason and imagination, asceticism and romanticism, common sense and poetry. Youth demands the colourful romantic idealism of service to a Mary Stuart, however much the force of reason may pull in another direction.

The Pirate (1821) is set in Shetland in the seventeenth century. It tells the story of two finely conceived contrasting sisters, Minna and Brenda Troil, one earnest and the other gay. Minna is a pale, dark-haired beauty with a passionate high-minded gravity, melancholy by temperament and acutely sensitive to the grandeur and sublimity of nature. Brenda has pale brown hair and a fresh complexion. She is less tall than her sister, has a lighter step, a more convivial, buoyant, and mirthful air. She is at once more trusting and more unselfish than her sister. If a comparison were to be made between the two sisters in *The Pirate* and the two sisters of Jane Austen's *Sense and Sensibility*, it would bring to light what constitutes Scott's allegiance to the Romantic movement. The Romanticism of Jane Austen's Marianne belongs to the eighteenth century; it is the sentimentality of Sheridan's Lydia Languish; but the Romanticism of Minna Troil belongs to the age of Byron and Wordsworth. It is mystical, primitive, and abandoned. Moreover, Scott's pirate, Clement Cleveland, is just as surely a product of the Romantic movement. A tough sailor, affecting bluntness and defiance in adversity, he assumes an air of superiority to all around him. He pretends to scorn women but has a successful way of handling them. His capacity for hatred — bitter, brooding hatred — is overwhelming. But then he has been bruised by the world and learned the hard way that a dash of humanitarianism in a buccaneer can be disastrous. In fact it brought him suffering and isolation which have hardened him into brutality and given him a sullen, moody ferocity and blackness of spirit. In short Cleveland is the Byronic hero, the Corsair of the North.

Redgauntlet (1824) deals with the supposed return of Prince Charles Edward twenty years after his defeat at Culloden. It brings to a conclusion Scott's long exploration of the conflict between the world of common sense and the world of romantic idealism, the world which has come reluctantly to terms with the practicalities of life under the House of Hanover and the anachronistic dreams of sentimental Jacobitism to which Scottish national feeling turned in nostalgia for the lost glories of independence.

Scott's first venture into English history, *Ivanhoe* (1819), deals with the struggle between Norman and Saxon in the reign of Richard I. Scott consciously set out to contrast the 'plain, homely, blunt manners, and the free spirit infused by their ancient institutions and laws', characterising the Saxons, and the 'high spirit of military fame, personal adventure, and whatever could distinguish them as the Flower of Chivalry', characterising the Normans. The central conflict is between honest, independent, primitive simplicity and the sophistication of a new artificial civilisation. In fact this antithesis is too little related to issues which arouse passion or moral fervour. Scott's pseudo-medieval dialogue degenerates at its worst into clumsy circumlocution such as:

'Nay but, rogue . . . this exceedeth thy licence. Beware ye tamper not with my patience.'

and even

'My knightly word I pledge; only come on with thy foolish self.'

Moreover, there is in this novel a cumbersome excess of detail in respect of clothes and accoutrements. Many a character seems to drag about with him the contents of a fair-sized medieval exhibition at a museum.

It is a pity that Scott's first venture into English history should have been so flawed artistically. Certainly there are fine things in *The Fortunes of Nigel* (1822), set in the reign of James I, especially the portrait of King James himself. *Kenilworth* (1821) deals with the secret marriage of Amy Robsart to the Earl of Leicester, secret because of the earl's position as favourite of Queen Elizabeth, and the mystery of Amy's sudden death. An authentic Elizabethan atmosphere pervades the book, partly because Scott seems to have conceived of the story of Leicester, Amy, and the villainous murderer Varney in terms of Shakespearean tragedy. *Woodstock* (1826) centres on the escape of Charles II after the battle of Worcester. All Scott's old skill in giving vitality to ideological and physical conflict is evident again, and the portrait of Oliver Cromwell is subtly and powerfully conceived.

But by far the finest of the non-Scottish historical novels is *Quentin Durward* (1823), set in fifteenth-century France at a time when 'the feudal system, which had been the sinews and nerves of national defence, and the spirit of chivalry, by which, as by a vivifying soul, that system was animated, began to be innovated upon and abandoned by those grosser characters' who openly avowed egotism as their 'professed principle of action'. Thus the conflict is between the romantic principles of chivalry and the Machiavellian opportunism of the new diplomacy. Charles Duke of Burgundy represents despotic feudalism, and Louis XI is the Machiavellian intriguer. There is a massiveness about the book which is more than a matter of word-count, for it presents a panorama of fifteenth-century life, epic in its fullness. Kings, courtiers, politicians, ecclesiastics, feudal lords, executioners, jesters, alchemists, gypsies, throng the pages. Not that we should accept Scott's historical reconstruction without reservation. Indeed, although in this novel all virtue seems to reside in the remnants of medieval attachment to principle which the new Machiavellian materialism is everywhere corrupting, when Scott returns to this period in *Anne of Geierstein* (1829), the solid worth of the new democratic spirit is shown up against the tyranny and decadence of the old feudal nobility.

Scott's eye for personality is matched by his eye for locality. What remains in the mind after reading the 'Waverley Novels' is both the people and their appropriate locales. One cannot think of the Master of Ravenswood without picturing his gaunt, towering fortress of Wolf's Crag, or of Norna of the Fitful Head in *The Pirate* without picturing her rough, primitive dwelling and its extraordinary accumulation of magical paraphernalia, cheek by jowl with her pet seal. The romantic stronghold of loyalty in *Old Mortality*, Tillietudlem, with its ceremony and its bounty, represents the last outpost of civilisation before the barren heaths take over; it is just the place for the reception and entertainment of Claverhouse and his army. By contrast we take our last look at Balfour of Burley, the black fanatic, where he lurks in a rocky hiding place, a cave pitched between the cataract and the whirlpool, utterly aloof from the society he longed to destroy.

It was once fashionable to denigrate Scott either as artist or as historian. But at its best his artistic imagination unifies the most varied and disparate material in an orderly vision, disciplining a far-reaching richness of human portraiture and scenic description as only the greatest writers have been able to do. We may let a historian speak for Scott the historian.

Waverley is still the best history-book on the Forty-five considered as a social phenomenon in its familiar time and place.

So writes G.M. Trevelyan, for whom Scott was 'the most learned of Scottish antiquaries'. The eighteenth-century historian Gibbon, Trevelyan tells us, 'conceived of mankind as essentially the same in all ages and countries'. Scott, however, changed all that. 'To Scott each age, each profession, each country, each province, had its own manners, dress, ways of thinking, talking, and fighting.' Thus the way in which Scott tried to 'see the real Cromwell by humanizing the man instead of dealing in generalities is typical of the new inspiration that Scott gave to history'.

Jane Austen

Jane Austen (1775–1817) was not a 'Romantic' and therefore, at first sight, consideration of her work might seem to be out of place in a book on Romanticism. There are two good reasons why she cannot be passed over. She is among the half-dozen most accomplished English novelists, and in the latter half of the Romantic period writers could no more be unaware of her than they were unaware of the poet Crabbe, another writer to whom the adjective 'Romantic' cannot properly apply. Moreover, Jane Austen was herself conscious of the Romantic movement and by their very distance from it her works shed light on its character and its contemporary influence.

There is an episode in Jane Austen's last novel, *Persuasion* (1818), in which Anne Elliot tries in conversation to comfort one Captain Benwick, who is mourning the loss of his betrothed. Anne discovers that he will give vent to his feelings when the subject of poetry is raised:

> — and having talked of poetry, the richness of the present age, and gone through a brief comparison of opinion as to the first-rate poets, trying to ascertain whether *Marmion* or *The Lady of the Lake* were to be preferred, and how ranked the *Giaour* and *The Bride of Abydos*, and moreover, how the *Giaour* was to be pronounced, he showed himself so intimately acquainted with all the tenderest songs of the one poet, and all the impassioned descriptions of hopeless agony of the other; he repeated, with such tremulous feeling, the various lines which imaged a broken heart, or a mind destroyed by wretchedness, and looked so entirely as if he meant to be understood, that she ventured to hope he did not always read only poetry, and to say she thought it was the misfortune of poetry to be seldom safely enjoyed by those who enjoyed it completely; and that the strong feelings which alone could estimate it truly were the very feelings which ought to taste it but sparingly.

Anne Elliot is a strong-minded young woman who has learnt to endure disappointments with a brave face, and she encourages Captain Benwick to read more prose memoirs and letters of the kind 'calculated to rouse and fortify the mind by the highest precepts and the strongest examples of moral and religious endurance'.

Gently, wryly, slyly, here and elsewhere, Jane Austen pricks the bubble of romantic inflation of the tenderer and the more self-indulgently anguished emotions. By force of contrast she highlights the outlines of romantic extravagance. She was the daughter of a country parson, and her life was the outwardly uneventful and unsensational life of a middle-class family, mostly spent at Steventon, Bath, and Chawton. She did not cast her mind over life in other ages or other centuries. She dealt with what she knew at first hand. And her literary allegiances were to those eighteenth-century novelists who had avoided the dramatic high jinks of Fielding and the coarse cartoonery of Smollett, namely Richardson and Fanny Burney. In *Northanger Abbey* (1818) she speaks scathingly of those who disparage novels.

> 'And what are you reading, Miss —?' 'Oh! it is only a novel!' replies the young lady; while she lays down her book with affected indifference, or momentary shame. 'It is only *Cecilia*, or *Camilla*, or *Belinda*'; or, in short, only some work in which the greatest powers of the mind are displayed, in which the most thorough knowledge of human nature, the happiest delineation of its varieties, the liveliest effusions of wit and humour, are conveyed to the world in the best chosen language.

Jane Austen was proud to remember every separate moment of Sir Charles Grandison's history. (*Cecilia* and *Camilla* are by Fanny Burney (1752–1840), *Belinda* by Maria Edgeworth (1767–1849), and *Sir Charles Grandison* by Samuel Richardson (1689–1761).)

Jane Austen's material is framed within the 'marriage plot'. This centres action on the advances, retardations, hesitations, doubts, and intrigues involved in love affairs. The 'marriage plot' has perhaps been most successfully managed from the feminine point of view, in that social conventions have refined feminine delicacy to the point of modest reticence about the stronger feelings of the heart. In Jane Austen's work the emotional, intellectual, and imaginative resources are concentrated on everyday events of local life. The high spots in the work of Scott may occur when armies clash and thrones are shaken, when life or honour hangs in the balance, when heart and head are rent in bitter strife. In Jane Austen the crises are of the ball-room and the drawing-room, and the agonies are smothered behind the daily performance of domestic duties. The core of a situation of anguish may lie in a word unspoken, a letter unwritten, a visit postponed, or a glance unreciprocated.

In *Sense and Sensibility* (1811) the two sisters, Elinor and Marianne Dashwood, both suffer the shock of losing the young men on whom they have set their hearts. But while Elinor is a girl of good sense who struggles to control her feelings privately, Marianne's romantic sensibility is such that she gives way to uncontrollable and inconsolable grief. By the most painful of processes in the awakening of her understanding Marianne learns that instead of falling a sacrifice to an irresistible passion for a dashing young man, who turns out to have a record of dissipation and cruelty, she must give her hand to a solid, sensible, but aged man of thirty-five 'who still sought the constitutional safe-guard of a flannel waistcoat'. The lesson learned between the ages of seventeen and nineteen may be called an 'anti-romantic' one, but in essence it is not very different from the lesson learned by Edward Waverley. He likewise has to expunge from his heart the images of both Prince Charles Edward and Flora MacIvor and settle down to domesticity with the practical, reliable Rose Bradwardine.

In Jane Austen, however, we never get lost by night on mountains or over moors, we hear neither the plunge of the dirk nor the clatter of the Lochaber axe, we never sight in the distance 'the shattered, thunder-splitten peaks of Arran', we visit no castles, no dens, no prisons, no Highland hide-outs. There are neither romantic backcloths nor romantic dramatis personae. 'You are now collecting your people delightfully,' Jane Austen wrote to a niece with literary ambitions, '3 or 4 Families in a Country Village is the very thing to work on.'

Jane Austen worked on them with the talents of a rare genius — a delicious ironic detachment, a winning sense of humour, and a deft epigrammatic turn of phrase. She is perhaps the most quotable of our novelists. No one naturally remembers the first sentence of *Waverley* or *The Heart of Midlothian*, but everybody remembers the first sentence of *Pride and Prejudice* which we quoted in our 'Introduction':

It is a truth universally acknowledged, that a single man in possession of a good fortune, must be in want of a wife.

By her subtle phrasing, Jane Austen can throw even into a situation of tension or anguish a comment pregnant with a sly detachment that brings a twinkle to the eye. At the most testing moment for Elinor in *Sense and Sensibility*, when she is overcome with confusion at the unexpected arrival of the man she has dearly loved but seemingly lost, she sits down and talks of the weather.

When Elinor had ceased to rejoice in the dryness of the season, a very awful pause took place.

The contrast between the heroine's desperate recourse to the subject of the weather in an attempt to conceal her embarrassment and the author's coolly deflationary summary of the effort as rejoicing 'in the dryness of the season' is characteristic of Jane Austen's comic irony. The reader often finds himself rejoicing in the dryness of the authoress.

Pride and Prejudice (1813) is a family novel concerning the five daughters of Mr and Mrs Bennet. There are enough foolish or half-foolish characters in the book to give appetising play to Jane Austen's sly agility in puncturing sham or hollow postures and transfixing pretentious humbugs with shafts of wit. In no novel is there a more searching exploration of how an intelligent young woman can be embarrassed by the behaviour of her nearest and dearest. Mr Bennet, a father with a dryly sarcastic tongue and a natural tendency to escape to his library from the overwhelmingly feminine environment, has nevertheless, in his winningly candid way, a distinct affinity with his daughter Elizabeth, who at least inherits his sense of humour. Mrs Bennet is foolish and empty-headed. The 'prejudice' of the title is the distinctly unfavourable view which Elizabeth forms and clings to in respect of a young man, Darcy, whose 'pride' offends her. The general silliness of some members of her family provides some excuse for Darcy's attitude, but aloof hero and independent heroine come together at last. Elizabeth's common sense, good-heartedness, sense of humour, and resilience make her a charmingly vivid character.

Charlotte Brontë complained of Jane Austen's evasion of the emotional heights and depths. 'The passions are perfectly unknown to her.' Yet an undercurrent of gravity runs through *Mansfield Park* (1814), in which the wealthy Sir Thomas Bertram takes over the upbringing of nine-year-old Fanny Price. She is Lady Bertram's niece, and comes from a poor and crowded home. Fanny's modesty, unselfishness, and firmness of character contrast with the prevailing worldliness and shallowness of most of the family, though her cousin Edmund recognises her qualities and the two fall in love. During Sir Bertram's absence the young people engage in private theatricals, rehearsing Mrs Inchbald's *Lovers' Vows* with a freedom and carelessness of conduct between the sexes which Fanny cannot condone. A distinctive personality is Aunt Norris, sister of her mother and of Lady Bertram, a thoroughly odious woman determined to keep the poor relation in her place.

'I am going to take a heroine whom no one but myself will much like,' Jane Austen said when she set about writing *Emma* (1816). Indeed Emma Woodhouse, mistress of her father's home, believes she has every reason to be pleased with herself, to accept her status as permanent, and to begin organising the lives of others. She starts with Harriet Smith, a rather foolish village girl, dissuading her from marrying a suitable local farmer and grooming her rather as the future partner of the vicar, Mr Elton. When her schemes misfire, Emma is ready with alternatives. It takes her some time to learn to know herself and her limitations. Her father is an amiable hypochondriac, the source of much gentle humour. Jane Austen achieves a great feat of comic irony in making her heroine at once a self-willed busybody, totally unconscious of the conceit implicit in her itch for doing good from above on her own predetermined terms, and yet at the same time immensely likeable.

Persuasion (1818) is a novel with an underlying earnestness which brings a toning-down of the ironic spirit. The story of Anne Elliot's love is believed to be based on Jane Austen's own experience. Some regard it as the best of her novels. Sylvia Townsend Warner calls it 'the most compelling and the weakest of Jane Austen's novels'. It is true that Anne Elliot is held by her creatrix in a deeply sympathetic and indeed compassionate gaze. The subtler exploration of psychological deeps in the development of love leaves little space for the lightness of spirit prevalent in *Emma*, but the satiric vein is still operative.

It was more operative still in *Northanger Abbey* (1818), written many years before it was finally published. It begins as a burlesque of the mystery novel popularised by Mrs Radcliffe's *The Mysteries of Udolpho*. In this respect it turns into comic absurdity the collision between 'Romanticism' and realism with which, in its various forms, so much current literature was concerned. Catherine Morland, daughter of a clergyman, meets Henry Tilney in Bath and is invited to the Tilneys' family home at Northanger Abbey. Catherine's reading has given her a romantic turn of mind and expectations of adventure not easily encountered.

> But from fifteen to seventeen she was in training for a heroine; she read all such works as heroines must read . . .

But alas:

> There was not one family among their acquaintance who had reared and supported a boy accidentally found at their door; not one young man whose origin was unknown.

Over-influenced by her familiarity with Mrs Radcliffe's mystery novels, Catherine allows her imagination to run away with her in the ancient Northanger building. The horrifically gruesome deeds suspected in her speculations turn out of course to be nothing more than figments of her dreams.

James Hogg

We return to Romanticism proper and to the Scottish scene. James Hogg (1770–1835), the Ettrick Shepherd, whom we met as a poet, published his novel *The Brownie of Bodsbeck* in 1818. It deals with the lot of the Covenanters whom Scott had depicted in *Old Mortality*. Scott told Hogg that he did not like it, 'because it is a false and unfair picture of the times and the existing characters altogether'. Scott's *Old Mortality* had been published in 1816, and his representation of the fanaticism of the Covenanters evoked hostility from those who regarded them as the defenders of religious freedom and the Presbyterian cause. Hogg claimed that he had written *The Brownie of Bodsbeck* before Scott's *Old Mortality* was published, but there is evidence which throws some doubt on this claim. Be that as it may, the Covenanters and those who aid them are sympathetically presented by Hogg, while Claverhouse and the Royalists are pictured as monsters of brutality.

The period is just after the battle of Bothwell Bridge, when defeated Covenanters were driven to hide in remote recesses in the hills of the Border country. A well-to-do, honest farmer, Walter Laidlaw, finds a pack of them hiding in the hills on his land. He sympathises with their plight but is no adherent of their cause. It is dangerous to help them, but he nevertheless supplies them with food and does not drive them away. What he does not know is that his daughter Katharine has stumbled upon a number of them holed up in a hidden underground den, and has been tending and feeding them. Walter's wife is a staunch episcopalian in principle, and this complicates the dilemma. The local superstitious belief in the antics of a brownie, a preternatural being, is quite naturally encouraged when strange things happen by night, and Katharine, who has nocturnal meetings with the men she is helping, is even assumed to have come into the brownie's keeping. In this work the seeming preternatural events, though convincingly utilised throughout the story, turn out to have a thoroughly natural explanation at the end. The more realistic tensions of the story arise when Claverhouse descends upon the farm in his pursuit of the scattered Covenanters, is annoyed by Walter's independent refusal to be bullied, suspects him of harbouring fugitives, and has him arrested. The narrative is somewhat clumsily put together. The book is at its best in colourful passages of dialogue and of personal narration by the characters; but it is precisely in these sections of the work that the Sassenach reader must have recourse to a glossary.

By contrast, *The Private Memoirs and Confessions of a Justified Sinner* (1824) is cunningly put together. Once more the struggle between Covenanter and Royalist provides a background to the tale, but there is certainly no inclination to favour the cause of religious fanaticism. An incongruous (perhaps symbolic) marriage between a Tory laird and a Covenanting religious fanatic produces an heir, George, and a second boy, Robert. The latter is suspected of being the son of the lady's spiritual director and takes his surname, Wringhim. The first part of the novel tells the story of the rivalry of these two brothers from the point of view of George, whom Robert persecutes by perpetually shadowing him, and eventually murders.

The second section of the book is the Memoirs of Robert, dug up from his suicide's grave long after his death. Robert tells how, on a crucial day in his life, 25 March 1704, at the age of eighteen, he came to believe himself one of God's elect:

That I was now a justified person, adopted among the number of God's children — my name written in the Lamb's book of life, and that no by-past transgression, nor any future act of my own, or of other men, could be instrumental in altering this decree.

In the rapture of his spiritual exultation he feels like 'an eagle among the children of men, soaring on high, and looking down with pity and contempt on the grovelling creatures below'. In this mood he makes a new and mysterious acquaintance whom he assumes to be a powerful prince and who is really the Devil. The Devil, of course, encourages him in the doctrine of the 'infallibility of the elect'. He leads him by his arguments to believe that he can do God's work best by killing his brother and taking his estate. Thus the basic tenets of human decency and the natural family affections are seen as carnal weaknesses to be subdued in the interests of the Christian duty to punish and destroy the wicked. All moral virtues are gradually turned topsy-turvy. When another is condemned for the murder he has himself committed, it is final proof of his righteousness. 'How could I doubt, after this, that the hand of Heaven was aiding and abetting me?'

Hogg plumbs the psychological deeps in tracing the mental disintegration of Robert Wringhim. But there is no question here of removing the idea of supernatural possibilities from the readers' heads. The relationship between the sinner and the Devil is so close that their identities may be confused. Moreover, the Devil can on occasion assume the appearance of another person. Robert is eventually reduced to a state in which he does not know whether he has indeed committed all the crimes with which he is ultimately charged, or whether he has lived through periods of alcoholic amnesia. He is hounded out of all security and peace, a hunted outlaw, terrified of the one whose presence has so long overshadowed his days. The Devil's influence is such that any dawning realisation of what is really happening is regarded as a fatal lapse of faith in his sacred calling.

John Galt

Another Scottish contemporary who, like Hogg, was offended by Scott's *Old Mortality* was John Galt (1779–1839): he published his novel *Ringan Gilhaize* (1823) to set the record straight. So he reveals in his *Literary Life* (1834):

> The book itself was certainly suggested by Sir Walter Scott's *Old Mortality*, in which I thought he treated the defenders of the Presbyterian Church with too much levity, and not according to my impressions derived from the history of that time. Indeed, to tell the truth, I was hugely provoked . . .

Galt's true forte, however, lay in a different genre. His *Annals of the Parish* (1821) records the doings in the country parish of Dalmailing, as chronicled by the Reverend Micah Balwhidder. Its successor, *The Provost* (1822), deals with small-town life from the point of view of James Pawkie, a tailor who rises in the local community to be appointed Provost three times. Neither of these books has a shapely plot. Each is episodic in construction. Galt saw himself as an innovator in this respect.

They would be more properly characterised . . . as theoretical histories, than either as novels or romances.

So he wrote, noting that his books lack the 'consistent fable' which is 'as essential to a novel as a plot is to the drama'.

The action of *The Provost* involves details of the personal politicking and intriguing by which town dignitaries are appointed, decisions made on such matters as the upkeep of roads, the town fairs, the appointment of a pastor, the activities of the press-gang, the installation of street lamps, the election of a Member of Parliament, and the raising of volunteers for the Napoleonic wars. The charm of the book lies in the ironic overtones unwittingly sounded by the narrator in his unselfconscious revelations of the ulterior motives of self-interest continuously operative in what he sees as his life of service to the community. The solemn self-importance of the man leads him into hilariously disproportionate judgments. When his plan to renew the seating in the kirk runs into opposition led by Mr Smeddum, the tobacconist, he declares:

The spirit by which the Smeddumites were actuated in ecclesiastical affairs, was a type and taste of the great distemper with which all the world was more or less inflamed, and which cast the ancient state and monarchy of France into the perdition of anarchy and confusion.

It is in throwaway touches of utter honesty that Pawkie gives himself away, as when he says of another opponent 'I found . . . a way of silencing him, far better than any sort of truth or reason'. Yet Pawkie is *not* unlovable, and herein lies Galt's mastery; in addition he has the gift of registering the comic and absurd with a laughable clarity which never degenerates into clownery.

Galt's masterpiece is *The Entail* (1823), a full-length novel which, if it lacks the engineering of a dramatically contrived plot, has an inner cohesion of theme and character-study which makes it one of the greatest novels, not only of its own period, but of our literature as a whole. It is a chronicle covering three generations in the life of a Glasgow family over some forty years. Claud Walkinshaw was brought up in poverty by a faithful old family retainer, knowing that his grandfather, the Laird of Kittlestonheugh, tried to revive the sinking family fortune by sending his son to die on a disastrous colonial venture, and all the family resources were risked and lost. Young Claud grows up determined to retrieve the family honour and the family estate. Launched as a pedlar, he builds up his own business to become a wealthy Glasgow merchant, and begins to buy back the lost estate. He marries the daughter of a landowner who, not having a son of his own, is ready to bequeath his estate to Claud's son, but insists that the inheritor must take his own name, Hypel. Claud refuses to allow his eldest son, Charles, to be so committed, and therefore Hypel bequeaths the estate to the next son, Walter. In fact the legal document is badly framed and Walter is able to succeed without changing his name. This first irony is intensified by the fact that Charles is an open, honest, generous young man and Walter is both peevish and mentally subnormal. When Charles insists on marrying Isabella Father-lans, even though her father has just been ruined, Claud's anger streng-thens his peculiar obsession with establishing a large, secure family estate, and he makes a will with an entail cutting Charles out from his due inheritance and leaving everything to Walter. This is the basis of a powerful human study in the havoc wrought by a tragic obsession. Claud goes through agonies of guilt and remorse as Walter's character deteriorates, Charles's misfortunes accumulate, and this once favourite son dies of a fever after the shock of learning from the family solicitor exactly what his father has done to him. There is penetrating psychologi-cal analysis of Claud's shifting moods and of the collision between fondness for Charles and recognition of Walter's mental unreliability on the one hand, and the over-ruling determination to hand on to a son the inheritance which he himself was denied. Illnesses and deaths play their part in intensifying the ironies. The births of daughters instead of sons complicate further plans for putting right in the next generation (by the marriage of cousins) what has gone wrong in the first generation. The scheme of *The Entail* defies any attempt to sum it up briefly. What gives the later part of the book the kind of cohesion which the study of Claud gives to the first half is the study of the Leddy Grippy. She is a subserviently innocuous figure during her husband's life-time. After his death her outrage at the numerous injustices legal decisions have inflicted on her and her family turns her into a formidable, commanding person-ality through whose efforts the worst inequities are rectified.

It was Galt's earlier books, especially *The Annals of the Parish* and *The Provost*, which won praise and admiration from Scott, Byron, and Coleridge. These books extended the range of the novel in their opening-up of the world of small-town politics. But *The Entail* has tragic grandeur and intensity which put it in the same class as Scott's *The Heart of Midlothian*, George Eliot's *Middlemarch*, and Hardy's *The Mayor of Casterbridge*. Only the use of Scottish dialect by some of the main characters has prevented general recognition of this fact.

Susan Ferrier

Scott added a note to the Reader at the end of *A Legend of Montrose* signifying that the 'Tales of My Landlord' were at an end. He had now done what he could to exhibit varieties of the Scottish character to southerners, but others were now showing talent in the same field.

> If the present author, himself a phantom, may be permitted to distinguish a brother, or perhaps a sister shadow, he would mention in particular the author of the very lively work entitled 'Marriage'.

Scott was later to get to know the author, Susan Ferrier (1782–1854), to feel high admiration for her work, and to enjoy her company for her spiritedness and lack of affectation. Susan Ferrier was the youngest of ten children of an Edinburgh Clerk of Sessions. She never married, but ran her father's house after her mother's death in 1797. Her father's connections included the Duke of Argyll, and Susan saw life in aristocratic houses as well as in metropolitan Edinburgh. She published her first novel, *Marriage* (1818), anonymously, and it has generally been accounted better than its successors, *The Inheritance* (1824) and *Destiny* (1831). Its appeal lies in its liveliness, especially its comic and satiric portraiture. In later works the authorial moralising is more ponderous. Scott linked Susan Ferrier with her Irish and English counterparts: 'Edgeworth, Ferrier, Austen have all given portraits of real society, far superior to anything man, vain man, has produced of the like nature,' he recorded in his Diary.

Jane Austen's good-humoured acceptance of the social mores of her day provides a sounding-board against which her wit resonates in judicious irony. By contrast John Galt assaults the ethic of parentally devised marriages of materialistic convenience, that are made in defiance of true love and compatibility, with a passion that represents anguish and indeed total inner disintegration as the cost of such wilfulness. Susan Ferrier steers a neat course between these contrasting attitudes.

In *Marriage* the Earl of Courtfield arranges for his seventeen-year-old daughter, Lady Juliana, to marry the Duke of L. Juliana is horrified, finding the proposed suitor aged and odious.

> Educated for the sole purpose of forming a brilliant establishment, of catching the eye, and captivating the senses, the cultivation of her mind, or the correction of her temper, had formed no part of the system by which that aim was to be accomplished.

Thus ill-prepared for life, 'the sport of every passion', she elopes with a lover as thoughtless as herself, and is cut off by her father. Her lover is the second son of a Highland laird and dependent on a well-meaning bachelor guardian. When Juliana is whisked to the Highlands, her romantic visions of the future are dashed by the crude reality of a grim home in a gloomy countryside, inhabited by her husband's sisters and aunts. Susan Ferrier has great fun with the rustic notions and crude idiosyncrasies of well-meaning Highlanders, but even greater fun with the ignorant snobbery of their ill-spirited English visitor. Juliana soon repents her marriage, and her husband escapes to service abroad. Of their twin daughters, Juliana herself brings up Adelaide in England to disastrous effect. The other, Mary, is rescued and brought up by her aunt in Scotland. Adelaide reverses the fate of her mother, breaking from the man she loves and marrying the wealthy but oafish Duke of Altamont to gain status and pleasure. But she soon discovers 'that of all yokes, the most insupportable is the yoke of an obstinate fool', and runs away into the arms of her lover and into social disgrace.

The novel thus explores a series of misalliances, while correct conduct is exemplified by Mary, for whom duty can never be sacrificed to love nor love to worldly advantage. The authorial voice repeatedly presses home the moral. Headstrong passion, haughtiness, self-will, filial disobedience, and all kinds of calculating self-interest bring unhappiness. Mary is saved by her sense of duty, her readiness always to weigh other people's interests against her own, and her refusal to have her head turned; above all the principles inculcated by a religious upbringing taught her not to nourish extravagant expectations of the possibilities of happiness on earth, rather to expect full happiness only hereafter. Susan Ferrier's satirical humour is sharp. Garrulous, self-opinionated women with absurd fads and obsessions have a hilarious fluency. Bitchy dialogue conducted in velvet gloves is brilliantly recorded. And even ostentatious name-dropping and poetic quotation by ladies with shallow literary pretensions come in for ridicule. By contrast Mary believes that 'learning, like religion, ought never to be forced into conversation; and that people, who only read to talk of their reading, might as well let it alone'.

Mary Brunton

The question whether religion ought to be brought into conversation could scarcely have occurred to Mary Brunton (1778–1818), for whom religion was the mainspring of her thinking. Brought up in the Orkneys, and married to Alexander Brunton, she lived for a time in Bolton and Edinburgh, and died in childbirth. Her novel *Self-Control* (1811) traces the long pursuit of a chaste heroine across the world by a wickedly persistent Lothario. It touched Jane Austen's sense of humour by its improbabilities. 'My heroine shall not merely be wafted down an American river in a boat by herself, she shall cross the Atlantic in the same way . . .', she said. But there is no such extravagance in Mary Brunton's second novel, *Discipline* (1814), which Jane Austen not only admired but was seemingly influenced by in writing *Emma*.

It is autobiographical in form and tells the story of Ellen Perry, daughter of a wealthy London merchant, who loses her mother in childhood and her father when she is seventeen; for his business collapses into bankruptcy and he commits suicide. Ellen is a spoilt child who in her earliest years has learned to manipulate her parents and to get her own way. She tells her story from the point of view of a grievously chastened and reformed character, and like all converts she tends to overstress the wickedness of her ways in her unregenerate youth. Her progress is from a life of self-indulgence, in which personal enjoyment and especially satisfaction of her vanity take precedence over any duty or obligation to others, through bereavement, poverty, and experience of extreme brutality, to utter resignation of herself to God's will, the attainment of humility, self-denial, and peace found in service to others.

If it all sounds very much like a sermon, it is. Ellen's good angel is a loyal old friend of her mother's who promised to keep an eye on her, and whose lectures in morality and piety take a naturalness from her sincerity and her fatal affliction. In the background is a Scotsman in his thirties, Maitland, who is all that Mr Knightley is to Jane Austen's Emma and much more, for Maitland has a tougher customer to deal with than Emma Woodhouse. Ellen is a ravishing beauty. She makes the most of it, and is only rescued at the last moment from running off clandestinely with Lord Frederick de Burgh.

What gives the novel a continuing vitality is Mary Brunton's subtlety and penetration in revealing how insidiously vanity and self-interest can corrode even the seemingly most harmless or indeed virtuous intentions. The way Ellen's vanity, her wilfulness, and her impulsiveness entangle her by sly gradations into indelicate obligations to an unprincipled young man, and into being manipulated by a dissipated society woman, shows gifts of human insight that anticipate Trollope. The fact that such developments are seen, not only as imprudently destructive of future happiness and security (as Trollope or for that matter even Jane Austen would have seen them), but more deeply in terms of eternal salvation, adds a spiritual dimension rare in the English novel. Nevertheless Mary Brunton is no puritanical kill-joy. She can turn an aphoristic phrase with the eloquence of Jane Austen:

> By some untoward fate, the government of husbands generally falls into the hands of those who are not likely to bring the art into repute . . .

She can plant a shaft of satiric humour with delightful casualness:

> Jessie was a pretty, playful creature, with capacity enough to show that talents are not hereditary . . .

Mary Brunton's wit, her sly humour, her subtlety in the analysis of psychological motivation, and her devastating acuteness in satirical portraiture of silly and unprincipled women make Jane Austen's admiration wholly understandable. She belongs of course with the Scots, for indeed Ellen's conversion to health of mind and soul is completed only in the Highlands, where at Castle Eredine she finds herself received into a small feudal society as ideal as Sir Charles Grandison's. Its unpretentious genuineness contrasts sharply with the dissipation and frivolity of the London society in which Ellen was brought up. Thus in two respects Mary Brunton belongs clearly among the Romantics. In the first place she makes the Scottish Highlands the appropriate scenic background for escape from the shallowness of a worldly civilisation. In the second place she brings moral and spiritual dimensions into the novel such as Wordsworth brought into poetry.

Maria Edgeworth

Scott saw Maria Edgeworth (1767–1849) as the writer who had done for Ireland what he was doing for Scotland. One of her earlier Irish stories, *Castle Rackrent* (1800), has been called 'the first Anglo-Irish novel', though in length and substance it is rather a long short story. It charts the decline of an Irish estate through four generations of irresponsibility and extravagance. What gives it a powerfully ironic bite is that the narrator, Thady Quirk, an old retainer, records his reminiscences as a plain-spoken, simple fellow for whom the dignity and prosperity of the family are of central importance. Thus the obvious sufferings of the tenants from mismanagement, corruption, and extortion are taken as read. A double irony arises from the fact that Thady's own son, Jason, has become the family agent, and has managed by cunning to get hold of the estate for the Quirks. But no such words as 'cunning' or 'extortion' deface Thady's chronicle. And Maria Edgeworth adds a Postscript to drive the ironies home:

> The Editor could have readily made the catastrophe of Sir Condy's history more dramatic and more pathetic, if he thought it allowable to varnish the plain round tale of faithful Thady.

It was not *Castle Rackrent*, however, but *Belinda* (1801) which drew commendation from Jane Austen; and if *Castle Rackrent* looks forward to the future in its use of a narrator too involved in what he is recounting to be totally unbiased and reliable, *Belinda* looks back to the eighteenth-century models provided by Fanny Burney and Samuel Richardson, with a dash of 'mystery' incorporated from Mrs Radcliffe. Yet everything is subject to control by subservience to a moral scheme. Belinda goes up to town but keeps clear of its follies and dissipations. She falls in love with Clarence Hervey, around whom mysteries and suspicions gather. He appears to be keeping a mistress, but in fact he is idealistically bringing up his young ward, Virginia St Pierre, on the principles of Rousseau. A child of nature, she shall be free of contamination by the vices and vanities of society. Her name indicates an intention to ridicule notions expounded in Bernardin de St Pierre's *Paul et Virginie*. Maria Edgeworth wrote with understanding on this matter, for her father, Richard Lovell Edgeworth (1744–1817), had endeavoured to educate his eldest son on the principles laid down in Rousseau's *Emile*, and the experiment was a failure. He was a wiser man when he came to write *Essays on Practical Education* (1797) with Maria's assistance.

Another theme in *Belinda* traces the reform of Lady Delacourt, a dissipated woman around whom also mysteries and suspicions gather. She hints at a blighted life. All are denied access to her boudoir except her servant Marriott, who exercises an uncanny power over her. Ultimately the blight turns out to be an injury to the breast resulting from a most unladylike duel. Lady Delacourt has to be recalled to true religion, 'mild and rational', after a delirious orgy of Methodism. For the moral themes pressed home turn again on the contrast between what indulges the feelings and the taste for extravagance and what is subject to control by reason and by religious precept. Maria Edgeworth is close to Susan Ferrier in her insistence that fashionable society, being dissipated, is unhappy, and that true contentment lies in the calm pleasures of domestic life. Vincent, the frank, warm-hearted, failed aspirant for Belinda's hand, is unfortunately weak on 'principle' and clings to the guidance of natural good feeling. As a result he becomes a gambler and goes to the bad. Harriot Freke, feminist scorner of convention and prejudice, learning and principle, is ridiculed for her crude self-advertisement and her offences against decorum. Meanwhile there are exhortations to beware the friendship of fashionable beaux who might duck you in the Serpentine, to scorn the absurd belief in first love, and to shun youthful reading of romances which can ruin earthly life.

It is not surprising that Scott's praise of Maria Edgeworth centred on the Irish novel *The Absentee* (1812). This is a novel designed to show the misery of the Irish tenantry caused by the absentee landlords and oppressive deputies, and also to recommend the happiness of a good landlord's life lived on his own estate among his tenants. Such dignified domesticity is contrasted with the misery of dissipated fashionable life in London, which is rotten with the petty rivalries of extravagant women and impoverished husbands. Maria Edgeworth ridicules the Irish gentry who ape English society and decry everything Irish. She is genuinely touching in showing the real sufferings of poor peasants face to face with extortionate demands from agents who are both lining their own pockets and financing the London dissipations of their masters. Lady Clonbony, a stupid, vain woman, is ruined by her ambition to belong to the inner ring of London society. The more money she spends on parties, and the more painfully and absurdly she tries to disguise her Irish accent, the more rebuffs and mockery she receives from those she apes and entertains. The hero, Lord Colambre, spies incognito on nefarious agents and comes to the rescue of the down-trodden peasantry. But for a time he faces an emotional conflict between his love for the admirable Grace Nugent and the belief that she is illegitimate.

Semi-mysterious impediments to marriage represent one of Maria Edgeworth's favourite devices. Obstacles stand in the way of the hero's marriage to the heroine in *Harington* (1817), for Berenice's father, Mr Montenero, has been told a false story that Harington is insane, while Harington believes that Berenice is a Jewess. At the end Berenice turns out after all to be a Christian, just as Grace Nugent turned out to be legitimate. Nevertheless the novel makes a fervent plea for tolerance. Maria Edgeworth analyses old Mr Harington's irrational anti-semitism and the antipathy to Jews instilled in his son in boyhood. The representation of the hero's early days in psychological detail for the purpose of explaining his character in later life is done with technical assurance by Maria Edgeworth, who was herself an expert educationalist. No doubt she appreciated what Scott had done in this respect in *Waverley*.

Perhaps the most enjoyable of Maria Edgeworth's novels is *Ormond* (1817), though again there are absurdities in its pivotal plot. Young Ormond reads Fielding's *Tom Jones*, and its immediate effect is to inspire him to live the life of the popular, frank, impetuous rake, and to involve him in a dangerous affair with a village girl, Peggy Sheridan. Such damage can accrue from reading Fielding. Fortunately Richardson comes to the rescue. Ormond reads *Sir Charles Grandison*, and its effect is wholly beneficial. He is inspired to emulate the conscientious gentleman whom women love for his virtue. The vitality of *Ormond* lies in its busy portrayal of life in a variety of settings and at vastly different social levels, from the pompous, if faded, society life of Ireland's struggling aristocracy to the activities of wreckers on the Irish coast. Maria Edgeworth does not close her eyes to controversy. She extended the scope of the novel to include public issues, political, religious, and social, which could stimulate the mind and stir the conscience.

Lady Morgan

The earthy, workaday Ireland of Maria Edgeworth's novels is a subject for social concern rather than for romantic idealisation. What she did for Ireland may have matched what Scott did for Scotland in the way of informing the English public about its life and conditions, but if we look for an author who sought to do for Ireland what Scott had done for Scotland in the way of presenting its scenery and culture as alive with romantic and historic glamour, then we must turn to Lady Morgan

(?1776–1859). Born Sydney Owenson, the daughter of an Irish actor and his English wife, she began her literary career with an epistolary novel, *St Clair* (1802). It is a passionate and tragic love story clearly derived from both Goethe's *Werther* and Rousseau's *La Nouvelle Héloïse*, books with which Lady Morgan's hero is very familiar. A few years later she achieved immense fame with her novel *The Wild Irish Girl* (1806), and six years after its publication married Sir Charles Morgan, physician to the Viceroy, Lord Abercorn. The couple lived in Dublin until 1837 and then moved to London. Lady Morgan had travelled about Ireland in her early days, experienced the life of the aristocracy, and travelled on the Continent.

The Wild Irish Girl is told in the form of letters, but in the last chapter an omniscient authoress intrudes to disentangle the not very taxing mysteries she has contrived. The narrator, Horatio, is son of Lord M., who sends the young man to look at his Irish estate. He goes, expecting to find a crude and barbarous people, but from his first arrival in the splendid city of Dublin he gradually learns to shed his prejudices. And the reader, subjected to a sometimes rather laboured course in Irish culture and Irish history, is suitably indoctrinated by a genuinely enthusiastic devotee of Irish ways, critic of English injustice, and advocate of national renewal. An accident brings Horatio into the decayed castle of an aged eccentric — Mr O'Melville to the ignorant, but to the local Irish the descendant of a noble house, and Prince of Inismore. It is his ancient lands which Horatio's father now owns, for Horatio's ancestor, one of Cromwell's generals, was awarded them after the butchery of the prince's ancestor. Horatio's need to tread carefully adds suspense as he succumbs, stage by stage, to the charms of the prince's daughter Glorvina, the 'wild' Irish girl. She plays the harp, has grace, culture, learning, and benevolence. Every time Horatio asks a question about things Irish, he receives a sustained reply, rich in illustration and quotation, and to make the course as thorough as possible Lady Morgan bespatters her text with lengthy footnotes.

In the background there is the familiar conflict between prudence and romance, and between realism and dream. But a new dimension is given to such personal issues by the symbolic character of the encounter between the Englishman and the Irish girl, and by the plea their relationship ultimately represents for an end to patronising and domination, and for harmonious mutual understanding. There is, however, a strongly 'Romantic' element in Lady Morgan's work that is both extravagant and melodramatic. The Irish scenery is painted with Radcliffean luxuriance and Gothick excess. Glorvina's beauty and mystic grace are portrayed in overpoweringly repetitious superlatives. Moreover, the degree of sensibility exhibited is cloyingly excessive. On one occasion of parting, after falling at Glorvina's feet, Horatio is eventually locked in her embrace and that of the family priest at the same time in a sobbing threesome.

It was a blissful agony; but it was unsupportable. Then to have died would have been to have died most blest.

These and sometimes even worse emotional convulsions overtake hero and heroine. It is not just that feelings are everywhere indulged, but they are also everywhere talked about. There cannot be a touching air played or a lovely scene witnessed without mutual congratulation on the fineness and delicacy of the sensibilities aroused and the nobility of the souls involved. It was no doubt this aspect of Lady Morgan's work which drew a sly mid-winter riposte from Jane Austen: 'If the warmth of her language could affect the Body it might be worth reading in this weather.'

As a writer Lady Morgan alternately fascinates and infuriates the modern reader. Her wit, her intelligence, her breadth of vision, and her capacity to make what is absurd look triply absurd, give her best passages a thrust that is unforgettable. Yet they are all but submerged in a bog of surrounding wordiness as undistinguished as it is redundant. Nowhere is the contrast more evident than in *The O'Briens and The O'Flaherties, A National Tale* (1827). Here Lady Morgan fastens on the period just prior to the rising of 1798 in the attempt to give a kaleidoscopic picture of Irish life from the aristocratic circles in Dublin to the remote rural recesses of Connaught. A military review in Phoenix Park, a viceregal dinner party in Dublin Castle, a secret meeting of the newly formed United Irishmen at which the hero Murrough O'Brien rubs shoulders with Hamilton Rowan, T.A. Emmet, and Napper Tandy, a city riot, a visit to a Connemara convent, trips to Galway beauty spots, and night meetings in graveyards all form a rich tapestry. The hero has been subjected to a part-Catholic, part-Protestant upbringing that makes him ripe for development into an Edward Waverley of the Emerald Isle. Yet, in spite of name-dropping in relation to political personalities, whether it be Grattan and Curran or Robespierre and Mirabeau, the historical canvas remains transparently thin. A plot of extravagantly fanciful complexities intermittently puts in an appearance amid acres of frothy dialogue and frothier description. Its implausibilities are absurd. Yet the sheer vitality that flows from the pen when, for example, the Countess of Knocklofty gets the conversational bit between her teeth, speaks volumes (many volumes) for the zest and spiritedness of the writer. The influence of Scott is everywhere glimpsed in such a way that the reader is continually reminded how brilliant Scott was, how thorough, how disciplined, how comparatively exact in historical chronology and allusion. Lady Morgan's fundamental good-heartedness and magnanimity nevertheless shine through. Her scathing denunciation of the damage wilfully done to the Irish by penal laws and discrimination, by Protestant bigotry, by corruption and paranoia in high places is compelling now, and it had its effect in her own day. She exemplifies a Romanticism run riot in a worthy cause.

Ann Radcliffe

In the history of literature it is generally major writers who exercise the greatest influence on the course of that history. But the Gothick movement in English literature, in its concern with the preternatural, and in its determination to exert pressure on the reader's feelings by picturing the awesome, the horrific, the mysterious, the exotic, and the sublime, was initiated by writers of no more than second-rate talent. Horace Walpole with *The Castle of Otranto* (1764), Clara Reeve (1729–1807) with *The Old English Baron* (1777), and William Beckford with *Vathek* (1786) all played their influential part in the Gothick movement, but none so forcefully as their successor Ann Radcliffe (1764–1823). Works which constitute 'literary landmarks' are not always also literary masterpieces, and they may even be very faulty by strict literary standards, but innovation is crucial in literary history.

Scott very perceptively put his finger on Mrs Radcliffe's most significant innovation:

Indeed, the praise may be claimed for Mrs Radcliffe, of having been the first to introduce into her prose fictions a beautiful and fanciful tone of natural description and impressive narrative which had hitherto been exclusively applied to poetry.

Her novel *The Mysteries of Udolpho* (1794) is a *tour de force*. It tells the story of Emily de St Aubert, who finds herself after her parents' death entrusted to the guardianship of a harsh, selfish, dissipated aunt, Madame Cheron. Mme Cheron marries Signor Montoni, a sinister, overbearing figure who ultimately turns out to be a kind of mafia godfather. A palpably awesome and frightening person, he carries Emily off to his mountain retreat, a grim castle in the Apennines. Thus Emily is torn away from the young man, Valancourt, on whom she has set her heart, and deposited in a sombre Gothick fortress lavishly equipped with trap-doors, secret passages, sliding panels, and all the paraphernalia of horror. Here strange figures glimpsed in the darkness, spine-chilling groans heard where no one is to be seen, and even a terrifying spectacle of human decomposition help to build up a massive array of liabilities in the shape of unsolved mysteries. At the end the authoress has to step into the novel herself to unravel the tangle. Yet the reader cannot but be aware that the author's characters have not all had the benefit of hearing the whole story recounted from the beginning. In short, their combined knowledge, if freely pooled, would be inadequate to remove all the terrifying doubts that have darkened their days.

Thus, although Mrs Radcliffe's forte is the mystery novel, she is not particularly adept at the craft which produces the modern detective novel. Her strength lies in the way she plays upon the reader's feelings as mysteries are encountered. Scott made the point that, however crude may be the dénouement that disinfects and cleans up the mysteries, this final clumsiness cannot detract from the reader's pleasure to date — 'the recollection of the powerful emotions of wonder, curiosity, even fear, to which we have been subjected during the currency of the narrative.' It is easy to make fun of *The Mysteries of Udolpho*. The story is supposed to be set in the sixteenth century, and indeed we hear the vesper bells from a convent and the midnight hymn of the monks, but anachronisms include a coach-and-six and detailed accounts of eighteenth-century dress and furniture, while the tone of social life and relationships is wholly of Mrs Radcliffe's own period.

Characters are not subtly conceived, but they are wrapped about by a poetic ambience which makes us 'feel' them. Emily has a capacity to act, a dangerous sensibility, an impulsive warm-heartedness and candour, and a melancholy vein of nostalgic reflectiveness. She also has a true piety — but it is not based on a rigid sense of duty, like Susan Ferrier's heroine's, rather it is sustained by a feeling for divine sublimity and majesty manifested through the forms of natural beauty. This is an aspect of Mrs Radcliffe's 'Romanticism'. She sees dissipation and vice as often nothing more than the consequences of boredom from which a healthy interest in literature and the arts can protect the sensitive soul. Ultimately she is with Henry Mackenzie in urging that the practice of vice brings dissatisfaction and the practice of virtue is pleasurable. Mrs Radcliffe's scenery is painted with a sensitivity to the grand, the sombre, and the terrifying in nature, which brings her close to the Romantic poets. Against the background of hills, rivers, and clouds, the occasional tower or château seems as timeless as they do. And it is not only crags and peaks, precipices and torrents, forests and solemn sunsets that are invested with mystic sublimity. When Emily first enters the Castle of Udolpho the surroundings are alive with tension. Every detail contributes to the atmosphere of lonely desolation and awesome mystery: the very size of the place, the gloomy signs of decay, the cold, and the noises of wind, door, and footstep are an ache in the heart.

The contemplation of nature is continually related to primal human feelings, as childhood memories and the recollection of the lost hopes of youth seep through the mind. Pervading all is a nostalgic awareness of the passage of time, leaving regret and bitter-sweet memories behind. It is near indeed to that healthy sense of life's transience and the littleness of human endeavour that permeates Scott's *The Antiquary*. Alongside this theme runs another, much of Mrs Radcliffe's period — the contrast between pastoral simplicity, purity, and peace and the vice, corruption, and dissipation of the fashionable world.

Matthew Gregory Lewis

The Monk (1796) by Matthew Gregory Lewis (1775–1818) has achieved the status of the archetypal Gothick horror novel. 'Monk' Lewis was twenty years old when it was published, and its success was sensational. Lewis found Mrs Radcliffe's *The Mysteries of Udolpho* 'one of the most interesting books that has ever been published', and after reading it he rushed through the composition of *The Monk*. There is a marked contrast between the two works. Mrs Radcliffe's ventures into the world of the mysterious and the preternatural depend for their effectiveness on postponing the true explanation of what fills the reader with awe and apprehension. The reader experiences something of a let-down when the commonplace character of what were seemingly uncanny and paranormal events is ultimately made clear. Lewis has no truck with any such prudery. He throws off all restraints of common sense and rationality in exploiting whatever marvels the machinery of ghostly terror, legendary superstition, and preternatural phenomena can supply.

Lewis was the son of a wealthy father with estates in the West Indies, who was for a time Deputy Secretary at the War Office, and Matthew himself became a diplomat and later a Member of Parliament. His literary work gained him the admiration of Byron and Shelley, whom he visited in Italy. His connection with Scott began in 1798, when he planned a collection of 'marvellous ballads' and sought to include some of Scott's own. Thus his *Tales of Wonder* (1801) includes both original ballads by Scott ('Glenfilas' and 'The Eve of St John' among them) and ballads which Scott had translated ('The Wild Huntsman').

This volume was the successor to Lewis's collection, *Tales of Terror* (1799), which, in a preliminary verse dialogue between 'Friend' and 'Author', includes a passionate defence of the Gothick vein. Lewis ridicules the current fashion for 'moral axioms', mournful sonnets, and 'leaden rules'. He wants to see the soul melted by pity, stormed by terror, and escaping the bonds of space and time.

> Oh! it breathes awe and rapture o'er the soul
> To mark the surge in wild confusion roll,
> And when the forest groans, and tempest lours,
> To wake Imagination's darkest powers!
> How throbs the breast with terror and delight,
> Filled with rude scenes of Europe's barbarous night!

He longs to exploit the superstitions of the Middle Ages:

To view the pale-eyed maid in penance pine,
To watch the votary at the sainted shrine;
And, while o'er blasted heaths the night-storm raves,
To hear the wizard wake the slumb'ring graves . . .

Lewis heads the first chapter of *The Monk* with an apt quotation from Shakespeare's *Measure for Measure*:

Lord Angelo is precise;
Stands at a guard with envy; scarce confesses
That his blood flows, or that his appetite
Is more to bread than stone.

Such a man too is the Capuchin Abbot Ambrosio, renowned for his piety and his asceticism. But it emerges that his monastic vocation has involved an unnatural repression of a vigorous, sensitive, and sociable personality. It is vanity alone that has kept him virtuous. A fiend in human form, Matilda, disguises herself as a boy and gains admittance to the monastery. There she cunningly sets about the seduction of Ambrosio by manipulating his chief weakness, his vanity. Once he has succumbed, Matilda gradually assumes domination of the monk, and he is led through an escalation of criminality, including the seduction of his beautiful, trusting penitent, Antonia, the murder of her mother Elvira, and eventually of Antonia herself. Since it emerges that he is Elvira's lost son, his crimes have culminated in incest and matricide.

The strange blend of psychological insight and moral orthodoxy with every kind of sensational excess in the way of lust and brutality gives the central theme a lurid effectiveness. If Ambrosio's career begins like that of Shakespeare's Angelo, it ends like that of Marlowe's Dr Faustus. Faced by the Inquisition, he makes a final desperate bid for safety by the sale of his soul, but infernal agents grab him and dash him to pieces, the agony of remorse torturing his heart. There is a faint Elizabethan flavour about the book at many points. Like Shakespeare's Juliet, Antonia takes a sleeping-potion and wakes up in the charnel-house beneath the monastery.

The main point of contrast with Mrs Radcliffe is Lewis's reversal of the progress from apparent mystery to workaday clarification. Matilda's seemingly naturalistic seduction of Ambrosio turns out to be the work of the Devil. Where the seemingly supernatural turned out in *The Mysteries of Udolpho* to be a matter of natural agencies after all, in *The Monk* the seemingly natural turns out to be in fact the supernatural. This is remarkably so in the sub-plot of Don Raymond and his beloved Agnes, whose aunt has imprisoned her in a castle and intends her for the convent. There is a superstition that every fifth year on the fifth of May a haunted chamber of the castle opens and a ghostly bleeding nun walks out with lamp and dagger to descend the stairs and cross the hall. 'On that night the porter always leaves the gates of the castle open . . .' The lovers regard the story as superstitious nonsense and plan to make use of the general belief in it for Agnes to escape her imprisonment in the dress of the nun. On the night in question Don Raymond receives his 'Agnes' into his arms and drives away with her. As the pace of the horses quickens and the drivers are hurled headlong to the ground, as wind, thunder, and lightning tear at the darkness, the awful truth dawns on the reader that the motionless figure in Raymond's arms is the despised phantom at whom the lovers scoffed. And so it proves to be. Agnes's fate is to be condemned to the convent in Madrid. She is later declared dead, though in fact she has been imprisoned in a secret underground vault, there to starve to death. The surroundings of the momentous adventures are remote indeed from those of contemporary England. 'Medieval' Europe is stocked with Gothick fortresses, robber-infested forests, and charnel-vaults, where sorcery and exorcism, magic mirrors and charmed potions are the order of the day.

Lewis has a gift for whetting the appetite in management of narrative by continually leading the reader to the pitch of excitement or curiosity — then delaying immediate resolution. Mysteries, shocks, discoveries, dramatic interviews, and crude adventures in blood and sex tumble on top of each other in a wild, crowding tide that sweeps the reader to the end. It is all riotously extravagant, and the polysyllabic artifices of style might well be used in instruction as examples of how not to write. Nevertheless the work amply deserved its success and it remains fascinatingly readable.

Mary Shelley

Of all Gothick horror novels the one that has survived most durably, to be widely read and filmed in our own century, is *Frankenstein, or the Modern Prometheus* (1818) by Mary Shelley (1797–1851). A period of bad weather in Switzerland bred a compact between Byron, Shelley, and Mary Shelley, that each should write a ghost story. Byron confirmed this version of the origin of *Frankenstein*, 'a wonderful work,' he said, 'for a girl of nineteen — *not* nineteen, indeed, at that time'. James Ballantyne gave it as evidence of Scott's 'delusions as to the merits of his own works', that 'he greatly preferred Mrs Shelley's *Frankenstein* to any of his own romances'. Frankenstein, a Swiss scientist, discovers how to give life to what is inanimate, manufactures a human form from fragments of corpses, and then turns it into a living being. It is, of course, a monster hideous to look at, which terrifies all who set eyes on it, yet it is not essentially evil but rendered so by envy of the happiness it is denied. In its solitude it educates itself by books to an understanding of the life of the emotions. It demands a female mate, and Frankenstein cannot bring himself to repeat his tragic experiment. In vengeful fury the monster embarks on a career of murder and even kills Frankenstein's bride on their wedding night. After suffering a mental collapse, Frankenstein determines to destroy his monster, pursues it across the world, and dies. The monster survives long enough to bewail its creator's end before going off to its own destruction.

Mary Shelley's subtitle suggests the mythic dimensions of her fable, and these are developed in the story itself. A correspondence is drawn between Frankenstein's manufacture of his monster and God's creation of the angel who was to turn into Satan. God's making of man is also at issue in the epigraph Mary Shelley takes from *Paradise Lost*:

> Did I request thee, Maker, from my clay
> To mould Me man?

Frankenstein's monster declares, 'I was benevolent and good; misery made me a fiend.' Thus the fable enquires into the responsibility of the Creator for the misery and evil in his created world. It is obvious too that an implicit critique of the damage advanced scientific technology could do can be read into the fable. Moreover, the book has lent itself to the search for psychological readings in terms of Mary Shelley's relationship to the mother who died after her birth and the brilliant father whose affection she longed for.

Charles Robert Maturin

If the Gothick horror novel reached its fullest vitality in Lewis's *The Monk*, it was magnificently revitalised a quarter of a century later in *Melmoth the Wanderer* (1820) by Charles Maturin (1782–1824). Maturin, a Dubliner, was educated at Trinity College, Dublin, and was then ordained into the Church of Ireland. He first tried his hand at Gothick horror in *The Fatal Revenge* (1807), and Scott, noting the 'powers of imagination and expression' displayed, thought it a remarkable instance of 'genius degraded' in an unworthy task. Maturin then tackled intrinsically Irish material, taking a leaf out of Lady Morgan's book with *The Wild Irish Boy* (1808), and displaying a Radcliffean sensibility in relation to wild romantic scenery in *The Milesian Chief* (1811). But Maturin himself came to recognise that these books lacked '*external* interest' and were too much the product of an imagination insufficiently nourished by real life.

Melmoth the Wanderer astonishes by its sheer fluency and extravagance. There is in Irish literature a brand of lavish excess which writers such as James Joyce have both revelled in and mocked. Maturin is a master at indulging it in such a way that the reader is carried along on a tide of profusion that never becomes tedious, and Maturin escapes any charge of affectation because, in the back of his mind, the reader senses that the writer does not take himself or his task too seriously. That said, it must be added that the horror and the terror, the torment and the agony, indeed the awe and the mystery are real enough.

Young Melmoth, a Dublin student, having inherited the estate of a miserly uncle, learns by the discovery of a manuscript and by the rescue of a Spanish nobleman wrecked on the Wicklow coast, that an ancient ancestor of his lives still. He sold his soul to the Devil in the seventeenth century in return for prolongation of life. He has roamed the world ever since, Melmoth the Wanderer, endowed with supernatural control of his movements, and desperately seeking someone who will take his place before his doom closes in upon him. The records of his various attempts to find a substitute are spilt out in series as the narrator, at first the Spanish nobleman, Alonzo di Monçada, unfolds story within story; then sub-contracted narrators emerge with a tale to tell or a manuscript to read. The stories abound in horror and suffering. There is Stanton, falsely identified as insane, imprisoned in a lunatic's cell, and entertained day and night by the imbecilic ravings of other inmates. Melmoth appears, door-key in hand, offering him an immediate escape 'into life, liberty, and sanity'. There is Monçada himself, who was tricked into the monastic life and whose resistance brings all manner of physical and mental torture at the hands of his superiors. In the very depths, when the Inquisition has him at its mercy, he rejects Melmoth's offer. So does Walberg, when poverty has reduced his loved wife and children to starvation. So does Elinor Mortimer, when treachery has destroyed all hope of married happiness with the man she loved. So finally does Isidora di Aliaga, whom Melmoth has, as she believes, 'married', and whom he has betrayed.

The moral is clear enough. 'I have traversed the whole world in the search and no one, to gain that world, would lose his own soul,' Melmoth finally concludes. What gives the book its power is, firstly, the intensity which Maturin's unfailing verbal thrust injects into accounts of the victims' sufferings. There are horrific torments of all kinds, squalid, sickening, and sadistic. There are long drawn-out agonies of neglect and brutality, seasoned with subtle treacheries and refined hypocrisies. Maturin's prose does not flag in stoking up the fire of emotional involvement. A second factor in the book's appeal is the cunning extravagance of the machinery of torment, whether physical or mental, which can be enthusiastically attributed by a Protestant to the world of Catholic intrigue. A third factor in the book's appeal is the poetic exuberance of the scenic backgrounds which enrich moments of love or rapture, misery or tragedy, with appropriate resonances from the environment. Moreover, the satanic figure of Melmoth is surrounded by an insidiously awesome ambience, Byronic in its flavour of the sinister and the perverted. When his 150 years run out at the end of the tale, his physique is suddenly transformed into that of an old man.

It is interesting that Oscar Wilde, whose mother had a family connection with Maturin, should have chosen after his downfall to call himself 'Sebastian Melmoth'. Interesting, not only because of the act of romantic self-dramatisation involved, but because Wilde's most subtle work of prose fiction, *The Picture of Dorian Gray*, is *Melmoth the Wanderer* condensed, secularised, and disinfected. Nor is this the only instance of Maturin's long-term influence. The Inquisitor in Bernard Shaw's *Saint Joan* speaks with the accents of Maturin's amiably tyrannical ecclesiastics.

Elizabeth Inchbald

Having followed the course of the Gothick horror novel to its culmination in the work of Maturin, we turn back to the 1790s to consider some literary innovations of a very different kind. Elizabeth Inchbald (1753–1821) was the wife of an actor and painter; she herself worked as an actress and wrote a number of plays. But more remarkable than any of them is her novel, *A Simple Story* (1791); it seems to have pioneered the theme of the chastening of a wilful heroine which served Susan Ferrier so well in *Marriage* and thereafter Jane Austen in *Emma*. The heroine of *A Simple Story* is Miss Milner, to begin with — and, alas, the reader never learns her Christian name. Even her husband keeps it to himself. But it is chiefly in such trivialities of etiquette that the book strikes the modern reader as artificial. Maria Edgeworth praised its convincing realism with eloquent superlatives.

Miss Milner's father is a Roman Catholic and her deceased mother was a Protestant. On his death, worried about her future, Mr Milner consigns his daughter at the age of eighteen to the guardianship of a thirty-year-old Roman Catholic priest, Mr Dorriforth. Opposed as the two are in temperament and conviction, Miss Milner falls in love with her guardian. In the first half of the novel the development of this situation is nicely managed. Dorriforth, a highly rational and restrained personality who can control his own impulses with rigorous discipline, is required to deal with a vital, impulsive, warm-hearted ward too little prepared by her upbringing to have sense not to give her beauty and charm full rein for the satisfaction of her vanity. However, Dorriforth's elder brother, Lord Elmwood, dies unexpectedly. As heir, Dorriforth is expected to get permission to resign his orders, and he does so. The two contrasting characters, after much tension and suffering, manage to come together in honest satisfaction of their mutual passion, and marry. There are seventeen years of happy domesticity until Lord Elmwood goes abroad to attend to family estates, and his wife's hold on domestic fidelity fails when his absence extends to three years. On his return, Lord Elmwood challenges her lover to a duel, then banishes his wife and her daughter Matilda for ever from his presence. Lady Elmwood dies, and the second half of the novel deals with the young Lady Matilda's life under the painful interdict banning her from her father's presence. Eventually a happy ending is contrived, and Mrs Inchbald is at pains to point out that Lady Matilda, unlike her mother, has been brought up in the hard school of constraint, learning early to cope with deprivation and injustice without losing her sympathy even for those who ill-treat her.

To that extent the novel is about the importance of education. The frank, explicit moral is that Mr Milner would have done better to leave his fortune elsewhere than to his daughter, rather than to have failed to bestow upon her 'A PROPER EDUCATION'. For the 'school of prudence — though of adversity — in which Matilda was bred' ensures her in the long run a happy marriage.

What is remarkable about the novel is that Mr Dorriforth, the 'older' hero to whom the young heroine eventually succumbs and submits, is not a faultless being like Emma's Mr Knightley (in Jane Austen's *Emma*) or Ellen Perry's Mr Maitland (in Mary Brunton's *Discipline*). Dorriforth is himself a man in need of just as great a psychological shake-up as is his ward. His refusal to open up with candour when the emotional atmosphere is uneasy, his repeated recourse to aloofness and outraged taciturnity as weapons of masculine domination, his pride in making and keeping rash punitive decrees, his sheer lack of either humour or self-knowledge — all these defects make him at least as responsible as his ward for the failures of mutual understanding that bedevil their relationship. Although somewhat caricatured, Mrs Inchbald's study of the damage that rigidly insensitive masculinity can do is striking and discerning.

Yet her later novel, *Nature and Art* (1796), lacks any comparable fluency of psychological investigation. It is a rigidly planned parable, contrasting the careers of two brothers, Henry and William, the one abounding in natural affection and sincerity, the other in pretentiousness and ambition. Decency takes the former into privation and danger abroad, and calculating conformity brings the latter ecclesiastical preferment at home. The contrast is intensified in the careers of their respective sons, young Henry and young William. Yet throughout the rather stilted presentation of this heavily didactic fable there runs a vein of true romantic indignation at the differences of treatment and judgment meted out to rich and poor.

> Lord and Lady Bindham, strenuous opposers of vice in the poor, and gentle supporters of it in the rich, never played at cards, or had concerts on a Sunday . . .

There is no truck here with the notion that sincerity and good-heartedness necessarily bring their own reward. They are as likely to bring calamity to the needy as self-centred calculation is to bring prosperity to the well-to-do. The tale calls feelingly for a new order in the final cry of the hero:

> Let the poor then no more be their own persecutors — no longer pay homage to wealth — instantaneously the whole idolatrous worship will cease — the idol will be broken.

William Godwin

Such sentiments make it understandable that Elizabeth Inchbald should have been one among the admiring ladies who gathered around William Godwin (1756–1836) when his *Enquiry concerning Political Justice* (1793) brought him fame and veneration. Fellow admirers included Mary Hays and Amelia Alderson (later Mrs Opie), as well as Mary Wollstonecraft, for the injustices which Mrs Inchbald revealed with a touching, if naïve, sensitivity were explored by Godwin with a thoroughness and acumen that made an immense impact on his contemporaries. Although, like Inchbald's *Nature and Art*, Godwin's novel *Caleb Williams* (1794) is designed with an ethical symmetricality too rigidly simplistic to sustain overall imaginative authenticity, yet Godwin gives a philosophic dimension to his presentation of the human lot in the current social environment, and his protest has a fervent logic. The full title of his most substantial and influential novel is *Things as They Are, or The Adventures of Caleb Williams*, and he wrote in his Preface:

> It is but of late that the inestimable importance of political principles has been adequately apprehended. It is now known to philosophers, that the spirit and character of the government intrudes into every rank of society.

But books of philosophy are not within everyone's reach, he adds.

> Accordingly it was proposed, in the invention of the following work, to comprehend as far as the progressive nature of a single story would allow, a general review of the modes of domestic and unrecorded despotism by which man becomes the destroyer of man.

So we find Caleb Williams, a warm-hearted, genuine young man, taken as secretary into the employment of Falkland, a wealthy local squire. He admires Falkland but is bewildered by his strange neurotic behaviour. The first part of the novel presents Falkland's past career as that of a noble-minded, honourable, generous, cultured gentleman, much taxed by the boorish arrogance and brutality of a neighbouring squire, Tyrrel, who is insanely jealous of Falkland's local pre-eminence. Tyrrel is a bully whose tyranny and malignancy drive an honest farmer, Hawkins, and his son into poverty and bring about the death of his own dependent niece, Miss Melville. He collides with Falkland over these brutalities, and a long-simmering hostility reaches its climax at a public assembly where Tyrrel, a big man, knocks Falkland repeatedly to the floor and kicks him. Within hours Tyrrel is found murdered. Whispered suspicions about Falkland are discredited by his manly self-defence. Hawkins and his son are arrested and executed.

This is the background to the central story of Williams's misfortune in first suspecting Falkland's guilt, then having it confirmed from his own mouth, and being bound to secrecy under the most devastating threats. The weakness of the plot is that Falkland, at first the model of honour and rectitude, and the champion of the weak against the strong, has to be transformed into the archetypal wealthy persecutor of the innocent. He makes Williams's life a misery, and when Williams manages to get away, pursues him with an obsessively vengeful malignancy. He frames Williams on a false charge of theft, and has him imprisoned. When Williams manages to escape he finds himself a notorious criminal whose wicked doings are the talk of the nation. Thus Godwin engineers a state of moral topsy-turvydom in which the wicked persecutor maintains his unsullied reputation, and his innocent victim is subjected to the most injurious defamations. The weakness of the story lies in the questionable motivation for Falkland's behaviour, as he himself sees it:

I have sworn to preserve my reputation, whatever be the expense . . . I love it more than the whole world and its inhabitants taken together!

And Williams is outraged:

I saw treachery triumphant and enthroned; I saw the sinews of innocence crumbled into the dust by the gripe of almighty guilt.

The most impressive thing in the book is perhaps the powerful irony indulged by Godwin when, on the run from gaol, Williams falls under the protection of a gang of thieves. For their captain treats him with a decency which overwhelms him, and shows up the rottenness of the national institutions by contrast. 'We who are thieves without licence,' says the robber captain, 'are at open war with another set of men who are thieves according to law.' He is an idealist in a world of corruption, who can exclaim, 'If fidelity and honour be banished from thieves, where shall they find refuge upon the face of the earth?'

Godwin struck a chord with his contemporaries when he attacked 'the power which the institutions of society give to one man over another' and lamented 'that law was better adapted for a weapon of tyranny in the hands of the rich, than for a shield to protect the humbler part of the community against their usurpations'. But his forcefulness as a propagandist militated against fictional authenticity. The reader cannot but be aware that the desperately iniquitous situations which most surely illustrate his message are the product of literary engineering that turns characters into puppets.

Thomas Holcroft

One of the men closest to Godwin in friendship and ideology was Thomas Holcroft (1745–1809), a personality of astonishing vitality and power. He was the son of a cobbler and had educated himself, working as a shoemaker, a teacher, a strolling player, and a journalist. Writing eventually took over. He wrote and adapted plays performed in London from the 1780s to the early 1800s. In his novels he sought to use fiction as Godwin used it, as a vehicle for his radical critique of the current political set-up. Two of the novels merit mention, but the first of them, *Anna St Ives* (1792), suffers from the kind of diagrammatic structure exemplified in Mrs Inchbald's *Nature and Art*. Anna, the virtuous heroine, is sought in marriage by two contrasting suitors. One, Coke Clifton, is an unprincipled aristocrat out to satisfy his vicious tastes; the other, Frank Healey, is the son of the steward employed by Ann's father, but he is a virtuous and rational idealist. The victory of social radicalism over corruption is symbolised in the union of the virtuous couple — somewhat illogically, for Frank looks forward to the time when the tyrannical and selfish despotism of marriage will be no more.

The Adventures of Hugh Trevor (1794–7) is less rigidly patterned, and it represents a comprehensive condemnation of the political and social iniquities which obstruct the path of the would-be virtuous idealist. 'Men do not become what by nature they are meant to be, but what society makes them,' Holcroft averred. He saw 'generous feelings and higher propensities of the soul . . . shrunk up . . . violently wrenched, and amputated, to fit us for our intercourse in the world'. Where Caleb Williams's long pilgrimage of persecution is so generalised that it assumes the philosophical character of a critique of the human condition, Hugh Trevor's career brings him into particularised contact with the contemporary agents of injustice wherever Holcroft can locate them. The most astonishing aspect of the book is the seeming thoroughness of Holcroft's knowledge of the contemporary world. We may turn to *Caleb Williams* to share a deeply felt outrage at current injustice, but certainly not to learn what was actually happening in the academic world, the literary world, the legal world, or the ecclesiastical world. For this kind of insight we must turn to *Hugh Trevor*.

The novel is autobiographical in form and suffers from some consequent crudities of the 'I-did-not-know-this-at-the-time-but-was-later-to-discover-it' variety. Indeed it is a rambling picaresque novel, exploiting some of the most hackneyed devices of earlier eighteenth-century fiction. Repeated coincidences enable Hugh Trevor to be at hand to save his beloved Olivia's life with a too strenuous frequency. When things are at their worst there will be a convenient bleeding stranger at the roadside, the victim of thugs, to be rescued in the nick of time and to turn out to be a long lost but vastly wealthy uncle looking for a worthy heir. As a work of art, in short, *Hugh Trevor* is full of defects, but for sociological interest the hero's experiences are captivating.

Hugh is a gifted boy who manages at first to rise in life by the display of his talents. But in whichever direction he turns, he soon finds that some kind of dishonest compromise of principle is necessary if he is to keep his footing. On those occasions when he does compromise he finds himself led deeper into the net of worldly intrigue. He must either commit himself fully to hypocrisy and falsehood, or he must ruin himself by taking on the powers-that-be. He goes to Oxford only to discover that the much dreamed-of university is riddled with corruption, that learning is at a discount, and dissipation the order of the day. He prepares for a career in the Church and wins the favour of a bishop who first preaches one of Hugh's sermons as if it were his own, then proceeds to publish a theological work by Hugh under his own name. He serves the Earl of Idford's cause by writing violent anti-government articles for the press under a pseudonym, but revolts when the earl, having accepted government patronage, requires him to write as virulently on the other side. He is shunned and persecuted when he protests against such iniquities, for he cannot conceal his outrage at the prevalence of hypocrisy and injustice in high places.

> Did not the history of the world proclaim that, he who would attain wealth and power must turn the prejudices of mankind to their own harm?

It is not only the Church and the governing aristocracy whose corruptions are analysed. The literary world's indifference to true talent is scathingly exemplified. The chicaneries to which members of the legal profession commit themselves are devastatingly exposed. Society's tyrannous mechanisms of possession are put under judgment. The falsification of true human virtue and value implicit in military aggrandisement and in the cult of the heroic is proclaimed. Holcroft's satirical vein is rich. It pulses with life. Every effort is made to avoid over-simplification in that Hugh has to be argued out of his illusions by fellow idealists. There are pages of dialectical analysis of the issues raised which make *Caleb Williams* look thin by comparison, but they do not enhance the readability of *Hugh Trevor* as a novel.

Holcroft, like Godwin, like Mrs Inchbald, has a touching faith in education: 'The world is unjust ... because it is ignorant.' In the eyes of the dedicated idealist Turl, it is ultimately as simple as that: 'Ignorance is the source of all evil.' But the psychological sinewiness of the book lies in the thoroughness with which realistic practical dilemmas facing the would-be reformer are analysed, in particular the question how far compromise is necessary in the attempt to achieve a position from which influence can be exercised. It is the wrestling with such realities which gives the book its inner force and its sturdiness of substance.

Robert Bage

The protest novel of the 1790s expresses the aspirations and frustrations of a decade during which the enthusiasm aroused among radicals by the French Revolution was tempered by disillusionment at the Reign of Terror of Robespierre. Official worry in England about the possible infectious influence of the Revolution produced a government clamp-down on supposedly seditious literature and organisations. Moreover, since England was formally at war with France from February 1793, radical propaganda and radical agitation could readily be interpreted as treachery. Thomas Holcroft was among a group of members of the Society for Constitutional Information who were briefly held in the Tower on a charge of high treason while the composition of *Hugh Trevor* was in mid-career. A letter was written to the *Morning Chronicle* by William Godwin, coolly analysing the charges against the prisoners and defending their sincerity in exercising what was assumed to be an English right, and in fact the charges against most of them were dropped.

There are echoes of the public hysteria that could be released at this time against suspected agitators in the best of the novels by Robert Bage (1728–1801), *Hermsprong, or Man as He Is Not* (1796). Bage was the representative of an older generation than either Holcroft or Godwin, and though he turned to novel-writing only late in his career as the owner of a paper mill in Derbyshire, most of his novels belong to the 1780s and are in the tradition of Fielding and Smollett. But he produced two novels in his sixties, *Man as He Is* (1792) and *Hermsprong, or Man as He Is Not* (1796), and the latter is alive with contemporary awareness not only of the social situation in England but also of the outside world — France and America in particular. Bage is a witty satirist who gives the impression of a man who plies the trade of writer with consummate ease. He can detach himself from his narrative and indulge in sly asides on either the activities of his characters or the author's task in dealing with them, in a way which recalls Sterne's *Tristram Shandy*. But his technique is not without the deficiences of the minor novelists of the period in respect of highly artificial plotting.

Bage makes use in *Hermsprong* of a situation exploited by Voltaire in his fable 'L'Ingénu'. The situation had already been used by Mrs Inchbald in the story of Young Henry in *Nature and Art*, and Bage may well have known both works. A noble savage, brought up abroad, comes into contact with European civilisation, and his reaction of genuine shock at attitudes offensive to reason and decency shows up the hypocrisies of supposedly civilised manners and institutions. Deeply injured by a family quarrel and treachery, Hermsprong's father emigrated, and Hermsprong was brought up among the American Indians. His father's sour experience of the world led him to inculcate only principles of utter truth and integrity. At the age of sixteen Hermsprong returns to France, thence to England, and expresses himself thus:

> It is six years since I have been endeavouring to acquire European arts. Of my progress I cannot boast. I cannot learn to offer incense at the shrines of wealth and power, nor at any shrines but those of probity and virtue. I cannot learn to surrender my opinion from complaisance, or from any principle of adulation. Nor can I learn to suppress the sentiments of a freeborn mind, from any fear, religious or political. Such uncourtly obduracy has my savage education produced!

Hermsprong collides with the powerful personalities representative of the aristocracy and the Church. He saves the life of Lord Gondale's beautiful daughter, and then thoroughly offends the peer by his refusal to bow the knee. On this basis the well-worn theme of conflict in a young lady's heart between the duty of obedience to her father and love for a seemingly totally unsuitable wooer is developed with a difference; for the threat to paternal authority is enriched by overtones of radical challenge to political and social stability. Hermsprong's outspokenness, his ironic critique of what he encounters, and his French connection make it possible for Lord Gondale to try to frame him as a spy.

The heroine, Caroline, has a close orphan friend, Maria Fluart, who on the feminine side, by sheer wit, spiritedness, and common sense, represents a challenge from within to the mores and presuppositions on which Lord Gondale's shallow and ponderously unimaginative world depends. Her conversation sparkles. Her sense of irony is devastating. She can prick the bubble of pomposity and pretence with a deft aphoristic scintillation:

> Our obligations to men are infinite. Under the name of father, or brother, or guardian, or husband, they are always protecting us from liberty.

Bage's work is significant as a part of the body of literature putting society under scrutiny and expressing the kind of outraged disgust at its corruptions that Shelley so eloquently voiced. But whether the cruel, tyrannical, testy, and utterly self-indulgent Lord Gondale is in fact to be considered any more authentic in his day than, say, Richardson's idealised

Sir Charles Grandison was in his day, is open to question. Scott, who recognised Bage's qualities and included three of his novels in Ballantyne's Novelists' Library, was quick to point out that the man of perfection, whose wisdom and virtue all emanate from the force of individual reason within, is a figment of the imagination. But the projection of this inspired individualism into collision with the cramping, fettering fashions and codes and institutions of a corrupt society is one more aspect of the Romantic spirit. It is as significant as the concept of the Byronic hero, and socially far more relevant.

Mary Hays

'While the institutions of society war against nature and happiness, the mind of energy, struggling to emancipate itself, will entangle itself in error.' So speaks the heroine of *Memoirs of Emma Courtney* (1796), the novel by Mary Hays (1760–1843). Emma has imbibed the principles of contemporary radical protest and gives them a distinctive feminist orientation. 'Every vice is the error of the understanding; crimes and prejudices are brothers; truth and virtue sisters,' she declares. Mary Hays, a friend and admirer of Mary Wollstonecraft, turned herself into a symbol of extreme, aggressive feminism and a ready target for ridicule by her uninhibited pursuit of men who failed to respond. Her Emma Courtney gives an account of her disastrously unreciprocated devotion to a young man whose intelligence and culture feed the flames of her passion, but whose mysterious sexual aloofness drives her to a frenzy of self-analysis and self-justification. She breaks all the conventions by declaring her love for him (by letter) and by continuing to pour out heart-felt pleas for responsiveness and understanding. Since she knows that Augustus Harley will lose a legacy if he marries, she offers herself as mistress; for calamities flow, she argues, 'from chastity having been considered as a sexual virtue'. In this respect it is not nature but 'the barbarous and accursed laws of society' which deny women full independence and freedom of action.

It is true that Emma Courtney looks back self-critically on her own past. In a happy childhood her days flew by in joy and innocence. In adolescence she devoured 'from ten to fourteen novels in a week'. She did not aspire to a rational independence but rather became 'a continual victim to the enthusiasm of [her] feelings; incapable of approving, or disapproving, with moderation'. In short, 'my own boasted reason has been, but too often, the dupe of my imagination'. In some respects this survey of an upbringing in which sensibilities have been allowed too free a play is interestingly in line, on the feminine side, with the account of the upbringing of Scott's Edward Waverley. But Emma's conviction that 'vice originates in mistakes of the understanding' unites Mary Hays with her radical contemporaries. Indeed a peculiar fascination of *Emma Courtney* is that the reader is made to feel that he has dropped in on a living conversation in which questions of human behaviour are being tossed about. The character of Mr Francis, Emma's trusted mentor, is a portrait of Godwin, and Godwin's words are incorporated in the advice he gives. There are quotations too from Thomas Holcroft's *Anna St Ives*, and there are references to Mary Wollstonecraft and to Rousseau's *La Nouvelle Héloïse* ('Ah! with what transport, with what enthusiasm, did I peruse this dangerous, enchanting work!'). The reader never loses the sense that Emma is waging a campaign, is engaged in a life-or-death struggle, is bursting with the inner turmoil of an obsessive passion. She pours out a stream of deeply felt pleas and claims, demands and pressures, only to encounter a seemingly strange human deadness at the heart of the man she idolises.

The trouble with the novel is that Augustus Harley is such a wet fish that it is difficult to understand how an intelligent woman could lose her heart to him. After all, if we are honest, it is not the moral codes and conventions of the ages that Emma is up against, but the pedestrian incompatibility of a self-protective individual. Nevertheless the book is a moving document. The feminine demand for admission to areas of fuller activity and for release from cramping assumptions about the role of women is eloquently voiced. And Emma Courtney's own repeated warnings against the danger of passion unregulated by reason saves her record from seeming self-indulgent.

Amelia Opie

Central to the thinking of novelists such as Mary Hays, who voiced feminist unease about current mores, was *A Vindication of the Rights of Woman* (1792) by Mary Wollstonecraft (1759–97). The book makes a forceful assault on the tradition of educating girls to notions of duty and propriety which keep them in a state of servile dependence. The follies and vanities of women are bred of a system which denies them proper intellectual stimulus and encourages them instead to interpret their roles in terms of pleasing men. Mary Wollstonecraft had been a teacher and private governess. Her work naturally brought her to the attention of radical contemporaries such as Godwin and Holcroft. She was familiar with the teaching of Rousseau. She went to Paris in 1792 and met a former American soldier turned merchant, Gilbert Imlay, cohabited with him, and bore him a daughter, Fanny, in 1794. Imlay did not share Mary's idealistic view of their relationship, which led her to believe that the union needed no marriage to cement it. He was not faithful, and he lost interest in her. Deeply bruised, she twice attempted suicide. Godwin, in his *Memoirs of Mary Wollstonecraft* (1798), describes with seeming delicacy how Mary came into his life in 1796, and there was a gradual growth of intimacy between them. Mary in fact took the initiative in visiting him.

> Her visit, it seems, is to be deemed a deviation from etiquette; but she had through life trampled on those rules which are built on the assumption of the imbecility of her sex.

Indeed Godwin is at pains to point out that the relationship grew with equal advances on either side. 'One sex did not take the priority which long-established custom has awarded it, nor the other overstep that delicacy which is so severely imposed.' Thus friendship slowly ripened into love.

> We did not marry. It is difficult to recommend anything to indiscriminate adoption, contrary to the established rules and prejudices of mankind; but certainly nothing can be so ridiculous upon the face of it, or so contrary to the genuine march of sentiment, as to require the overflowing of the soul to wait upon a ceremony, and that which, wherever delicacy and imagination exist, is of all things most sacredly private, to blow a trumpet before it, and to record the moment when it has arrived at its climax.

In fact, when Mary became pregnant, a somewhat shame-faced concession to convention was made, and the couple married. Mary Godwin, the future wife of Shelley, was born in August 1797, and within a few days the mother died.

Amelia Opie (1769–1853) was on such terms with Godwin that he proposed to her (as Amelia Alderson) only a few weeks before becoming Mary's lover. And it was Mary's experience that inspired Mrs Opie to the composition of her novel *Adeline Mowbray* (1804). Adeline's mother, Mrs Mowbray, is left a wealthy widow when Adeline is ten. Mrs Mowbray is a foolish, impractical woman who loves to stuff her head with all the latest theories, philosophical, political, and educational, chiefly as an equipment for drawing attention to her distinctiveness. She is an armchair theoretician, and Adeline imbibes from her a good deal of nonsense which might have rendered her an idle blue-stocking, were it not that her maternal grandmother, Mrs Woodville, instructs her, behind her mother's back, in all the useful accomplishments of housewifery. Thus Adeline manifests a queer mixture of theoretical idealism and practical good sense. She is very beautiful. Mother and daughter come into contact with a notorious contemporary thinker, Frederic Glenmurray, who has 'attacked the institution of marriage', praising by contrast 'the superior purity, as well as happiness, of an union cemented by no ties but those of love and honour'. Glenmurray, of course, represents Godwin. He and Adeline fall in love, and Adeline feels it the highest honour to put into practice the noble ideals of her beloved mentor. Mrs Mowbray is horrified and cuts off her daughter from any future connection.

Adeline is a noble-minded woman capable of great self-sacrifice, generous, and overflowing with sympathy and help for the poor and the sick. She and Glenmurray share a tender mutual devotion, but external contacts repeatedly bring home to Adeline that, in the eyes of respectable society, she is a fallen woman unfit for converse. The couple go abroad. Amiable and intelligent new acquaintances drop them in horror when the truth reaches them. Back home, Adeline experiences the humiliation of discovering that she is assumed by men to be sexually available. You cannot be a kept mistress and assume the status of a wife. Two contrasting modes of address and treatment separate the roles. When Adeline becomes pregnant she is horrified to stumble upon a scene where an illegitimate child is mocked and shunned by other boys. And when her own servant-maid seems to regard her philosophy as a ticket to illicit liaisons, she is overcome with guilt.

There is much that is technically crude in the book, but Mrs Opie handles the psychological effects of Adeline's disillusionment with skill and subtlety. Time after time Glenmurray eagerly offers to marry her, but Adeline believes wrongly that this would involve for him a sacrifice of principle made purely out of sympathy for her. She is too unselfish to accept any such sacrifice. Thus both partners make themselves miserable through being locked in a refined unselfishness which is mutually damaging. Yet Mrs Opie never presses the absurdity of this situation so as to destroy the reader's sympathy for Adeline.

In the upshot, of course, Adeline learns her lesson. She concludes that marriage is the only bulwark against unbridled licentiousness.

> . . . Marriage is a wise and ought to be a sacred institution; and I bitterly regret the hour when, with the hasty and immature judgment of eighteen, and with a degree of presumption scarcely pardonable at any time of life, I dared to think and act contrary to this opinion and the reverend experience of ages, and became in the eyes of the world an example of vice, when I believed myself the champion of virtue.

Thomas Love Peacock

The novel of interlinked conversations was the medium used by Thomas Love Peacock (1785–1866). Having settled his characters after a good dinner or on a country walk, he would present their talk in the form of dramatic dialogue. His literary affinities were with the eighteenth-century satirists. Indeed he would have no place in a book about the Romantics were it not for two facts. He was a life-long friend of Shelley, and he satirised the Romantics engagingly. In his relationship with Shelley he displayed both a warm affection for him as a fascinatingly fervent personality and, at the same time, a keen relish of the absurdities and impracticalities of Shelley's idiosyncrasies and enthusiasms.

Peacock's sense of the absurd was exercised at the expense of fashionable notions abroad in the current political, literary, and cultural scenes. In *Headlong Hall* (1816), Harry Headlong, a dilettante, invites a group of guests from the literary and philosophical worlds to his home in North Wales. There they walk, eat, and talk. Mr Foster is an optimistic believer in progress, Mr Escot a pessimist convinced that the world is going to the dogs, and Mr Jenkinson is convinced that human nature neither improves nor deteriorates. Dr Gaster, a gourmet cleric, and Mr Milestone, a picturesque landscape gardener, complete the circle. Inevitably their conversation reflects topical debates. A slapstick element intrudes when Mr Milestone blows up a section of the estate in an attempt to render it more picturesque.

This pattern was adopted with modifications and with increasing attention to plot in *Melincourt* (1817) and succeeding novels, but it was in *Nightmare Abbey* (1818) that Peacock turned his ridicule specifically on the Romantic poets and on Shelley in particular. Christopher Glowry Esquire lives at Nightmare Abbey, a picturesque, semi-dilapidated mansion in Lincolnshire. His son and heir, Scythrop, inhabits the south-east tower, and at the beginning of the book he is deeply distressed by the marriage of his beloved to the Hon. Mr Lackwit. But he is soon the 'easy conquest' of Miss Marionetta Celestina O'Carroll, a skilled and provoking coquette who becomes distant whenever she elicits the warmth she carefully stokes up. Scythrop is Shelley. Marionetta keeps him feverishly entangled. But he is joined in his tower by a mysterious young lady calling herself 'Stella', a fan of Scythrop's treatise 'Philosophical Gas; or a Project for a General Illumination of the Human Mind'. She is 'seeking refuge from an atrocious persecution' and has at last recognised a kindred mind in the author of the pamphlet. (Did she but know it, the persecution she flees — as the reader soon guesses — is her father's determination to marry her to Scythrop.) Stella's conversation reveals 'a highly cultivated and energetic mind, full of impassioned schemes of liberty, and impatience of masculine usurpation'.

Alas, Scythrop discovers that his soul has a larger capacity for love than Marionetta alone can fill. He has to face the fact that he is in love, at the same time, with 'two damsels of minds and habits as remote as the antipodes'. Marionetta knows nothing of the world: her life is 'all music and sunshine', while Stella can share 'all his romantic and philosophical visions'. Peacock was in fact intimately acquainted with Shelley's temporarily simultaneous passions for Harriet and for Mary, and had sympathy for the former, but seriousness is not allowed to intrude into the novel. Scythrop loses both women, 'Stella' (Celinda is her proper name) to Mr Flosky. Flosky is a comic portrait of Coleridge, a man who forever loses himself in metaphysical disquisition, but stops conclusively when he finds himself 'unintentionally trespassing within the limits of common sense'. He is at work on a book about the distinction between fancy and imagination, and has already written 'seven hundred pages of promise to elucidate it'. Lord Byron pays a visit in the person of Mr Cypress. He is to go abroad, having quarrelled with his wife and consequently adopted poses which Peacock culls from *Childe Harold*:

> We wither from our youth; we gasp with unslaked thirst for unattainable good; lured from the first to the last by phantoms — love, fame, ambition, avarice — all idle, and all ill — one meteor of many names, that vanishes in the smoke of death!

Part 4

Romantic prose

William Hazlitt

William Hazlitt (1778–1830) gives the reader the feeling conveyed by the greatest of his contemporaries — Wordsworth, Scott, Byron, and Keats — that the Romantic movement would have been incomplete without him. What the poets did for English poetry Hazlitt, and to a lesser extent De Quincey, did for English prose, revitalising its cadences and replenishing its figurative resources. Hazlitt was a dynamic force for verbal renewal. He was a wild enthusiast for the French Revolution and greeted it as Wordsworth first greeted it:

> Youth then was doubly Youth. It was the dawn of a new era; a new impulse had been given to men's minds, and the sun of Liberty rose upon the sun of life . . .

But this enthusiasm was to last a life-time, and in Hazlitt's eyes those like Wordsworth and Coleridge who changed their attitude with the changing times were guilty of betrayal. In this respect, as in others, Hazlitt was at loggerheads with current opinion. He could be an uncomfortable presence socially. Coleridge spoke of him as 'brow-hanging, shoe-contemplative, strange . . . jealous, gloomy and of an irritable pride'. We catch the picture from those who knew him of a man at once superficially shy, sullen, graceless, introspective, and yet blazing with inner passion, zest, and even joy.

Hazlitt has a quadruple significance for us as a 'Romantic' prose writer. In the first place he voices radical political and social idealism and does so with the thoroughness and persistence of a writer for whom such enthusiasms are a basic and unalterable part of his philosophy. In the second place he is at one with the Romantic poets in his reverence for earlier English literature and in particular for Shakespeare. In his *Characters of Shakespeare's Plays* (1817) he plunges into the heart of the emotional and psychological complexities, bringing flashes of illumination to bear on the human substance of the plays. Much of what he has to say may seem obvious to twentieth-century readers, but we have to bear in mind that it was Romantic critics such as Hazlitt and Coleridge who first opened people's eyes to what are now commonplaces of analytical criticism of Shakespeare's characters, and who first supplied a vocabulary appropriate to this kind of commentary.

In the *Lectures on the English Poets* (1818) Hazlitt deals with major writers from Chaucer onwards. He shares with Keats the revived appreciation of Edmund Spenser, showing a keen sensitivity to Spenser's imaginative appeal.

> But he has been unjustly charged with a want of passion and strength. He has both in an immense degree. He has not indeed the pathos of immediate action or suffering, which is more properly the dramatic; but he has all the pathos of sentiment and romance — all that belongs to distant objects of terror, and uncertain, imaginary distress.

In his final lecture Hazlitt turns to living poets. And this brings us to the third crucial significance of Hazlitt's work as a Romantic. For here and in his critical work *The Spirit of the Age, or Contemporary Portraits* (1825) he examines contemporary writers with rare acumen. Of Scott, as a poet, he writes:

> He never wearies or disappoints you. He is communicative and garrulous; but he is not his own hero . . . [This, in Hazlitt's eyes, differentiates him from Wordsworth.] He is very inferior to Lord Byron in intense passion, to Moore in delightful fancy, to Mr Wordsworth in profound sentiment; but he has more picturesque power than any of them.

Hazlitt is the most quotable of critics; for he excels in shedding shafts of sudden illumination in vivid image or telling aphorism.

> Mr Coleridge talks of himself, without being an egotist, for in him the individual is always merged in the abstract and general.

He does justice to 'The Ancient Mariner' as 'unquestionably a work of genius' and to the 'brilliancy and richness' of Coleridge's talk, but criticises his prose for its dullness, 'prolixity and obscurity', and laments the wasteful dissipation of Coleridge's talent through the undisciplined character of his speculations.

It is characteristic of Hazlitt that he pays a heartfelt tribute to Scott the novelist for the sheer range and variety of his imaginative world. 'His works (taken together) are almost like a new edition of human nature.' He then turns on Scott with a virulent denunciation of his political attitudes, and the rhetoric froths and foams with calumniating vituperation. A page or two later, the literary aspect reasserts itself as Scott is compared to Byron.

> We like a writer (whether poet or prose-writer) who takes in (or is

willing to take in) the range of half the universe in feeling, character, description, much better than we do one who obstinately and invariably shuts himself up in the Bastille of his own ruling passions. In short, we had rather be Sir Walter Scott (meaning thereby the Author of Waverley) than Lord Byron a hundred times over.

Hazlitt commends Byron's 'intensity', the way his verse 'glows like a flame', the way he 'grapples with his subject, and moves, penetrates, and animates it by the electric force of his own feelings'. But 'self-will, passion, the love of singularity, disdain of himself and others (with a conscious sense that this is among the ways and means of procuring admiration) are the proper categories of his mind . . .'. It is Byron's serious poetry that Hazlitt can commend. He thinks little of Byron's satirical work. Indeed *Don Juan* represents for him, as it did for Southey, a prostitution of the poet's talents.

For Hazlitt Wordsworth is 'the most original poet now living'. His 'genius is a pure emanation of the Spirit of the Age'.

No one has shown the same imagination in raising trifles into importance: no one has displayed the same pathos in treating of the simplest feelings of the heart . . . Remote from the passions and events of the great world, he has communicated interest and dignity to the primal movements of the heart of man . . .

It will be evident that Hazlitt's gifts as a critic are those of a vigorous, penetrating, combative mind equally capable of magnanimity and of bitter hostility. As a free-wheeling essayist, when politics and prejudice can be laid aside, Hazlitt comes fully into his own, a 'Romantic' in the most fruitful of all his personae. And here lies his fourth significance for us. Throughout his life he contributed essays to current journals, and later gathered them into collections. In his essays there is little on the surface of the literary contrivances adopted by Charles Lamb. Rather, the tone of Hazlitt's essays suggests the spontaneous spilling-out of ideas and anecdotes from a vast reservoir of vital inspiration. In the celebrated essay 'On Going a Journey' (from *Table Talk*, 1821–2) there is a breathless outpouring of sheer delight in solitary walking, 'the clear blue sky over my head, and the green turf beneath my feet, a winding road before me, and a three hours' march to dinner . . .'. In the equally celebrated essay 'The Fight' (*New Monthly Magazine*, February 1822) the bustle and excitement, the tension and the drama of a knock-out prize fight at Hungerford are realised with an immediacy which drags the reader to the ring-side and pummels him with a description of the smashing, smearing, stunning crudities of the tussle. By contrast 'The Letter-Bell' (*Monthly Magazine*, March 1831) weaves a charming sequence of reflections around the daily arrival of the postman, vividly recreating personal hopes

and delights and disappointments attendant on this simple event, and
endowing the mundane with poetry and drama.

Charles Lamb

In a light and playful essay 'On Great and Little Things' (*Table Talk*,
1821–2) Hazlitt looks back to the night in December 1806 when his
friend Charles Lamb heard his farce *Mr H—* hissed off the stage at
Drury Lane Theatre.

> Mr H—, thou wert damned! Bright shone the morning on the playbills
> that announced thy appearance, and the streets were filled with the
> buzz of persons asking one another if they would go to see Mr H—,
> and answering that they would certainly: but before night the gaiety,
> not of the author, but of his friends and the town was eclipsed, for
> thou wert damned!

The playfulness of tone adopted for this post-mortem on Lamb's failure
as a dramatist seems appropriate. It was observed that Lamb himself
joined in the audience's hissing at the crucial climax when Mr H—'s
embarrassing name turns out to be Hogsflesh. Lamb's many friends
acknowledged his gaiety and his sterling moral worth.

> And Lamb, the frolic and the gentle,
> Has vanished from his lonely hearth.

So Wordsworth wrote when lamenting the loss of his friends in his poem
on the death of James Hogg.

Lamb spent most of his life in the Accountants Office of the East India
Company. That it was in external respects an uneventful life was partly
the result of what he called 'a day of horrors' in September 1796 when
he returned from the office to find his sister Mary holding a carving knife
in her hand, with which she had just killed her mother. Charles nobly
took over the care of his sister, whose life was punctuated by periods of
madness, and the two were alone together after their father's death in
1799. Lamb's hopes of marriage were spoilt. When he proposed to the
actress Fanny Kelly in 1819 she could not face the domestic situation.
Lamb was much visited by contemporary writers, however, and his
conversation delighted them.

Like Hazlitt, he played his part in the renewal of interest in past
literature. The *Tales from Shakespeare* (1807), designed for young readers,
was largely the work of his sister Mary, and was for long in popular use.
His *Specimens of English Dramatic Poets* (1808) drew attention to long-
neglected Elizabethan and Jacobean dramatists whose names are now
widely known. His essay 'On the Tragedies of Shakespeare' argues that
it is the poetry and the characters that give Shakespeare his appeal and

that his plays can be fully relished in the study. Their performance scarcely matters.

Lamb produced a handful of poems which have found their way into anthologies. The lament 'The Old Familiar Faces' has a prosaic directness of phrase and rhythm which gives it a plaintive pathos. Side by side with the jaunty couplets of 'A Farewell to Tobacco' it seems to encapsulate the extremes of Lamb's persona which Wordsworth pinpointed in the contrast between 'the frolic and the gentle' and 'the lonely hearth'. But it is as an essayist that Lamb excels. He began to write regularly for the *London Magazine* in 1820, using the pseudonym 'Elia' (the name of a fellow-clerk in his first post). The collections, *Elia* (1823) and *The Last Essays of Elia* (1823), gathered material from the *London Magazine* and elsewhere.

Where Hazlitt as an essayist is all gusto and spontaneity, Lamb is all poise and contrivance. Lamb relished Elizabethan literature and the prose of such fanciful seventeenth-century stylists as Sir Thomas Brown, and he happily incorporated archaic turns of phrase into his highly posturing prose. The artifices are amusing because they smack of self-parody and can be loaded with irony. But comedy often consorts with melancholy. The external lightness of tone can seem like a veil covering a pathos too deep to be allowed to surface. The submergence of emotion under rhetorical extravagance, the distancing of reality by the adoption of pose and gesture, both serve to intensify the intimacies they seemingly protect, and, ironically, the reader may feel strangely closer to Lamb for the great verbal charade in which he performs. If Hazlitt drags you to his side by tugging at your arm, Lamb lures you into companionability by the winning gracefulness of his courtesies.

> I like to meet a sweep — understand me — not a grown sweeper — old chimney-sweepers are by no means attractive — but one of those tender novices, blooming through their first nigritude, the maternal washings not quite effaced from the cheek — such as come forth with the dawn ... I reverence these young Africans of our own growth — these almost clergy imps, who sport their cloth without assumption; and from their little pulpits (the tops of chimneys), in the nipping air of a December morning, preach a lesson of patience to mankind.
>
> *(Elia)*

It would be absurd to pretend that the verbal devices here militate against genuineness. Rather they somehow charge the utterance with a controlled undercurrent of tenderness.

There is a converse pose in which the essayist calls out the reader's sympathy for himself as innocent victim. In 'A Bachelor's Complaint of the Behaviour of Married People' he explains that it is not the quarrels of married couples that offend him, but the aggressive way in which they parade their amorousness and mutual content. If a man were to accost a plain woman of his acquaintance and tell her bluntly she was not good enough to be his wife, it would be considered grossly ill-mannered —

> Just as little right have a married couple to tell me by speeches, and looks that are scarce less plain than speeches, that I am not the happy man, — the lady's choice. It is enough that I know I am not: I do not want this perpetual reminding!

Ironic self-justification, self-deprecation, and self-mockery are all modes of opening up a wounded heart to the reader. The rich range and versatility of Lamb may be sampled in such celebrated essays as 'Recollections of the South Sea House', 'Old China', 'A Dissertation upon Roast Pig', 'Mrs Battle's Opinions on Whist' and, perhaps most entrancing of all, 'The Superannuated Man'.

Thomas De Quincey

In an article in the *North British Review* in November 1848 Thomas De Quincey (1785–1859) denied the claim that Hazlitt was a 'great thinker'. 'Hazlitt had read nothing,' he argues. He was 'not eloquent because he was discontinuous'.

> Hazlitt's brilliancy is seen chiefly in separate splinterings of phrase or image which throw upon the eye a vitreous scintillation for a moment, but spread no deep suffusions of colour, and distribute no masses of mighty shadow. A flash, a solitary flash, and all is gone.

De Quincey goes on to criticise Lamb's 'extravagant admiration of Hazlitt'. Indeed, while conceding Lamb's 'exquisite genius', he finds 'his own constitution of intellect' guilty of the same 'habit of discontinuity'. With Lamb De Quincey judged it to be a matter of personal temperament. The 'excess of his social kindness' was such that he always kept open house, and in consequence 'all his life . . . he must have read in the spirit of one liable to sudden interruption'.

De Quincey himself was a great reader and a writer whose prose style was consciously designed to combine a highly patterned architectural structure with a symphonic, indeed often contrapuntal, interplay of configuration and reverberation. He theorised with rare sensitivity both on techniques of style and on the imaginative and emotional resources they can liberate. In a memorable article in the *London Magazine* for March 1823 ('Letters to a Young Man whose Education Has Been Neglected') he attacks the simplistic division of books into those that *instruct* and those that *amuse*.

> The true antithesis to knowledge, in this case, is not *pleasure*, but

power. All that is literature seeks to communicate power; all that is not literature, to communicate knowledge.

Shakespeare and Milton are cited to illustrate what is meant by communicating power. It is what happens when the reader —

is made to feel vividly, and with a vital consciousness, emotions which ordinary life rarely or never supplies occasions for exciting, and which had previously lain unawakened, and hardly within the dawn of consciousness — as myriads of modes of feeling are at this moment in every human mind for want of a poet to organise them.

De Quincey was an eager devotee of Wordsworth from his boyhood. He went to live at Grasmere in 1809 and took over Dove Cottage in succession to Wordsworth. That coolness developed between the two men was in some respects discreditable to De Quincey and in other respects discreditable to Wordsworth. De Quincey's increasing addiction to opium and its effect on his manner of life were all too reminiscent of Coleridge's degeneracy. Moreover, De Quincey's marriage to a local farmer's daughter, Margaret Simpson (after making her pregnant), was regarded by Wordsworth as a social descent unbefitting a gentleman. Perhaps the chequered character of the relationship between the two writers ought to be borne in mind when the reader turns to the substantial articles about the Lake Poets which De Quincey wrote in journals over many years and which were eventually published collectively this century as *Recollections of the Lake Poets* (1948). It is a captivating volume, a blend of imaginative literary comment, perceptive analysis of character, and vividly recaptured pictures of the poets in their home settings. Certainly De Quincey, for all his Wordsworthian enthusiasms, is no idolater. How far his differences with the poet affected the reliability of his record is questionable. But there are fascinating anecdotal tit-bits which bring the great one down to earth.

For instance, De Quincey paints a somewhat unflattering picture of Wordsworth's physique: 'His legs were pointedly condemned by all female connoisseurs in legs.' They were serviceable enough. De Quincey calculates that they must have 'traversed a distance of 175,000 to 180,000 English miles', but —

the Wordsworthian legs were certainly not ornamental; and it was really a pity, as I agreed with a lot of ladies in thinking, that he had not another pair for evening dress parties.

De Quincey goes on to describe a walk in which he and Dorothy followed behind Wordsworth and a toweringly tall and well-built clergyman:

At intervals Miss Wordsworth would exclaim, in a tone of vexation, 'Is it possible, — can that be William? How very mean he looks!'

De Quincey affects a level-headed candour. His analysis of Dorothy Wordsworth's character in its strengths and its deficiencies is a subtle and penetrating one. His picture of Mary Wordsworth dwells directly and frankly on her 'obliquity of vision' and her plainness, but only to wonder how she could nevertheless 'exercise the practical fascination of beauty, through the mere compensatory charms of sweetness all but angelic'.

The witty satirical streak in De Quincey perhaps achieved its fullest expression in a brilliant *tour de force* originally written for *Blackwood's Magazine*, 'On Murder Considered as One of the Fine Arts'. A masterpiece of irony, it is presented in the form of a lecture delivered before The Society of Connoisseurs in Murder. The lecturer notes that his task might have been easy enough centuries ago 'when the art was little understood, and few great models had been exhibited', but now that 'masterpieces of excellence have been executed by professional men' the public will look for a corresponding improvement in critical theory on the subject.

> Practice and theory must advance *pari passu*. People begin to see that something more goes to the composition of a fine murder than two blockheads to kill and be killed — a knife — a purse — and a dark lane. Design, gentlemen, grouping, light and shade, poetry, sentiment, are now deemed indispensable to attempts of this nature.

Most readers make their acquaintance with De Quincey through his celebrated work *Confessions of an English Opium Eater*. This work first appeared in the *London Magazine* in 1821, was published in book form in 1822, and was revised and expanded by De Quincey in 1856, three years before his death. In it we can read his story from his own mouth. He was the son of a well-to-do Manchester businessman who died when Thomas was seven, leaving small inheritances to his wife and children. The widowed Mrs De Quincey moved first to Bath, then to Chester. Thomas was sent to Manchester Grammar School in 1801, from where he was expected to get an exhibition to Oxford. He found the school intolerable, though the main reason he gives for this — that he could not indulge his passion for long country walks — is rather unconvincing. However, he ran away, then persuaded his mother to let him go walking in Wales. A bare minimum of money was allowed him, and this time he ran away to London and tried to borrow money on his expectations while living in the utmost poverty on the streets. De Quincey, looking back, finds his failure at this time either to earn money or to appeal to his family as inexplicable as the reader finds it today. He found solace in a sixteen-year-old street-walker, Ann, whose surname he never learned and whom therefore he lost sight of when he renewed contact with his family. He went up to Oxford in 1803 for five years of study; he searched vainly for Ann in his vacations, and she haunted his imagination for long years afterwards.

It was in 1804 that excruciating toothache and neuralgia drove him first to take opium, and he became for eight years an intermittent user of the drug, often taking it deliberately twice a week. He writes lyrically about its beneficent effects, insisting that whereas wine 'disorders the mental faculties, opium . . . introduces amongst them the most exquisite order, legislation, and harmony'. It substitutes composure for agitation, concentration for distraction, puts the moral affections 'in a state of cloudless serenity; and high over all the great light of the majestic intellect'. But in 1813, at Grasmere, he became more gravely addicted, taking a massive daily dose. He pictures himself in his cottage among the mountains of a winter evening, with his 5000 books around him, a blazing fire, a tea-table with two cups and saucers, and a decanter holding a quart of ruby-coloured laudanum. It is a picture of happiness to which he had to bid a long farewell, and the section headed 'The Pleasures of Opium' is succeeded by 'The Pains of Opium'. The record of suffering is truly harrowing. The horrific dreams, the total torpor, the unutterable gloom, and the constant consciousness of failure make the succeeding three years a continuous torment. The climax of the misery comes when the dreams of vast buildings and landscapes, of lakes and oceans, become horribly peopled.

> The sea appeared paved with innumerable faces, upturned to the heavens; faces, imploring, wrathful, despairing; faces that surged upwards by thousands, by myriads, by generations; infinite was my agitation; my mind tossed, as it seemed, upon the billowing ocean, and weltered upon the weltering waves.

De Quincey was strong-willed enough to achieve a vast reduction of dosage and indeed periods of total abstinence from the drug. He moved to Edinburgh in 1828 and worked thereafter for *Blackwood's Magazine*, *Tait's Magazine*, and other journals.

Leigh Hunt

Making a living by writing for journals appears not to have been too precarious a matter at this time. The age of the Romantics coincided with an age in which periodical magazines of a high quality were open to aspiring essayists. Hazlitt, Lamb, and De Quincey were able to succeed as such only because there was a ready outlet for them. The history of the various periodicals, some long-lasting, others short-lived, is a study in itself. A key figure whose name recurs repeatedly in this field was Leigh Hunt (1784–1859). An indefatigable journalist and editor, he launched *The Examiner* in 1808 with his brother John. This proved to be a highly successful magazine, and Hunt edited it for thirteen years. It supported current progressive causes such as the abolition of slavery, Catholic emancipation, and legal reform. Its radicalism on such subjects as flogging in the army from time to time threatened to get the Hunt brothers into hot water, and when they published an attack on the Prince Regent in March 1813 they were both fined heavily and imprisoned for two years. The attack was a sharp one.

> The delightful, blissful, wise, pleasurable, honourable, virtuous, true and immortal Prince was a violator of his word, a libertine over head and ears in debt and disgrace, a despiser of domestic ties, the companion of gamblers and demireps, a man who has just closed half a century without one single claim on the gratitude of his country or the respect of posterity.

Leigh Hunt thus achieved the status of a martyr for freedom in the eyes of idealists such as Shelley. Yet political passion did not distort Hunt's thinking to the extent that it distorted Hazlitt's. His literary significance lies in the opportunities he gave to worthy contemporaries. He displayed considerable perception in his advocacy of poets such as Shelley and Keats.

It was in *The Examiner* in November 1817, January and March 1818 that Hunt published extracts from Shelley's *The Revolt of Islam*, elucidated the poem, and praised it with comparisons to the work of Dante and Lucretius. Keats's poetry too was pressed upon the public. Indeed the hostility to Keats manifested by the *Quarterly Review*, a Tory journal, was fuelled by Keats's association with Hunt. In 1818, after the publication of Keats's *Endymion*, the *Quarterly Review* damned the young poet as 'a disciple of the new school of what has been somewhere called Cockney poetry' of which 'Mr Leigh Hunt . . . aspires to be the hierophant'. Keats is dismissed as Hunt's 'simple neophyte'. Other, short-lived journals which Hunt edited were *The Reflector* (1810–11) and *The Indicator* (1819–21).

Such was the respect of Shelley and Byron for Hunt's work in the periodical field that they planned a new magazine, *The Liberal*, and invited Hunt over to Italy to forward the project. In fact *The Liberal* (1822–3) lasted through only four issues, of which the first contained Byron's *Vision of Judgment*. Shelley had pressed Hunt eagerly to join them in Italy and had obtained a loan from Byron to make the journey possible. The venture seems to have been doomed from the start. Shelley was drowned soon after the Hunts arrived in Italy in July 1822. Byron agreed to house the Hunts on the ground floor of his villa, but he soon found Hunt boring and his numerous children a terrible trial. 'They are dirtier and more mischievous than Yahoos,' he wrote to Mary Shelley on 6 October 1822. 'What they can't destroy with their filth they will with their fingers.'

Hunt came back to England in 1825 to continue his copious journalistic and editorial work.

As a creative writer, Hunt has claims both in poetry and in fiction (one novel). He dedicated to Byron *The Story of Rimini* (1816), a poem based on the Paolo and Francesca story in Dante. Byron commented on the matter in a letter to Tom Moore in 1818.

When I saw *Rimini* in MS, I told him that I deemed it good poetry at bottom, disfigured only by a strange style. His answer was, that his style was a system, or *upon system*, or some such cant; and, when a man talks of system, his case is hopeless . . .

If Hunt the poet is remembered today, it is not for his substantial works such as this and *Hero and Leander, and Bacchus and Ariadne* (1819), but for a couple of curiously brilliant throwaways, the verses 'Jenny kissed me' and 'Abou ben Adhem', which once every schoolchild in the country knew by heart.

We say 'curiously brilliant' because brilliance is not among Hunt's qualities either in verse or prose. Adjectives like 'competent', 'pale', and 'pedestrian' tend to spring to the lips of critics when categorising his work. But many of his occasional essays keep their interest in a quietly unexciting way, perhaps especially when he comments on the contemporary public scene in writing about such subjects as the theatre, or 'Seamen on Shore' ('He would buy all the painted parrots on an Italian's head on purpose to break them, rather than not spend his money'), or the fascination of London shops ('A poulterer's is a dead-bodied business, with its birds and their lax necks. We dislike to see a bird any where but in the open air, alive, and quick'), or the attraction of 'Coaches' ('The prettiest of these vehicles is undoubtedly the curricle, which is also the safest. There is something worth looking at in the pair of horses, with that sparkling pole of steel laid across them. It is like a bar of music, comprising their harmonious course').

Thus, in a mood of quietly reflective good humour, he turns an observant eye on the human scene under such headings as 'On Getting up on Cold Mornings', 'On the Graces and Anxieties of Pig-Driving', or 'English and French Fashions'. He never galvanises by his energy as Hazlitt does, nor delights by his easy virtuosity as Lamb does, nor dazzles by his flamboyance as De Quincey does. Hunt's is a workaday style and it serves his modest purposes effectively.

Walter Savage Landor

Leigh Hunt lived on well into the Victorian age, publishing an *Autobiography* in 1850 which many critics have regarded as his miscellaneous journalism at its best. He survived to achieve the dubious honour of being portrayed by Dickens in *Bleak House* (1852–3) as Harold Skimpole, a dreamy self-deceiver. In the same novel Dickens portrayed Walter Savage Landor (1775–1864) as the likeable, good-natured, but irascible Boythorn. Landor, whose poetry we touched upon earlier in this book (and whose drama we shall take note of later), manages to defy neat categorisation. A combative eccentric, he won admiration for his moral strength and for a devotion to conscious artistry which has generally failed to win him a wide readership. The artistry is indeed so conscious, the control of emotion so disciplined, that he fits uncomfortably among the 'Romantics'. On the one hand he was, in De Quincey's words, 'built by nature to animate a leader in storms, a martyr, a national reformer, an arch-rebel', and on the other hand he was a man of means inclined by birth to an austere cultural élitism.

As a prose writer he has been chiefly celebrated for the series of *Imaginary Conversations* published in 1824–9, in 1848, and in 1853. These deal with a wide variety of historic personages. In 'Henry V and Ann Boleyn' the king visits Ann just after she has been condemned to death, and she boldly resists his attempts to incriminate her for infidelities. In 'Essex and Spenser' the two men meet just after Spenser has escaped from Ireland, having had his house destroyed and his infant child burnt alive. In 'Oliver Cromwell and Walter Noble' Noble comes to remonstrate with Cromwell over the execution of Charles I. In 'Leofric and Godiva' husband and wife ride into Coventry and Godiva pleads for mercy on its rebellious citizens.

> Yea, Godiva, by the holy rood, will I pardon the city, when thou ridest naked at noon-tide through the streets.

More erudition is brought into play in such dialogues as 'Epictetus and Seneca', 'Boccaccio and Petrarc', 'Lord Bacon and Richard Hooker', and 'Diogenes and Plato'.

The twentieth-century reader, however, is bound to wince at the archaic artifices of style. Consider the opening of 'Queen Elizabeth and Cecil':

> ELIZABETH: I advise thee again, churlish Cecil, how that our Edmund Spenser, whom thou call'st uncourteously a whining whelp, hath good and solid reason for his complaint. God's blood! shall the lady that tieth my garter and shuffles my smock over my head, or the lord that steadieth my chair's back while I eat, or the other that looketh to my buck hounds lest they be mangy, be holden by me in higher esteem and estate than he who hath placed me among the bravest of past times, as well as safely and surely set me down among the loveliest of the future?
>
> CECIL: Your Highness must remember he carouseth fully for such deserts . . .

The stilted syntax, the 'ye olde' vocabulary, and the attendant verbosity devitalise the speakers and hinder any close engagement with their concerns. It is not difficult to understand the current neglect of Landor.

Thomas Love Peacock

We have considered Peacock's fictional satire of Romanticism. He also wrote an essay, 'The Four Ages of Poetry' (published in *Olliers's Literary Miscellany*, No. 1, in 1820), which is a half-serious and comically exaggerated onslaught on the Romantic poets. The clarity and concreteness of Peacock's attack gives the reader a vivid experience of the literary controversy of the period. The four ages are the ages of Iron, Gold, Silver, and Brass, representing respectively primitive bards, cultivated traditional national poetry, more sophisticated and fastidious artistry, and reversion to barbarism. In terms of English literature the four ages are represented by medieval romance, Shakespeare, Dryden and Pope, and the Romantics.

The Romantics reject authority. They say to themselves:

> Society is artificial, therefore we will live out of society. The mountains are natural, therefore we shall live in the mountains. There we shall be shining models of purity and virtue, passing the whole day in the innocent virtue of going up and down hill, receiving poetical impressions, and communicating them in immortal verse to admiring generations.

Peacock lays about him with such swingeing good humour that none could take offence, yet perceptive analysis of Romantic ways of thinking underlies his comic satire. Other thinkers may be advancing the progress of knowledge, he claims, but the poet is wallowing in the rubbish of the past.

> Mr Scott digs up poachers and cattle-stealers of the ancient border. Lord Byron cruizes for thieves and pirates on the shores of the Morea and among the Greek Islands. Mr Southey wades through ponderous volumes of travels and old chronicles, from which he carefully selects all that is false, useless, and absurd, as being essentially practical; and when he has a commonplace book full of monstrosities, strings them into an epic. Mr Wordsworth picks up village legends from old women and sextons, and Mr Coleridge, to the valuable information acquired from similar sources, superadds the dreams of crazy theologians and the mysticisms of German metaphysics.

So Peacock continues, arguing that 'a poet in our times is a semi-barbarian in a civilised community'.

The highest inspirations of poetry are resolvable into three ingredients; the rant of unregulated passion, the whining of exaggerated feeling, and the cant of factitious sentiment . . .

Such ingredients can nourish 'a morbid dreamer like Wordsworth', but can never make a philosopher or statesman or anyone of any practical and rational use in life.

Shelley was provoked by Peacock's assault to write *A Defence of Poetry*, which was published only posthumously in 1840. In it Shelley gives poetry a moral as well as an aesthetic significance. 'The great instrument of moral good is the imagination . . . Poetry enlarges the circumference of the imagination by replenishing it . . .' Man has conquered nature by his science only to remain himself a slave to social inequalities. Hence the need for the creative faculty which can translate knowledge into generous action. Poetry stands in relation to the selfish pursuit of money as God stands in relation to Mammon. It is an essential means of protecting human nature from the depredations of calculating selfishness. Shelley's inspiration carries him to the heights in his claims for his vocation.

Poetry is indeed something divine. It is at once the centre and circumference of knowledge; it is that which comprehends all science, and that to which all science must be referred . . . Poetry thus makes immortal all that is best and most beautiful in the world . . . Poetry redeems from decay the visitations of the divinity in man . . . Poets are the hierophants of an unapprehended inspiration . . . Poets are the unacknowledged legislators of the world.

In this lofty conception of poetry and poethood Shelley comes close to Wordsworth, whose inspiration took fire on the same topic in the Preface to the *Lyrical Ballads* (1800):

Poetry is the most philosophic of all writing . . . its object is truth . . . Poetry is the image of man and nature . . . Poetry is the breath and finer spirit of all knowledge; it is the impassioned expression which is the countenance of all Science . . . Poetry is the first and last of all knowledge — it is as immortal as the heart of man.

Nowhere can we sense more acutely the profounder aspects of literary Romanticism then when we contrast the high-spirited polemics of Peacock with the poetic credos of Shelley and Wordsworth.

Reviewers (Jeffrey, Gifford, Lockhart)

We have already caught sight of the flourishing world of periodical journalism in which Leigh Hunt's career was deeply involved. The student of the Romantic period will continually be confronted by reference to the various reviews in which the public dialogue about contemporary writers was kept alive and frequently flared up into bitter controversy. A good deal of the most vital reviewing came from Edinburgh. Francis Jeffrey (1773–1850), who rose to be Lord Jeffrey, a Judge of the Court of Session and a Member of Parliament, helped to found the *Edinburgh Review* in 1802 and remained its editor until 1829. Byron gave him pride of place in his assault upon critics in *English Bards and Scotch Reviewers*, recalling an episode in 1806 when Tom Moore was so offended by scornful treatment in the *Edinburgh Review* that he challenged Jeffrey to a duel. Fortunately the police emerged from hiding to arrest the would-be duellists.

Jeffrey's critical style was often provocatively patronising. 'This will never do,' he began his review of Wordsworth's *The Excursion*. Though he wrote appreciatively of Scott and gave a warm welcome to Keats's *Poems* (1820), he proved constitutionally incapable of doing justice to Wordsworth and 'the Lake School', as he called them in 1817. His imaginative limitations led him to call Wordsworth's 'Ode on the Intimations of Immortality' 'the most illegible and unintelligible part of the publication' when he attacked Wordsworth's *Poems in Two Volumes* in 1807. Over twenty years later, looking back in 1829, he saw the Romantic movement as spent.

> Since the beginning of our critical career we have seen a vast deal of beautiful poetry pass into oblivion . . . The tuneful quartos of Southey are already little better than rubble: and the rich melodies of Keats and Shelley, and the fantastical emphasis of Wordsworth, and the plebeian pathos of Crabbe, are melting fast from the field of our vision. The novels of Scott have put out his poetry. Even the splendid strains of Moore are fading into distance and dimness except where they have been married to immortal music; and the blazing star of Byron himself is receding from its place of pride . . . The two who have longest withstood this rapid withering of the laurel, and with the least marks of decay on their branches, are Rogers and Campbell . . .

The explanation for this is that 'fine taste and consummate elegance' have ousted the public's long flirtation with 'fiery passion, and disdainful vehemence'.

The *Edinburgh Review* was a Whig journal, and there were two Tory periodicals with which it had to contend. The *Quarterly Review* was founded in 1809 with the specific purpose of rivalling the *Edinburgh Review*. When Scott could not be prevailed upon to accept the editorship of the new journal, it was given to William Gifford (1756–1826). Gifford was called upon with some respect in Byron's *English Bards and Scotch Reviewers*:

Why slumbers Gifford? let us ask again.
Are there no follies for his pen to purge?

But it is a critical platitude that Gifford was not big enough for the post
and abused his power. One of the harshest 'hatchet-jobs' in literary
history was done at his expense by Hazlitt in *The Spirit of the Age*:

He is admirably qualified for this situation [as editor of the *Quarterly*]
... by a happy combination of defects, natural and acquired; and in
the event of his death, it will be difficult to provide him a suitable
successor.

The other Tory rival to the *Edinburgh Review* was *Blackwood's Maga-
zine*. As the *Edinburgh Review* was the nursling of Scott's publisher,
Archibald Constable (1774–1827), and the *Quarterly* of Byron's publisher,
John Murray (1778–1843), so *Blackwood's* was the nursling of William
Blackwood (1776–1834), whose list of authors included Susan Ferrier and
James Hogg. All three publishers were Scots. *Blackwood's Magazine*
began in 1817. It was in *Blackwood's* that attacks on the 'Cockney School
of Poetry' first appeared, in which Keats and Hazlitt, as well as Leigh
Hunt, were pilloried. Wordsworth and Shelley, however, received more
sympathetic treatment. These journals have had a continuing influence
in English literature. Leigh Hunt's *The Examiner* (1808) lasted some
seventy years until 1881. The *Edinburgh Review* survived until 1929, the
Quarterly Review until 1967, and *Blackwood's Magazine* until 1980.
    One of the critics early associated with *Blackwood's* was John Gibson
Lockhart (1794–1854), and he took over the editorship of the *Quarterly*
in 1825. Lockhart produced some entertaining sketches of Scottish life
and character in *Peter's Letters to his Kinsfolk* (1819). The depth of his
conservatism may be gauged from a passage in which he turns to resist
proposed changes in curriculum and regulation at Oxford and Cambridge.
(Lockhart himself had been at the Universities of Glasgow and Oxford.)
He stresses the value of a rich tradition to the student:

He studies in his closet the same books which have, for a thousand
years, formed the foundation of the intellectual character of Englishmen.

He even defends the requirement for membership of the 'National
Church'. Lockhart also wrote some novels, including *Adam Blair* (1822),
a book which has been compared with James Hogg's *Confessions of a
Justified Sinner* for its exploration of grave moral conflict. Blair is a
Scottish minister whose beloved wife has died, and an old friend of his
early days, Charlotte Campbell, now married, comes to see him. Eventually passion for her overcomes Blair, he faces disciplinary action, and is
unfrocked for misconduct. What gives the book its power is the analysis

of the agony and remorse which Blair suffers, and the delirious dreams of his disturbed imagination.

Today we know Lockhart chiefly as a biographer. His *Life of Burns* (1828) was highly praised on its publication, but has since been criticised for its over-delicate treatment of the poet's private life. His *Life of Sir Walter Scott* (1837–8) stands beside Boswell's *Life of Dr Johnson* as one of the fullest and finest biographies in our literature. Lockhart had married Scott's daughter Sophia and naturally had many personal memories of Scott. He displayed astonishing thoroughness in exploring the vast array of letters and papers, reducing them to order. Moreover, he managed, while working through them, to present Scott as a stirringly vivid character gradually emerging to his full stature, and to relate the events of his career as a shapely drama. Lockhart makes Scott both admirable and lovable. If, by modern standards of biographical rectitude, there is carelessness and even inaccuracy here and there, this scarcely detracts from the magnitude of the achievement in making the *Life* as a whole so moving and unforgettable.

William Cobbett

In 1819 in *Peter's Letters to his Kinsfolk* Lockhart was protesting against the vain attempt to improve Oxford and Cambridge, 'those great and venerable institutions', educating men destined in the future 'to discharge the most sacred and most elevated duties of English citizenship'. In his *Rural Rides* (1821) William Cobbett (1762–1835) saw Oxford differently, as a place full of drones and wasps noted for '*folly*, emptiness of head; want of talent' —

> and one half of the fellows who are what they call *educated* here, are unfit to be clerks in a grocer's or mercer's shop.

Cobbett, the son of a Hampshire farmer and innkeeper, and largely self-educated, was a combative, rebellious soul who frequently crossed swords with the powers-that-be. After serving with the army for six years in Canada, he produced evidence from the regimental accounts of dishonesty among senior officers and, fearful of being framed himself, took his bride to America in 1792. He had established himself as a journalist by the time he returned to London in 1800. In 1802 he began to publish his *Political Register*, which lasted until 1835. Cobbett's hostility to the short-lived Peace of Amiens (1802) brought a mob attack on his house; his attack on government policy in Ireland was punished by a fine; but he increasingly assaulted corruptions such as the abuse of pensions and sinecures, electoral bribery, and the need for reform of Parliament. His article on the flogging of mutinous militiamen in the *Political Register* for 1 July 1809 earned him a fine of £1000 and two years' imprisonment in Newgate. By this time Cobbett, who had started as a Tory, was a confirmed radical, and in 1831 he was brought to court again by the government over an article supposedly inciting rural disorder, but the prosecution failed. He became Member of Parliament for Oldham in 1832.

The work which has retained its popular appeal longest is his *Rural Rides*, published between 1821 and 1830. Cobbett set out to investigate the condition of life in the country. The Napoleonic wars had left a legacy of economic distress. Food prices had risen during hostilities, benefiting landlords and farmers, but not the labourers, and had fallen drastically with the coming of peace. Many were ruined. Speculators and newly rich industrialists stepped in to take over country estates. Cobbett was old enough to remember a time when tenant-peasants, yeomen, and landlords all worked within a community in shared use of common land, but in the last decades of the eighteenth century Enclosure Acts deprived cottagers of rights over the commons and facilitated the development of large estates in the hands of landlords who had credit and capital with which to update the exploitation of agricultural land. The gap between rich and poor widened, and as Cobbett toured the country he was outraged at the wretched poverty of rural labourers in many areas. He wrings the heart still when he cites actual cases, as for instance when he calculates that a Hampshire hedger's wages will not keep his family's bread consumption up to the level of the allowance in gaols (*Rural Rides*, 12 November 1825).

Cobbett took comprehensive swipes at what he saw as a conspiracy of government and aristocracy and finance against the common people. Inflated pensions and sinecures distributed by government, pluralist ecclesiastics, the vicious laws against poaching, and above all the 'Funds' — that is the National Debt vastly increased during the war — were among his targets. But he was no Swiftian lacerator of human folly, though his unadorned prose style, direct and lucid, sturdy and workmanlike, is in the Swiftian tradition. Cobbett has a touching sensitivity to the charms of the countryside, an observant eye for its beauties, natural and human. He has a heart of gold. When we hear him paying tribute to his beloved wife in his *Advice to Young Men* (1829), explaining how he said 'That's the girl for me' when at twenty-one he saw her as a girl of thirteen, and telling how they shared domestic labours in the early years of marriage, the reader knows he is in touch with one of the frankest, most unaffected, and indeed lovable men who ever opened their hearts on paper.

Critics have detected a Wordsworthian dimension in Cobbett's feeling for the countryside and its inhabitants. Hazlitt praised him eloquently. Carlyle put him at the side of Scott as epitomising the thoroughly 'healthy' man.

So bounteous was Nature to us; in the sickliest of recorded ages, when British literature lay all puking and sprawling in Werterism, Byronism, and other Sentimentalism . . . Nature was kind enough to send us two healthy Men . . .

Mary Russell Mitford

Cobbett, together with his wife, provoked a similarly warm tribute from a prosier and less exalted pen, that of Mary Russell Mitford (1787–1855); she stayed for a time near his home at Botley when he was at the height of his powers. She praised his 'unfailing good humour and good spirits' and the simplicity, kindness, and devotion of his wife in her *Recollections of a Literary Life* (1852). Miss Mitford had something in common with Cobbett in her love of country life and country people, her delight in the old-fashioned village community of pre-industrial England, and in the sturdy simplicity of her prose. But there is nothing in her to match his passion for greater justice and his indignation against the great and powerful. Yet what she lacks in vehemence and pugnacity Miss Mitford compensates for in shrewdness, humour, and irony. She has a sharp eye for the minutiae of human character and appearance, as well as of the natural environment.

Miss Mitford's father was an irresponsible physician who failed to practise and squandered money on gambling and extravagances. He came to Alresford, Hampshire, from the north, married an heiress, and by the time their daughter was ten he was imprisoned for debt. At this point Mary Russell Mitford began her lifelong career of rescuing her father. She had insisted on number 224 when a ticket for an Irish lottery was purchased. It won £20,000. The windfall went to her father's head, and a new estate was purchased at Gravely in Berkshire; but by 1820 the family were reduced to the level of tenants in an old cottage nearby at Three Mile Cross. Mary's pen was her means of supporting her wayward but beloved father.

Though (as we shall see later) she was ambitious to succeed in romantic historical drama in the style of Joanna Baillie, she fortunately began in 1819 to exercise her gifts on a less grandiose scale too, as occasional essayist in *The Lady's Magazine*, and this is where the first of her sketches of village life appeared. *Our Village* came out in book form in five volumes between 1824 and 1832.

In an early piece, 'The Primrose', Miss Mitford and her greyhound May walk by the comfortable house where she spent 'eighteen happy years'. But, although it nearly broke her heart to leave, now, three years later, she would not for the world be uprooted again even to be 'restored to the old beloved ground'. Miss Mitford gives voice to basic everyday feelings with infallible genuineness. Her portraits of village characters, each in their appropriate environment, shoemaker and blacksmith, shopkeeper and innkeeper, carpenter and gardener, curate and retired officer, are deftly sketched. There is a poise, a restraint, and a fineness of perception that give a winning gracefulness to a prose which, effortless as it seems, was in fact the product of conscious artistic application. Nowhere does the warmth of her personality come through more clearly than when she concedes her special affection for vividly pictured village boys in 'The Hard Summer'. Her imaginative range is considerable. In a piece, 'A Castle in the Air', where expectations of a welcome new occupant of a nearby house are excited only to be dashed, the artistry of the accomplished short-story writer is brought delicately into play. Equally finely shaped and packed with quiet humour is the celebrated piece 'Jack Hatch'.

It is true that Miss Mitford draws a veil over the seamy and squalid aspects of rural life. She has no social axe to grind. But her quiet humour, her shrewd touches of irony — even of irony at her own expense — save her from any possible charge of complacency. She is equally free of sentimentality. 'This sounds like a very tragical story,' she writes in 'Another Glance at Our Village' of the death of the drunken blacksmith. But the wife with 'a complaining, broken-spirited air, a peevish manner, a whining voice, a dismal countenance' is now another woman, a widow who 'talks and laughs and bustles about . . . She is a happier woman than she has been at any time these fifteen years, and she knows it'. The subsequent warning to village husbands about keeping away from the ale-house if they want their wives to be sorry when they die is as near as we get to didacticism. Miss Mitford found her impossible father lovable, and her appreciation of goodness wherever she can find it lights up her sketches.

Part 5

Romantic drama

Verse drama: the great poets (Wordsworth, Coleridge, Shelley, Byron)

It was perhaps natural that a literary movement which returned to the age of Shakespeare with new reverence and enthusiasm should have seen many attempts to revitalise poetic drama. Some of these attempts were mere 'closet drama', that is, poems in dramatic form which were never intended for production on stage. It might seem like splitting hairs to try to draw a clear line of distinction between dramatic pieces which were never intended for the stage and dramatic pieces which ought never to have been intended for the stage, especially since there is a third category, to which some of Byron's poetic dramas belong, namely dramatic pieces which were never intended by the writer for the stage but which the theatrical people insisted on performing. For this reason we shall consider in turn the poetic dramas of the great poets and of some lesser poets, though only a few by the latter made any great noise on the stage.

Wordsworth's *The Borderers*, composed in 1795–6, was certainly not intended for the stage. Wordsworth tells us in his Preface how the spectacles of wickedness of which he was an eye-witness during the French Revolution taught him that as 'sin and crime are apt to start from their very opposite qualities, so are there no limits to the hardening of the heart, and the perversion of the understanding to which they may carry their slaves'. The action of the play takes place during the reign of Henry III. Oswald is a rebellious spirit who was long ago deceived into leaving a sea-captain marooned on an island to starve. Early remorse has been swallowed up in a career of active challenge to the world's hatred by bold intellectual superiority to personal shame or public obloquy. Marmaduke is the idealistic leader of a band of borderers whose hearts are in the right place. Oswald finds in him 'a mirror of my youthful self' and determines to make him his equal now in guilt and in intellectual superiority to its significance. Thus he leads Marmaduke by a tangle of falsification into distrust of his beloved Idonea and vengeance on her supposedly guilty father, Herbert. Oswald has a good deal of Shakespeare's Iago and Edmund in him, and Herbert roams the stormy hills like a second King Lear. But Oswald's fabrications are so elaborate in contrivance that only a fool could fall for them. Marmaduke wallows in neurotic excesses at the instigation of a patent deceiver, and thus forfeits the reader's sympathy.

The obsession with guilt and with the question whether a villain should be punished recurs in Coleridge's one effective play, *Remorse*, which was put on at the Drury Lane Theatre in 1813. Coleridge goes to the Spain of Philip II to show Spaniards in civil strife with Moslem Moors in Granada. Don Alvar, elder son of Marquis Valdez, is as noble as his brother Don Ordonio is wicked, and he is critical of the Inquisition while Ordonio makes use of it. Ordonio has tried to have Alvar assassinated and to win his beloved Teresa for himself. Returning after three years' exile, Alvar, falsely persuaded that Teresa is now Ordonio's wife, agonises long over the need to bring his would-be assassin and once much-loved brother to a state of remorse and penitence. The play is in many ways a workmanlike effort. The blank verse is flexible and easy to listen to. The use of mystery and suspense is effective. Where Wordsworth's dramatic text sounds like the utterance of a single brooding voice, Coleridge's has the vitality of true dialogue. The villainous Ordonio is in some respects reminiscent of Wordsworth's Oswald. He is one who has walked alone —

> And phantom thoughts unsought-for troubled him.
> Something within would still be shadowing out
> All possibilities; and with these shadows
> His mind held dalliance.

There is a streak of wilful Byronic diabolism about the villains of Wordsworth and Coleridge.

Shelley's excursion into theatrical enterprise was crude by comparison with Coleridge's. He was fascinated by the story of Count Cenci, a man of great wealth, depravity, and cruelty, who indulged an incestuous passion for his daughter Beatrice. Aided by her stepmother and her brother, she plotted his death. In spite of urgent appeals to the Pope, the murderers were executed. These events took place in Rome in 1599. Shelley's play *The Cenci* (1819) was never performed in his life-time, the topic of incest being considered unfit for public treatment. Shelley thought highly of his study of Beatrice, a young woman of simplicity who is unbalanced by her suffering and turns coolly vengeful as a result. But Cenci himself is a pantomimically extravagant monster whose relish of brutality, sadism, and all manner of wickedness is voiced in orgies of hollow rhetoric. In Shelley's eyes, the Count, who buys off penalties for murderous crimes by contributions to the papal treasury, becomes an immense symbol of the privileged tyranny and injustice he never wearied of lambasting. Beatrice has good lines from time to time, but the play suffers from melodramatic excess and from structural crudities as well as from the verbal inflation to which Shelley was all too prone.

Byron's verse idiom was far more appropriate for dramatic dialogue than those of Wordsworth, Coleridge, or Shelley. He was master of a direct, crisp, forceful rhetoric that invites oral declamation, and he chose the dramatic form for a series of works, *Cain* (1821), *The Two Foscari* (1821), *Marino Faliero, Doge of Venice* (1821), and *Werner* (1823). But Byron did not want these plays to be acted. He was angry when *Marino Faliero* was put on at Drury Lane. The tragedy is 'fit only for the . . . closet,' he wrote to Tom Moore. 'I write only for the *reader*.' And later he told Moore, 'I am sorry you think *Werner* even *approaching* any fitness for the stage, which . . . is very far from my present object.'

In fact, after Byron's death *Werner, The Two Foscari*, and even *Manfred* were all produced on the stage. *Werner* proved a notable success, though the text was drastically mangled. And there is no doubt that Tom Moore was right to sense its actable qualities. The tragedy explores the theme of guilt and remorse dear to the other Romantic poets-turned-dramatists. It does so in terms of a troubled father-son relationship, and in this respect echoes *The Two Foscari*, where the father is Doge of Venice and has to acquiesce in his son's banishment for treason. Werner has been disinherited by his father for youthful extravagance and an imprudent marriage. He hides in impoverishment from his persecutor, Count Stralenheim, who has supplanted him as heir. Stralenheim unexpectedly and unknowingly meets Werner, his wife Josephine, and their son Ulric under the same roof. In a moment of vengeful weakness Werner steals some of Stralenheim's gold. It is an excusable lapse in an honourable man unbalanced by privation, himself the dispossessed victim of the man he robs — but it haunts Werner for the rest of his life. Stralenheim is murdered the same night, and his death restores Werner to his estate. What he does not know until late in the play is that his son Ulric was Stralenheim's murderer. Ulric has committed himself to evil after the pattern of Wordsworth's Oswald and Coleridge's Ordonio. 'Is it strange / That I should *act* what you could *think*?' he asks Werner.

> We have done
> With right and wrong; and now must only ponder
> Upon effects, not causes.

Verse drama: lesser poets (Baillie, Mitford, Hemans, Landor)

Two years before his marriage to Annabella Milbanke, we find Byron writing to her in flattering terms of her 'friend', Joanna Baillie (1762–1851), the Scottish dramatist and poetess.

Nothing could do me more honour than the acquaintance of that Lady, who does not possess a more enthusiastic admirer than myself. She is our only dramatist since Otway and Southerne . . .

Joanna Baillie's high reputation in her day was nourished by the publication of successive volumes of *Plays on the Passions* in 1798, 1802, and 1812, and by *Miscellaneous Plays* in 1836. In her light comedies she used prose, but her more serious plays are written in a stilted blank verse which seem to derive from the pseudo-Shakespearean tradition of eighteenth-century tragedy. Where it is simple it is both flaccid and awkwardly mechanical:

> CITIZEN: What sounds are these, good friend, which this way bear?
> SECOND CITIZEN: The brave Count Basil is upon his march,
> To join the emperor with some chosen troops,
> And doth as our ally through Mantua pass.
>
> (*Basil*, Act I, scene 1)

When passion or horror is called for the verse explodes into extravagance which smacks of burlesque:

> ETHWALD: . . . Thou rear'st thy stately neck,
> And while I list, thou flarest in men's eyes
> A gorgeous queen . . .
> Heaven warring o'er my head! there is in this
> Some fearful thing betoken'd . . .
> I am prepar'd to front thee and thy mates,
> Were ye twice numbered o'er . . .
>
> (*Ethwald*, Act V, scene 5)

It is difficult for us to understand the respect for Joanna Baillie's work shown by Scott as well as Byron. The verse moves lumberingly, the rhetoric tends to be second-hand. The plays are too lifeless for the closet, let alone the stage.

Joanna Baillie's success inspired others to emulate her. Among them was Miss Mitford, whose efforts in the most pretentious vein of verse drama stand in such sharp contrast to her work in prose; the latter breathes vitality and genuineness. Introducing her play *Julian* (1823) in the collected edition of her *Dramatic Works* (1854), she tells us that its story and characters 'are altogether fictitious', though classical readers will recognise her indebtedness at certain crucial points to Euripides and Sophocles. In her play a heroic son saves the life of his royal cousin (and young king) by wounding a would-be assassin. The assassin turns out to be his own father, now acting as regent. The guilty father survives from Act I to Act IV in seeming health, trying to claim the crown, before the wound gushes blood and the tragic deed can be called 'parricide'. The blank verse is clumsy metrically, the poetic substance trite and hollow. It is interesting, however, that the theme of guilt which destroys the relationship of father and son should recur, though here the father is the criminal and the virtuous son, Julian, refuses to recriminate him publicly at the cost of his own reputation and even freedom. He rebuffs the powerful nobles who demand corroboration of his father's guilt:

> Had ye no fathers,
> Had ye no sons, that ye would train men up
> In parricide? I'll not answer ye.

Apparently audiences revelled emotionally in such crises. The actor Macready, who played the part of Julian, later played the part of Byron's Werner and 'improved' Byron's play by extemporaneously rushing across the stage in Act V, scene 1, asking Gabor, who holds the secret of Ulric's guilt, 'Are you a father?', and whispering, 'Say 'No!' When Gabor obliged with a resounding shout, Macready burst out 'Ah, then you cannot feel for misery like mine!' and the audience responded with acclamation.*

Indeed Miss Mitford also tackled the father-son theme in her tragedy *Foscari*, performed at Covent Garden in 1826, explaining in her Prologue that her play was written before Byron's *The Two Foscari* was published:

> Deem not of it worse
> That 'tis a theme made sacred by his verse.
> Ere his bold Tragedy burst into day,
> Her trembling hand had closed this woman's play.

As her *Foscari* preceded Byron's play, so her tragedy *Rienzi* (produced 1825) preceded Bulwer-Lytton's novel *Rienzi, the Last of the Roman Tribunes* (1835), and Wagner used Miss Mitford's play as well as Bulwer-Lytton's novel in the libretto for his opera *Rienzi* (1842).

After the production of *Rienzi*, Miss Mitford tells us, 'Maria Edgeworth, Joanna Baillie, Felicia Hemans . . . vied in the cordiality of their praises', but her next play *Charles the First* remained unacted for a long time:

> The hindrance lay in Mr George Colman, the licenser, who saw a danger to the State in permitting the trial of an English Monarch to be represented on stage, especially a Monarch whose martyrdom was still observed in our churches. It was in vain that I urged that my play was ultra-loyal . . .

Miss Mitford regarded Felicia Hemans's praise of her work as especially generous, because the production of Mrs Hemans's *The Vespers of Palermo*

---

* The story is told in the *Revels History of Drama in English*, edited by Clifford Leech and T. W. Craik, Volume VI, *1750–1880*, p.195, Methuen, London, 1975.

(1823) at Covent Garden in the same year as *Julian* gave the two authoresses the status of potential rivals.

In fact *The Vespers of Palermo* was a total failure in London and was taken off after one night. A production in Edinburgh proved to have more staying power, but in his *Autobiography* (1850) Leigh Hunt commented scathingly on the contrast:

> A dispassionate reader of the present day ... will probably agree that the London audience showed at least as much discrimination ... as that in Edinburgh.

The twentieth-century reader is more likely to be astonished at the success of the successful plays, whether by Joanna Baillie or Miss Mitford, than at the failure of plays which scarcely excel them in absurdity.

To turn from the verse drama of Baillie, Mitford, and Hemans to that of Walter Savage Landor is to climb up to a totally different level of literary taste and expertise. Landor's verse dramas are frankly closet plays. 'None of these poems of a dramatic form were offered to the stage,' he wrote, 'being no better than *Imaginary Conversations* in metre.' (The word 'better' is odd.) The first and best of the plays, *Count Julian* (1812), is another exploration of a paternal-filial relationship soured by the anguish of guilt. But this time it is a father-daughter relationship, and the guilt is rather that of the daughter's seducer than of the daughter herself. Count Julian is overwhelmed with a torrent of emotional distress when King Roderigo of Spain dishonours his loved and innocent daughter Covilla. (The same situation is treated in Southey's narrative poem *Roderick, the Last of the Goths* (1814), but in Southey's version Julian's daughter is called Florinda.) Determined to avenge the wrong, Julian allies himself with Moorish invaders and Roderigo is defeated.

Awkward questions of motive and loyalty, private and public, bristle around these developments and are aired with force and eloquence. Up to the point of climax in the play Roderigo's intention is to divorce his wife Egilona and to make Covilla his queen. But in a devastating outburst Julian brings home to Roderigo the full shame of his guilt and the havoc he has wrought, and Roderigo begs for forgiveness. Julian imposes his conditions:

> I swerve not from my purpose; thou art mine,
> Conquer'd; and I have sworn to dedicate,
> Like a torn banner on my chapel's roof,
> Thee to that power from whom thou hast rebell'd.
> Expiate thy crimes by prayer, by penance.

Roderigo is allowed to betake himself to a hermitage, 'barefooted, bruised, dejected, comfortless, / In sackcloth', to do penance and seek peace. This is not of course what Julian's Turkish allies want for the tyrant they hate. Thus there is ample scope for dispute at the political and ideological level as well as for detailed exploration of mental processes and emotional cross-currents. Characters spend their time talking about each other and analysing themselves. There is no sense of dramatic action. There is indeed little direct clarification of what is happening at any moment. Instead, oblique references, buried amid tense personal interchanges and passages of brooding, leave the reader to infer what has happened as best he may.

Why then devote space to Landor's verse drama? The answer is simple. After the metric jog-trot and shallow, ready-made rhetoric of so many contemporary verse dramas, Landor's blank verse comes like a refreshing stream. Virile, intense, sinewy, and often compact, it is alive with psychological subtlety, imaginative richness, and emotional power. Moreover, it has philosophical dimensions that give profundity and universality to the moment-by-moment conflicts within and without. The reader in the closet may feel that he has been present at the meeting of a debating society rather than at the theatre or at a scene of action; but the debate explores the gravest and most moving issues. *Count Julian* was succeeded by historical dramas which increasingly rely on conversational rather than dramatic vitality, so that Landor's transition to the composition of pure *Imaginary Conversations* was a natural and logical one.

Gothick tragedy:
Charles Maturin, 'Monk' Lewis

At the opposite end of the artistic spectrum from Landor's is the verse drama of Charles Maturin. For Maturin has a sense of theatre, indeed a determination to exploit its resources to the maximum. His Gothick drama *Bertram* (1816) has all conceivable romantic ingredients — turreted castle on the crags overlooking the ocean and nearby monastery; and a storm at sea viewed from the rocks by monks holding torches, whilst a vessel sinks before their eyes and the monastic bell tolls. There are scenes on castle ramparts, in castle galleries, in dimly lit chambers, in convent chapel, and finally — 'A dark wood, in the back Scene a Cavern, Rocks and Precipices above'. The action is deftly presented. Count Bertram has been ruined and banished by the king who once favoured him, and his great enemy Lord Aldobrand has married Bertram's beloved Imogine who had to choose between watching her father die of hunger and accepting Aldobrand's hand. Now a melancholy woman, determined to be a good wife and mother, and struggling against her unforgettable passion for her lost Bertram, she suddenly finds Bertram, now leader of a band of outlaws, cast by shipwreck into her presence when her husband is absent on a crusade. Ultimately what is intended to be a last farewell

meeting with Bertram at night leaves her a faithless wife. The agonies
are piled on heavily before the final bloodbath.

Bertram is a Byronic figure.

> The grief that clothes that leader's woe-worn form,
> The chilling awe his ruin'd grandeur wears
> Is of no common sort.

So observes Imogine's maid. Bertram is a man disillusioned and embit-
tered, whose dark pride and brooding sternness electrify those he encounters. Small wonder that Imogine's senses blaze again and she totters into
his arms. Whatever else may be said of Maturin's verse, it is at least free
of the colourlessness and insipidity of Miss Mitford's and Mrs Hemans's.

> IMOGINE: Oh hang me shuddering on the baseless crag —
> The vampire's wing, the wild worm's sting be on me,
> But hide me, mountains, from the man I've injured.

Maturin's gifts were certainly not contemptible. His fluency and the
flamboyance of his vocabulary served him well. The vogue for Gothick
tragedy gave *Bertram* considerable popularity for a time. Indeed Coleridge
thought it worthwhile to devote several pages of his *Biographia Literaria*
to a thorough critical demolition of the play. Although allowances must
be made for an element of envy on the part of a verse-dramatist
disappointed of a comparable success, Coleridge's dissection of the play's
demerits is both surgically acute and rollickingly funny. Maturin's efforts
to build on this theatrical success were in vain. *Manuel* (1817), which
failed, has interest only as another exploration of complex father-son
relationships. Old Manuel accuses old De Zelos of having murdered his
son, and as the two old men are beyond duelling age, De Zelos's son
takes up his father's cause, believing him innocent. The assassin hired
by De Zelos is overcome with remorse, takes up Manuel's cause, and is
overcome. The unjust cause, in innocent hands, triumphs over the just
cause, in guilty hands. 'As heavy a nightmare as ever was bestrode by
indigestion,' Byron said of the play. 'It is the absurd work of a clever
man.'

But something more indigestible was to follow, the play *Fredolfo* (1819),
perhaps Maturin's most extravagant effort. A contemporary criticism
describes how at one moment in the production an actor with a grave
and solemn announcement to make precipitated the audience into a
fit of merriment. Certainly the dialogue contains prize specimens of
absurdity.

> BERTHOLD (*absorbed in malignity*): I could, such is my heart's o'erflowing
>   spleen
> To all that loved, and lovely are — methinks,

> I could, even with a look — as thus — dart through him
> The basilisk's eye-fang — dying on the throe.

Yet Maturin's *Bertram* stands up well to comparison with the general run of Gothick horror drama, perhaps chiefly because, with all Maturin's extravagances, it has at least one kind of economy, a unified and shapely plot. The critic can sum it up in a sentence or two. Now we should need a page or two to sum up the action of some of 'Monk' Lewis's plays. *The Castle Spectre* (published 1798), a prose melodrama, mixes together an indigestible brew of dramatic themes of rivalry in love, intrigue, usurpation, and murder, in a feudal castle equipped with the maximum in the way of subterranean passages, movable panels, and secret springs. The supposedly murdered rightful owner has been chained sixteen years in a dungeon below, and his murdered wife makes spectral appearances in white garments stained with blood. Complex intrigues produce meetings and misses, escapes and recaptures of staggering implausibility. The plotting technique would be more appropriate to farce.

What is perhaps even more remarkable is that the same excess of plotting appropriate to burlesque is to be found in Lewis's full-blown verse tragedy, *Adelgitha, or The Fruits of a Single Error* (produced 1806). It is the drama of a woman whose past returns to ruin her reputation and happiness after twelve years of faithful married life. At the age of sixteen she tended a wounded knight, who unscrupulously took advantage of her innocence and then was careless enough, in dying repentant, to leave evidence of what had happened where it could come into the hands of the world's worst villain. But to relate this is only to scratch the surface of an elaborate narrative structure of rebellion, usurpation, love and deception, intrigue and counter-intrigue. Lewis admits in his Preface that, having first concocted the story, he looked then for some historical characters on whom to peg it. Hence we are in Otranto in the year 1080 and Michael Ducas, Emperor of Byzantium-in-exile, is indulging in every conceivable wickedness at the home of Robert Guiscard, Prince of Apulia, who has nobly led a force to rescue him. Michael Ducas's malignant pride is such that he must do his utmost to ruin the man to whom he owes the greatest obligation. Adelgitha, Robert's wife, Princess of Apulia, with her hidden past, becomes the victim of his blackmail. The happiness of his great benefactor is ruined by the knowledge that his noble reputation is tainted by his wife's dishonour. At the end, once her husband's righteous anger has softened into forgiveness, Adelgitha stabs herself, glad to die now that his love is retrieved, and so doing, to free his name from the dishonour she has brought him.

> I'm happy! — Guiscard, Guiscard . . . thus I thank thee, (*embracing him*)
> And next *reward* thee thus! — (*stabs herself*)

Thus indeed she spares him the shame of loving where esteem is lost. And if anyone thinks Adelgitha's fate is too severe, Lewis insists, in a final note, that his object in writing the tragedy 'was to illustrate a particular point; viz. the difficulty of avoiding the evil consequences of a first false step'.

This is heavy-handed moralism indeed; and the verse conveying it has the artifice and prolixity we might expect from the author of *The Monk*:

Hark! 'twas the convent-bell! — and see, the Abbess
To chaunt their matins in yon chapel leads
Her white-robed team.

The paraphernalia of convent and shrine, abbess and nuns, were to become standard. Lewis's own influence in this respect was no doubt crucial. On the back page of the 1816 edition of *Adelgitha*, the publisher advertises such titles as *Confessions of the Nun of St Omer*, *St Botolph's Priory*, *The Monk of Udolpho*, and *The Monk and His Daughter*, all novels.

Restraint was never one of Lewis's characteristics. He had created a sensation at Covent Garden in 1803 with his monodrama, *The Captive*. The scene is a dungeon. The captive is a woman seemingly incarcerated by her husband as a lunatic. Harsh music, a rough gaoler delivering the daily ration of bread and water, and various horrible glimpses of madness and cruelty seen through a grated window and along a gallery above the cell provide a fit background to the woman's lament. As the horror mounts, the woman's tale of misery, with its repeated refrain, 'I'm not mad! I'm not mad!', culminates in a frenzied shriek, 'I'm mad! — I'm mad!' The play had to be taken off because of the agitation and dismay it provoked: ladies weeping, fainting, shrieking, while the more controlled members of the audience sat aghast with pale horror on their faces. 'Two people went into hysterics during the performance, and two more after the curtain dropped,' Lewis wrote to his mother, explaining that he had withdrawn the play, since it had proved 'too terrible for representation'.

Popular comedy: Thomas Holcroft, Frederick Reynolds, John O'Keeffe

Thomas Holcroft, author of the novel *Hugh Trevor*, played up to the vogue for extravagant Gothick melodrama when he wrote *A Tale of Mystery* (1802), adapted from a play by the French dramatist, Guilbert de Pixérécourt (1773–1844), himself an exploiter of the sinister and the bloodthirsty. Bad brother has ambushed and mutilated good brother to gain his fortune and his wife, and good brother keeps quiet, being too good to want to see his own brother pay the penalty. This is the bare bones of an elaborate network of mystery, tension, deception, and criminality, which embroils the next generation when they reach marrying age. The whole reads like a jumble of theatrical clichés.

Though Holcroft wrote over thirty pieces for the stage, it is generally agreed that only his comedy *The Road to Ruin* (1792) justifies the kind of attention that is given to his best work as a novelist. Here again is a crucial father-son relationship. Mr Dornton is a wealthy London financier. His son Harry comes near to ruining the firm by his extravagant dissipations. But he has an underlying genuineness of character and a real love for his father. So father alternately reviles and forgives him, wrings his hands in despair at his son's folly, and melts at signs of grace in him. When his father's firm ultimately seems to totter on the edge of disaster as a result of his dissipations, Harry finally sees the error of his ways. He plans to save his father by marrying a silly wealthy widow instead of his beloved Sophia. There is a certain vitality in the play, which brings convincingly to life the young gamesters, the scatter-brained widow, the empty-headed gold-digger, the seedy lawyers, and the various hangers-on of the fashionable contemporary world. But it would be idle to pretend that there is any element of social protest here such as is found in *Hugh Trevor*. Although the wasteful ways of the wealthy, their fripperies, extravagances, and dissipations are brought home, there is no representative here of a different ethic. Young Dornton is the lovable young wastrel with the heart of gold. Tradesmen who press for payment of debts are faintly ridiculous. Moral judgment is wholly focused on the theme of the father who has been too indulgent, but whose consequently wayward son turns up trumps at last. The scattered thousands of pounds are lightly forgotten.

Historians of the theatre regard the period between about 1785 and 1820 as a golden age for dramatists in pecuniary terms. Both Covent Garden and Drury Lane theatres were enlarged to meet the increasing demand for entertainment in the 1790s, and playwrights were able to demand higher payments for successful plays. Frederick Reynolds (1764–1841) told his own story in *The Life and Times of Frederick Reynolds* (1827), and boasted of his high earnings. He was a master of the farcical comedy of manners, and his lively play *The Dramatist, or Stop Him Who Can!* (1789) has been accounted his best. It is a genial and often witty comedy, making the most of conventional eighteenth-century artifices. There is a mature Lady Waitfort, desperate for a husband and ready to make do with Lord Scratch — though she has had her eye on the more youthful Harry Neville, who is in love with Louisa Courtney. Louisa is an heiress, courtesy of Lord Scratch, and various interested parties aspire to her fortune. There is a misdirected amorous letter to make Lady Waitfort look foolish, a plethora of minor deceptions, a good deal of hiding behind sofas and in closets, and a bungled attempt to carry the heiress off.

What gives notability to the play is the study of Vapid, a dramatist, who seems to belong to the company of the literati later burlesqued by Thomas Love Peacock. He despises Lord Scratch's peerage.

A Peer! psha! contemptible; — when I ask a man who he is, I don't want to know what are his titles and such nonsense; no, Old Scratch, I want to know what he has written, where he had the curtains up, and whether he's a true son of the drama.

Vapid's conceit is infinite. His composition of an epilogue shows him to be an ass. His excessive zeal in search of copy means that other people's confusions have to be exaggerated and their agonies have to be protracted in order to produce an 'incident' telling enough for inclusion in his next play. Even his own courtship of Marianne is as much a rehearsal as a reality. Reynolds contrives some hilariously comic interchanges on this basis. 'Go to her!' Vapid urges hero Neville at the climax —

Go to her, preserve the unity of action, — marry her directly . . . The women, dear creatures, are always ready enough to produce effect — but the men are so curs't undramatic — go to her, I tell you, go to her.

Another highly successful comedy of incident was *Wild Oats* (1791) by John O'Keeffe (1747–1833). O'Keeffe was born in Dublin, and spent some twelve years as an actor there. He began to turn out farces and operas, came to London, and became a regular supplier of such popular pieces for the London theatre. *Wild Oats* was justly considered a more ambitious work. 'This comedy is the only attempt of the author to produce a drama above opera and farce,' Mrs Inchbald wrote in *The British Theatre*, the collection of contemporary plays she edited. It is certainly a cunningly contrived piece of work. The theme of the lost heir and child of unknown origin, dearly beloved of novelists and dramatists from the time of Fielding's *Tom Jones*, is given a new twist. The 'wild oats' were sown long ago by Sir George Thunder, a sea captain, when he induced his seaman, John Dory, to procure a seeming clergyman to deceive the desired Amelia into a sham marriage. He called himself 'Captain Seymour' for this purpose, then deserted Amelia, married a wealthy lady under compulsion by his father, and was widowed.

Dory, however, now reveals that the clergyman was indeed in holy orders and the marriage is no sham. The basic pattern of deception and counter-deception is exploited in a convoluted series of intrigues involving Thunder's son, Harry, and Rover, an actor friend he has made while passing himself off as an actor ('Dick Buskin'). Harry's filial duty to woo and marry Lady Amaranth, and Rover's role in falling in love with her when he himself is believed to be 'Harry', produce a fetching imbroglio. There is a point at which Harry Thunder, known as 'Buskin', is telling Rover how he has been persuaded to pretend to be Harry Thunder. The succession of comic crises and reversals is given sauce and colour by a variety of lingos. There is nautical slang for the former seamen, a rich flow of quotations from Shakespeare and other dramatists for the actor, Rover, and a nice vein of biblical archaisms for Ephraim Smooth and other Quakers. This was a vein which was to become a mine of rich rhetoric and humour when Scott turned to portray Covenanters and the various Puritan sects in the Waverley novels.

Sentimental comedy: Mrs Inchbald, Thomas Morton

Sentimental moralism intrudes into *Wild Oats* chiefly in respect of a subplot in which a grasping Farmer Gammon tries to evict and imprison the impoverished Banks and his sister, and is shamed by the generosity of others. By comparison Elizabeth Inchbald's comedy of two years later, *Everyone Has His Fault* (1793), reeks of sentimental moralism. It explores the subject of marriage. Sir Robert Ramble has forced his faithful wife to divorce him, and it is interesting that this is possible only because the marriage took place in Scotland. Where English law allowed a husband to divorce a wife for infidelity, only Scottish law allowed a wife to divorce a husband for infidelity. There is a good deal of sentimentality and precious little psychological plausibility in the way Sir Robert is brought to his knees in penitence before his wronged wife.

His case is matched by that of the cruelly henpecked Mr Placid, who would dearly like to cast off his wife, but as he was unfortunately married in the home country, a judicial separation is the most he can hope for. By contrast the old bachelor, Mr Solus, would like nothing so much as a wife to cosset him, while the ideal loving partners, Mr Irwin and Lady Eleanor, are being reduced to destitution for the imprudence of their match, Lady Eleanor's father, Lord Norland, having cut them off. The Irwins have returned from America to find the hearts of London's society people locked against the appeal of former friends in dire need. This gives Irwin the opportunity to lose his balance and to snarl as sarcastically as Percy B. Shelley himself about the hypocrisy of the world's wealthy and powerful.

This is one of Mrs Inchbald's original plays. Like others of her contemporaries, she adapted the work of French and German dramatists. Her *Lovers' Vows* (1798), the play which causes all the fuss when it is rehearsed by the young people in Jane Austen's *Mansfield Park*, was in fact adapted from a play by the German dramatist August von Kotzebue (1761–1819), the same author from whom 'Monk' Lewis adapted *Rolla* (1799) and *The East Indian* (1799). Lewis, incidentally, also adapted *Rugantino: The Bravo of Venice* (1805) from the French dramatist Guilbert de Pixérécourt, from whom Thomas Holcroft derived *A Tale of Mystery* (1802). Whatever plays Mrs Inchbald adapted, it is generally agreed that she put on them the stamp of her own emphasis on the domestic virtues and the need to preserve them against the depredations of moral laxity, fashionable folly, and crude social taboos based on rank or wealth. The modern student is indebted to her for editing *The British Theatre, A Collection of Plays with Biographical and Critical Remarks*, published in twenty-five volumes in 1808, and followed by a new edition in twenty volumes in 1824.

Perhaps the most competent of the dramatists who turned their hands to comedy around the turn of the century was Thomas Morton (?1764–1838), and his most competent play was *Speed the Plough* (1800). It has a special interest for the literary historian in being the best comedy from a bad period for comedy. Moreover, it displays the intrusion of Romantic notions of grandeur and heroism, of nobility and moral rectitude, even of long-concealed criminality and long-endured remorse, into the world of eighteenth-century comedy.

The play opens in a rural world not vastly unlike that of Goldsmith's *She Stoops to Conquer*, but before long we are in a world more like that of Coleridge's *Remorse*. Realistic rustic scenes involving Farmer Ashfield and his family set the initial tone of things. It is homely and earthy. Dame Ashfield's talk is full of references to the local busybody she most dislikes for her pretensions and her opinionatedness. 'What will Mrs Grundy think?' Although Morton is responsible for 'Mrs Grundy', she has become something very different in modern usage. She is now the voice of puritanical respectability in the face of sexual freedom. In Morton she is simply a means by which Dame Ashfield registers her own prickly defensiveness and assertiveness in the face of feminine rivalry. Her husband tells her so:

DAME: And do you think I envy Mrs Grundy indeed?

ASHFIELD: What dant thee letten her aloane then — I do verily think when thee goest to t'other world, the vurst question thee't ax 'il be, if Mrs Grundy's there — Zo a be quiet, and behave pratty, do'ye —

The peasants mouth this stage Zummerset, but in their very home has been bred a young man of mysterious origin, Henry (the standard lost heir), whose agonising yearning to know his own father betrays a different level of education. Here he is, having just witnessed a ploughing accident:

I found him suffering under extreme torture, yet a ray of joy shot from his languid eye — for his medicine was administered by a father's hand — it was a mother's precious tear that dropt upon his wound — Oh, how I envied him!

A survey of the literary ingredients that go to make up this strangely attractive hotch-potch of a play would cross all boundaries of genre. The return of Sir Philip Blandford to the local castle opens up a complex tale of horror. Sir Philip stabbed his loved brother when he found him making love to his bride on the eve of marriage, and is now tormented by remorse. He imagines his brother dead and his own estate near ruin in the hands of mortgagees. But the brother has survived to atone secretly by being himself the mortgagee and laying Sir Philip's deeds and bills at his feet before the curtain falls. Henry, of course, is the brother's son, and he has not only won the prize at ploughing but has also carried Sir Philip's daughter from the blazing castle in his arms before the final curtain.

The oscillation between scenes of genuinely vital comedy and scenes displaying characters in states of deep anguish, bitter resentment, and even severe inner moral conflict does not make for artistic wholeness. Sometimes the investigation of moral tension is effected with an almost burlesque naïveté, as when Sir Abel Handy's son, Bob, sends Susan Ashfield away for a few moments while he ponders their future. And ponder he does through an extended soliloquy. Shall he make love to this farmer's daughter and be the proud possessor of a beautiful mistress? Ah, but what might be her fate if virtue yielded to love? Picture the converse, if she becomes his legal wife:

> I behold her giving to my hopes a dear pledge of our mutual love. She places it in my arms — down her father's face runs a tear, but 'tis the tear of joy.

So Susan is recalled, marriage proposed, and the audience breathes a sigh of relief.

Conclusion

The Gothick element which in *Speed the Plough* sits so incongruously alongside the stuff of rural comedy was to overflow the banks of artistic taste and plausibility as the Romantic period merged into the Victorian period. James Robinson Planché (1796–1880), who was to become one of the most productive and popular writers for the Victorian theatre, had his first success with *The Vampire* (1820), a melodrama adapted from the French of Pierre Carmouche (1797–?). The play opens with an 'Introductory Vision' in which Lady Margaret is seen sleeping on a rude sepulchre inside a cavern at Staffa. The Spirits of the Flood and the Air arise to warn her of the impending threat, and perform 'magical ceremonies' to bring the vampire into her dream. There is a pantomimic quality about the whole melodrama. Supernaturalism runs riot too in the melodramas of Edward Fitzball (1793–1873). In *The Flying Dutchman* (1827) we witness storms and mists, sinking ships and drowning sailors, and Vanderdecken, the doomed Dutchman 'with a demoniac laugh, rises from the sea in blue fire, amidst violent thunder' whilst a Phantom Ship appears in the sky behind. This might be all very well, were it not that the plot of the play, concerning the fate of Lestelle Vanhelm, sought in marriage by two solid men as well as by the phantom wanderer, involves numerous farcical antics in which people hide from each other in a sea-chest, and Lestelle's Dutch suitor, Peter, dresses up as a woman for all the world as though he were performing in *Charley's Aunt*. Both Planché and Fitzball, by the way, were among the numerous dramatists who adapted Scott's novels for the stage. Planché adapted *Kenilworth Castle* (1821), *The Witch of Derncleuch* (from *Guy Mannering*) (1821), *The Pirate* (1822), and *St Ronan's Well* (1824), while Fitzball did *The Fortunes of Nigel* (1822), *Peveril of the Peak* (1823), and *Waverley* (1824).

The popularity of stage adaptations of the Waverley novels is only one aspect of the Romantic influence on the theatre. 'Influence' is a key word. There was a full-blown Romantic novel produced by Scott, and there were full-blown Romantic poems produced by Wordsworth, Byron, Keats, and Shelley. In drama there is only a second-hand Romanticism derivative of the work of novelists and poets. We see it in the stage settings in caverns and forests, in castles and palaces, on rocky coasts and in dimly lit dungeons. We see it in the Gothick exploitation of the feudal and the monastic, the preternaturally horrific and the liturgically picturesque. We see it in the taste for larger-than-life heroics in selfless causes, noble gestures, and costly self-sacrifices. We see it in the masculinity of the men and the femininity of the women, in the gallantries and agonies involved in the preservation of maidenly chastity and wifely fidelity. We see it in the portrayal of prolonged anguish and remorse for guilt. When spectres rise, spirits float through the air, or ghosts stalk through moonlit galleries, above all when technical ingenuity is harnessed to produce spurts of flame or puffs of smoke from artifacts and from human beings, then we sense the determination of dramatists to transfer bodily to the theatre those effects which have stirred readers of poetry and novels in the quiet of the parlour or the garden.

Part 6

Suggestions for
further reading

WORKS BY the major writers discussed in this book are readily available, often in editions with introductions and notes for students. Of the lesser writers considered here, the novelists are almost all currently available in popular editions from Oxford University Press, Pandora or Virago (for women writers). The few minor poets treated here who are not readily available can be adequately sampled in anthologies such as *The Oxford Book of Nineteenth-Century Verse*, in which almost half the volume is devoted to our period. Verse dramas by the poets are of course included in collected editions of their poetry. Essayists and prose writers are well represented in volumes published by Dent (Everyman's Library), Oxford University Press, Penguin, and other publishers. The following lists of books on poetry and drama, the novel, and prose draw attention to biographical and critical studies which will extend the student's knowledge of the writers and appreciation of their works. Under the heading of 'General background' some books are recommended which will shed further light on the Romantic movement and on the age in which the Romantics wrote.

Romantic poetry and drama

BRENT, PETER: *Byron*, Weidenfeld and Nicolson, London, 1974.

CURRY, KENNETH: *Southey*, Routledge, London, 1975.

GITTINGS, ROBERT (ED.): *John Keats: Letters, a New Selection*, Oxford University Press, Oxford, 1970.

GITTINGS, ROBERT and MANTON, JO: *Life of Dorothy Wordsworth*, paperback edition, Oxford University Press, Oxford, 1988.

GUNN, PETER (ED.): *Byron: Letters and Journals*, Penguin, Harmondsworth, 1984.

HAMILTON, G. ROSTREVOR: *Walter Savage Landor*, Longmans, Green, London, 1960.

HAYWARD, JOHN (ED.): *The Oxford Book of Nineteenth-Century Verse*, Oxford University Press, Oxford, 1964.

HILL, ALAN G. (ED.): *Letters of Dorothy Wordsworth*, Oxford University Press, Oxford, 1981.

HILL, ALAN G. (ED.): *Letters of William Wordsworth*, Clarendon Press, Oxford, 1984.

HILL, JOHN SPENCER: *A Coleridge Companion*, Macmillan, London, 1983.

HOLMES, RICHARD: *Shelley; The Pursuit*, Penguin Books, London, 1987.

HOLMES, RICHARD: *Coleridge* (Past Masters Series), Oxford University Press, Oxford, 1982.

JACKSON, J. R. DE J.: *Poetry of the Romantic Period*, Routledge, London, 1980.

JERROLD, W. C.: *Thomas Hood, His Life and Times*, (reissue of the 1907 edition), Haskell House Publishers, Brooklyn, NY, 1982.

JUMP, JOHN: *Byron* (Author Guides), Routledge, London, 1972.

LEECH, CLIFFORD and CRAIK, T. W. (GENERAL EDS): *The Revels History of Drama in English*: Vol. VI, *1750–1880*, by Michael Booth *et al*, Methuen, London, 1975.

LEFEBURE, MOLLY: *Samuel Taylor Coleridge: A Bondage of Opium*, Gollancz, London, 1974.

LINDSAY, JACK: *William Blake*, Constable, London, 1974.

MARCHAND, LESLIE A. (ED.): *Lord Byron: Selected Letters and Journals*, John Murray, London, 1982.

MOORMAN, MARY (ED.): *Journals of Dorothy Wordsworth*, Oxford University Press, Oxford, 1971.

MOORMAN, MARY: *William Wordsworth: A Biography*, 2 vols, Clarendon Press, Oxford, 1957.

NEW, PETER: *George Crabbe's Poetry*, Macmillan, London, 1976.

PAGE, NORMAN (ED.): *Byron: Interviews and Recollections*, Macmillan, London, 1985.

QUENNELL, PETER (ED.): *The Journal of Thomas Moore 1818–1841*, Batsford, London, 1964.

SELINCOURT, E. DE (ED.): *William Wordsworth: A Guide to the Lakes*, 5th edition, Oxford University Press, Oxford, 1977.

TIBBLE, J. W. and TIBBLE, ANNE: *John Clare; A Life*, new edition, Michael Joseph, London, 1972.

TRINDER, B. W.: *Mrs Hemans* (Writers of Wales), University of Wales Press, 1984.

WALSH, WILLIAM: *Introduction to Keats*, Methuen, London, 1981.

WHITE, TERENCE DE VERE: *Tom Moore, the Irish Poet*, Hamish Hamilton, London, 1977.

WISCHUSEN, STEPHEN (ED.): *The Hour of One; Six Gothic Melodramas*, Gordon Fraser, London, 1975.

WORDSWORTH, JONATHAN: *William Wordsworth: The Borders of Vision*, Oxford University Press, Oxford, 1982.

WRIGHT, DAVID (ED.): *Trelawny's Recollections of Shelley, Byron, and the Author*, Penguin, Harmondsworth, 1973.

The Romantic novel

ANDERSON, W. E. K. (ED.): *The Journal of Sir Walter Scott*, Clarendon Press, Oxford, 1972.

BUTLER, MARILYN: *Maria Edgeworth; A Literary Biography*, Clarendon Press, Oxford, 1972.

CAMPBELL, MARY: *Lady Morgan; The Life and Times of Sydney Owenson*, Pandora Press, London, 1988.

CHAPMAN, R. W. (ED.): *Jane Austen: Selected Letters*, Oxford University Press, Oxford, 1985.

COTTOM, DANIEL: *Civilized Imagination: A Study of Ann Radcliffe, Jane Austen, and Sir Walter Scott*, Cambridge University Press, Cambridge, 1985.

CRAIK, W. A.: *Jane Austen: The Six Novels*, Methuen, London, 1965.

DAICHES, DAVID: *Sir Walter Scott and His World*, Thames and Hudson, London, 1971.

FENTON, FELIX: *Thomas Love Peacock*, Allen and Unwin, London, 1973.

GALT, JOHN: *The Member: An Autobiography*, ed. by Ian A. Gordon, Scottish Academic Press, Edinburgh, 1975.

GORDON, IAN A.: *John Galt: The Life and Work of a Writer*, Oliver and Boyd, Edinburgh, 1972.

HARDY, BARBARA: *A Reading of Jane Austen*, Peter Owen, London, 1975.

HEWITT, DAVID (ED.): *Scott on Himself*, Scottish Academic Press, Edinburgh, 1981.

HOGG, JAMES: *Memoir of the Author's Life and Anecdotes of Sir Walter Scott*, Scottish Academic Press, Edinburgh, 1972.

JOHNSON, EDGAR: *Sir Walter Scott; The Great Unknown*, 2 vols, Hamish Hamilton, London, 1970.

KELLY, G.: *The English Jacobin Novel 1780–1805*, Clarendon Press, Oxford, 1976.

LASKI, MARGHANITA: *Jane Austen and Her World*, Thames and Hudson, London, 1969.

LOUGY, ROBERT E.: *Charles Robert Maturin*, Bucknell University Press, Lewisburg, Pa, 1981.

SAGE, VICTOR (ED.): *The Gothic Novel; A Selection of Critical Essays* (Casebooks Series), Macmillan, London, 1987.

SIMPSON, LOUIS: *James Hogg; A Critical Study*, Oliver and Boyd, Edinburgh, 1962.

SOUTHAM, B. C. (ED.): *Jane Austen; The Critical Heritage*, Routledge, London, 1968.

TOMPKINS, J. M. S.: *The Popular Novel in England 1772–1805*, Methuen, London, 1932.

Romantic prose

BLAINEY, A.: *Immortal Boy; A Portrait of Leigh Hunt*, Croom Helm, Beckenham, Kent, 1985.

CASEBY, RICHARD: *The Opium-Eating Editor; Thomas De Quincey and the Westmorland Gazette*, Westmorland Gazette, Kendal, 1985.

CECIL, DAVID: *A Portrait of Charles Lamb*, Constable, London, 1983.

HART, FRANCIS RUSSELL: *Lockhart as a Romantic Biographer*, Edinburgh University Press, Edinburgh, 1971.

HOWE, PERCIVAL P.: *Life of William Hazlitt*, Greenwood Press, London, 1973.

INGPEN, ROGER (ED.): *The Autobiography of Leigh Hunt*, Constable, London, 1902.

LINDOP, GREVEL: *Opium-Eater; The Life of Thomas De Quincey*, Dent, London, 1985.

MARSHALL, PETER H.: *William Godwin*, Yale University Press, New Haven and London, 1984.

PRIESTLEY, J. B.: *William Hazlitt*, Longmans, Green, Harlow, 1960.

SUPER, R. H.: *Walter Savage Landor; A Biography*, Greenwood Press, London, 1977.

TOMALIN, CLAIRE: *The Life and Death of Mary Wollstonecraft*, Harcourt Brace Jovanovich, New York and London, 1974.

WILLIAMS, RAYMOND: *Cobbett* (Past Masters Series), Oxford University Press, Oxford, 1983.

General background

BRIGGS, ASA: *The Making of Modern England 1783–1867; The Age of Improvement*, Harper Row, New York, 1965.

BUTLER, MARILYN: *Romantics, Rebels, and Revolutionaries; English Literature and Its Background 1760–1830*, Oxford University Press, Oxford, 1981.

DE BEER, SIR GAVIN: *Jean-Jacques Rousseau and His World*, Thames and Hudson, London, 1972.

FORD, BORIS (ED.): *Pelican Guide to English Literature*, Vol. 5, *Blake to Byron*, Penguin, Harmondsworth, 1982.

HARRIS, R. W.: *Romanticism and the Social Order*, Blandford Press, London, 1969.

JACK, IAN: *English Literature 1815–1832*, *Oxford History of English Literature*, Vol. 10, Oxford University Press, Oxford, 1963.

KING, R. W. (ED.): *England from Wordsworth to Dickens*, Methuen, London, 1928.

PRICKETT, STEPHEN (ED.): *The Romantics* (Context of English Literature Series), Methuen, London, 1981.

QUENNELL, PETER: *Romantic England, Writing and Painting 1717–1851*, Weidenfeld and Nicolson, London, 1970.

RENWICK, W. L.: *English Literature 1789–1815, Oxford History of English Literature*, Vol. 9, Oxford University Press, London, 1963.

RICHARDSON, JOANNA: *The Regency*, Collins, London, 1973.

WATSON, J. STEPHEN: *The Reign of George III, Oxford History of England*, Vol. 12, Oxford University Press, Oxford, 1960.

Index

The index lists authors and selected works. Page numbers in **bold** indicate a main entry for a writer.

The author of this handbook

HARRY BLAMIRES is a graduate of the University of Oxford, where he studied English Language and Literature. He spent a large part of his teaching life as Head of the English Department at King Alfred's College, Winchester, but retired early to concentrate on writing in 1976. His publications include works of fiction and theology as well as literary history and critical books. He has contributed *Studying James Joyce* (1986), an introduction to Joyce's work as a whole, to the York Handbooks series, and in *The New Bloomsday Book* (Routledge, 1988) he has now updated his classic guide to Joyce's *Ulysses* which students have used for over twenty years. His *Short History of English Literature* (Methuen, 1974, revised edition, 1984) and his *Twentieth-Century English Literature* (Macmillan, 1982, revised edition, 1986), a volume in the Macmillan Histories of Literature (ed. A. N. Jeffares), have established his reputation as a literary historian. The present book succeeds *The Victorian Age of Literature* (1988), in the York Handbooks series, and *A Guide to Twentieth-Century Literature in English* (1983), which he edited and to which he contributed the articles on writers of the United Kingdom and Ireland.